London
1995

Merry Christmas

to

Dearest

Father

Love always,
Margot Paul, Elliott, Natasha
&
Anastasia

HENRY VIII
A EUROPEAN COURT IN ENGLAND

Henry VIII

A European Court in England

Edited by David Starkey

COLLINS & BROWN

IN ASSOCIATION WITH THE NATIONAL MARITIME MUSEUM, GREENWICH

First published in Great Britain in 1991
by Collins & Brown Limited
Mercury House
195 Knightsbridge
London SW7 1RE

A CIP catalogue record for this book
is available from the British Library

ISBN 1 85585 008 7 (Hardback)
ISBN 1 85585 013 3 (Paperback)

Editor: Juliet Gardiner

Edited and designed by Toucan Books Limited, London

Reproduction by Daylight, Singapore
Printed and bound in Italy by New Interlitho SpA, Milan

INITIALS OF CONTRIBUTORS

P.A.	Philip Attwood
J.M.B.	Janet Backhouse
R.C.D.B.	Robert Baldwin
P.B.	Peter Barber
R.D.B.	Robert Bell
A.C.	Alan Coates
T.C.	Tom Campbell
E.C.	Edward Chaney
P.C.	Paul Courtenay
P.G.	Philippa Glanville
P.H.	Peter Hacker
W.H.	Willem Hackman
M.J.	Mark Jones
C.K.	Candy Kuhl
X.L.	Xavier Lavagne
A.McG.	Arthur MacGregor
F.P.	Frances Palmer
A.S.	Arthur Searle
D.S.	David Starkey
H.T.	Hugh Tait
S.T.	Simon Thurley
A.V.	Alan Vince
S.W.	Susan Wabuda
K.W.	Karen Watts
H.W.	Hilary Wayment
R.W.	Rosemary Weinstein
G.W.	George White
R.W-S.	Robert Woosnam-Smith

All dimensions, unless otherwise noted, are in millimetres.

Jacket and title-page: Miniature of Henry VIII, 1525-7, by Lucas Horenbout. See page 91.

Back jacket: Canon in honour of Henry VIII, 1516, written round a finely painted Tudor rose. See page 154.

Contents

6   PREFACE

8   INTRODUCTION: The Legacy of Henry VIII by David Starkey

14   I GREENWICH AND THE RIVER
14   Early Tudor London by Rosemary Weinstein
20   Greenwich Palace by Simon Thurley

26   II THE FRIAR'S CHURCH: CHRISTENING AND MARRIAGE
28   Stained Glass in Henry VIII's Palaces by Hilary Wayment

40   III THE TILTYARD: THE JOUSTS OF JULY 1517
42   Henry VIII and the Founding of the Greenwich Armouries by Karen Watts
47   The Early Tudor Tournament by Steven Gunn

50   IV THE FIELD OF CLOTH OF GOLD, 1520

54   V THE BANQUETING HOUSE: THE RECEPTION OF 1527
58   Holbein as Court Painter by Susan Foister
64   The Banqueting and Disguising Houses of 1527 by Simon Thurley
70   Nicolaus Kratzer: The King's Astronomer and Renaissance Instrument-Maker by Willem Hackmann
77   A Diplomatic Revolution? Anglo-French Relations and the Treaties of 1527 by Charles Giry-Deloison
88   Illuminated Manuscripts and the Development of the Portrait Miniature by Janet Backhouse

94   VI THE ORDERS OF THE GARTER AND ST MICHAEL

100   VII THE GREAT HALL: A ROYAL CHRISTENING, 1533
104   Music at the Court of Henry VIII by Peter Holman
107   Anne Boleyn as Patron by Maria Dowling
112   Goldsmiths and their Work at the Court of Henry VIII by Hugh Tait

118   VIII ACTON COURT AND THE PROGRESS OF 1535
120   The Royal Visit to Acton Court in 1535 by Robert Bell

126   IX THE PRESENCE CHAMBER: NEW YEAR, 1538
131   Plate and Gift-Giving at Court by Philippa Glanville

136   X THE GENTLEMEN PENSIONERS, 1539

138   XI THE BEDCHAMBER: THE CLEVES MARRIAGE, 1540
140   Fatal Matrimony: Henry VIII and the Marriage to Anne of Cleves by Rory MacEntegart
145   Henry VIII and Mapmaking by Peter Barber
155   Greenwich and Henry VIII's Royal Library by James Carley
160   The Religion of Henry VIII by Diarmaid MacCulloch
163   The Sports of Kings by Simon Thurley

172   XII HENRY VIII AND THE NAVY
172   Henry VIII: the Real Founder of the Navy? by David Loades

182   NOTES TO THE ESSAYS

187   INDEX

Preface

FOR PEOPLE TODAY Henry VIII is most closely associated with Hampton Court Palace, and with the Tower of London. There were, however, two other places which undoubtedly meant more to him than either of these famous buildings. One was Nonsuch Palace, on which Henry lavished a fortune, and intended to be one of the wonders of his reign. The other was Greenwich Palace.

Henry VIII was born at Greenwich on 28 June 1491 and he spent about a third of his life among the rambling red brick buildings along the waterfront. It was at Greenwich that he married Catherine of Aragon, his first wife, and here his daughter, the future Queen Elizabeth I, was born. He entertained foreign ambassadors in the palace, hunted in the royal park, held tournaments in the tiltyard, and established the armouries which manufactured the celebrated Greenwich armour. It is therefore appropriate that Greenwich should be the location for a major exhibition to commemorate the 500th anniversary of the birth of Henry VIII. This catalogue has been designed to accompany the exhibition but also sheds new light on many aspects of the reign, and will remain an important contribution to Tudor studies long after the exhibition has closed.

Nothing now remains of the Tudor palace at Greenwich, but archaeological investigations and recent research have provided valuable information about the buildings and the life of the court that went on among them. One of our aims has been to assemble pictures and artifacts associated with the palace, the tiltyard and the royal park and to recreate some of the events which took place here.

The response to our requests for loans has been extraordinarily generous. Public institutions and private individuals have lent some of their rarest and most valuable treasures. The names of lenders appear with the catalogue entries. We are grateful to all of them for their co-operation, but my Trustees and I would particularly like to thank the following:

Her Majesty the Queen has graciously agreed to the loan of fourteen Holbein drawings, as well as miniatures, artifacts and four major paintings; the Dean and Chapter of the Chapel Royal, Windsor have lent the magnificent Black Book of the Order of the Garter; the Duke of Buccleuch, the Duke of Devonshire, the Duke of Norfolk and the Earl of Yarborough have lent major items from their great collections; the Worshipful Company of Goldsmiths has lent one of its greatest treasures: the royal clock salt; the British Museum has lent no less than thirty items; the British Library has lent twenty-seven manuscripts and charts; the Public Record Office, and the Victoria and Albert Museum have each lent eighteen items. This gives some indication of the response, and in all cases lenders have been patient and helpful with the inevitable paperwork and administrative details surrounding each loan.

The high value and quality of the items on display has had a considerable bearing on the cost of mounting the exhibition. We are therefore particularly grateful to Mrs Coral Samuel for her most generous and timely contribution towards the display costs, and for her personal interest and support for the project from the beginning. Likewise we are grateful to the *Sunday Express* for agreeing to become sponsors of the exhibition. In addition to their financial support, which came at a crucial time, they have been closely involved with publicizing and marketing the exhibition, and we have much valued their ideas and their assistance.

Dr David Starkey was appointed historical adviser to the exhibition at the outset, and has proved an inspiration to all involved with the project. He has given his time unstintingly, and his detailed knowledge of the subject, his enthusiasm and his ideas have been absolutely invaluable. He drew up the concept brief, selected the exhibits and played a key role in the design of the exhibition. David Starkey's historical expertise has been complemented by the flair and professionalism of the design team at Event Communications led by Steve Simons and Celestine Phelan. We are grateful to all of them for their commitment, and in particular to Rachel Townshend, the project manager, who has worked long hours and cheerfully overcame all difficulties to produce the show on time. Our thanks are also due to Charles Giry-Deloison for agreeing to act as our French historical adviser and for his contribution in negotiating the French loans.

Overall co-ordination of the exhibition has been the responsibility of Dr David Cordingly, Head of Exhibitions. Working to an extremely tight schedule he and his team have overcome a succession of financial, security, conservation and transport problems and produced one of the most magnificent exhibitions to be shown at Greenwich. David Cordingly has been ably assisted by James Taylor who has been involved with all aspects of the exhibition and the accompanying catalogue. Particular thanks go to John Meek and Jane MacAndrew, respectively designer and managing editor of the catalogue. Rosalynd Whitford has been in charge of the conservation side, and Claire Nunns has dealt with loans, transport and insurance. Susan Barber has looked after publicity and the press, Robin Scates has handled visitor services, and the educational programme has been in the hands of Susan Millar and Margaret Lincoln. John Falconer has assisted with the catalogue and exhibition texts, and Lisa Edge has worked on the graphic design side. Patrick Roper, the Museum's Development Director, has been closely involved throughout the project and played a key role in marketing the exhibition to a wide audience and in encouraging the British Tourist Authority to establish a year of celebrations under the title 'Henry VIII Five Hundred'. I would also like to acknowledge our debt to Helen Miles for promoting the idea of a Henry VIII celebration at Greenwich.

It is a pleasure to acknowledge in addition the kind co-operation and assistance of Dr W.C. Allan, Dr N. Andernach, François Aunt, Dr Janet Backhouse, Stuart Bailley, Robert Baldwin, Dr Peter Barber, David Beasley, R.D. Bell, Dr Bruce Barker Benfield, Andy Bodle, General Raymond Boissau, Christopher Bornet, R.D. Buchanan-Dunlop, Francis Cheetham, Francis Collard, J.R. Chichester-Constable, Mary Clapinson, Terry Corbett, Simon Daives, Dr Philip Dixon, M. Jean Favier, Christopher Foley, Dr Helen Ford, Dr J.P. Filedt Kok, Peter van Geersdaele, Jane Gibson, Chris Gregson, A.V. Griffiths, Philippa Glanville, Dr Christian Geelhar, Dr Peter Hacker, Dr W.D. Hackmann, Kate Hannah, Colonel A.B. Harfield, Felix Holzapfel, Peter Jackson, Mark Jones, Raymond Keaveney, Ann de Lara, Xavier Lavagne, Gillian Lewis, Arthur MacGregor, Dr J.M. Maddison, Helene Mitchell, Theresa Mary Morton, J.D. Money, Isabelle du Pasquier, Brian Pilkington, A.G. Pilson, Sydney Sabin, Dr Roger Schofield, Gary Stewart, Philip Sugg, Hugh Tait, Simon Thurley, Karen Watts, Guy Wilson, Dr Hilary Wayment, Rosemary Weinstein, Victoria Williams, Robert Woosnam, and R.C. Yorke.

Richard Ormond
Director, National Maritime Museum

The Legacy of Henry VIII

BY DAVID STARKEY

EVERYONE KNOWS that Henry VIII had six wives. But how many are aware that he had fifty-five palaces, or that these were furnished with over two thousand pieces of tapestry - 'the largest documented collection ever formed', over one hundred and fifty panel paintings, besides canvases and terracottas, and 2,028 items of plate, with 1,450 books in the libraries at Whitehall and 329 at Greenwich (XI.24-9)? Or that the King's personal wardrobe included forty-one gowns, twenty-five doublets, twenty-five pairs of hose, twenty coats, eight cloaks, fifteen Spanish capes, eight walking staves and forty girdles? Or that in his personal armoury there were ninety-four swords, thirty-six daggers (XI.34), fifteen rapiers and twelve woodknives (XI.33)? Or that his guards were equipped with over a thousand parcel gilt and velvet trimmed partisans? Or that from 1538-9 he fortified the whole southern coast from the Thames to Milford Haven in a scheme costing (together with the northern border and Calais) £376,500 and larger in scale than anything attempted till the twentieth century (XI.10)? Or that these fortress were equipped with 2,250 pieces of ordnance, with the Tower, the main arsenal, having another 400 guns and 6,500 handguns (XII.7)?

Henry VIII, in short, built and accumulated more than any other English king; he also demolished, destroyed and dispersed more. The cost, human and material, was immense: Henry executed two Queens, a cardinal, a lord chancellor, a duke, a marquess, two earls, a countess, a viscount and viscountess, four barons and dozens of lesser fry; while between 1536 and 1540 the 563 English monasteries and other religious houses were dissolved, the 9,000 monks and nuns pensioned off, and their lands, worth £120,000 a year, seized. By the end of the reign, the profits of the dissolution amounted to £1,300,000. The losses, in terms of despoiled beauty and ruined lives, can scarcely be calculated. But some attempt at arithmetic must be made. For our judgment of the reign depends on the balance we draw between what the King broke down and what he built up. How do we weigh the monastic libraries, the loss of which John Bale, who approved of the dissolution, castigated as 'a most horrible infamy' (below, p.155), against Henry's royal library; 563 monasteries against fifty-five palaces, or the plough-shares of the monastic lands against the swords and guns and ships and fortifications of the King's re-armament programme?

There is no easy answer, for we are dealing also with a calculus of values. On the rightness or wrongness of Henry's religious policies the historian as such can have nothing to say on one side or the other. But there is a subtler problem. Most modern historians dislike war, and they disapprove of conspicuous consumption even more. They can also apparently call on Thomas Cromwell, Henry's great minister, to support their prejudices. In a speech prepared for the 1523 Parliament Cromwell denounced the conquest of Thérouanne, the flower of Henry VIII's first campaign in France, as having cost 'more than twenty such ungracious dogholes could be worth' (*LP* III ii, 2958); while in 1534, now in the heart of government, he deplored the burden of the King's insatiable building: 'What a great charge it is to the King to continue his buildings in so many places at once ... and if the King would spare for one year, how profitable it would be to him' (*LP* VII, 143). But what historians have seen as statements of principle were only criticisms of particular policies, and when Cromwell came, probably in 1536, to draw up a general account of 'things done by the King's highness sithens I came to his service', a document which necessarily embodies values, the values were entirely traditional. Cromwell lists the lands the King had purchased; the great ships he had rebuilt; the bows and brass ordnance he had

The French confirmation of the treaty of Amiens, 1527 (V.27) See page 78

'made ... here in England'; the palaces he had 'newly builded' at Hampton Court and Whitehall, 'with the tennis plays and cockfight, and walled the park with a goodly wall'; and finally the 'most costly charge' he had borne in the meeting with Francis I at Boulogne in 1532, the coronation of Anne Boleyn the following year (*LP* X, 1231) and in his 'great wars' in Scotland and Ireland. In other words, magnificence in peace and glory in war were the proper business of kings; the task of ministers like Cromwell was only to find the means.

Seeing Henry's material achievements in a light that would have been intelligible to a contemporary is a problem; seeing them at all is perhaps a greater one. For time has dealt harshly with his works. Many of the ruins of the monasteries Henry dissolved and half demolished still stand and their 'cold, bare ruined choirs' have been a mute indictment of his policies from Shakespeare's days to ours. On the other hand, of his gigantic total of fifty-five palaces, there survive substantial portions of only two: Hampton Court and St James's. Whitehall is only a name, and Nonsuch is scarcely even that. To recover any sense of their grandeur we must rely on archaeology and a handful of drawings by the mid-sixteenth-century Flemish artist, Wyngaerde. The rot had set in early under Henry's children, Edward, Mary and Elizabeth. But it was the Civil War of the mid-seventeenth century, and the revolution in artistic taste of the Restoration, that dealt the *coup de grâce*. The dispersal of Henry's vast collection of plate, art and artifacts followed much the same course, though here the fecklessness of the Stuarts played as big a part as the iconoclasm of the Regicides: it was the latter who broke up Henry's crown jewels; it was the former who had first pawned and then melted down his plate.

But, despite the scale of the losses, much survives. Here we assemble some of the most important and representative examples of stained glass, sculpture, armour, weapons, tapestry, painting, manuscripts, miniatures, gold and silver plate, jewellery, clocks and scientific instruments, maps, books and the hundred and one items of everyday life. That of course is what any exhibition might be expected to do. But here it becomes the manifesto for a particular historical approach, and a justification for the independent status of this book. In effect, we offer an echo of Cromwell's memorandum of 1536: we view the King through his buildings and their furnishings, his munitions and ships, his triumphs in war and peace. But, for the sake of coherence, we narrow the perspective to the single palace of Greenwich. Here Henry was born; spent about a third of his time, and last visited only three weeks before his death at Whitehall. And here occurred some of the most important and dramatic events of his reign. The palace itself is long vanished but, as far as possible, we reconstruct it, to give a vivid sense of time and place both to the visitor to the exhibition and to the reader of this book. Each section represents a part of the palace or its environs. The sections are arranged in a sequence, going from exterior to interior: from the Friars' Church, through the tiltyard and banqueting house, into the palace with its suite of more and more private rooms. Each section also represents the events of a particular day at Greenwich: in the tiltyard, the jousts of 7 July 1517; in the banqueting house, the reception of the French ambassadors on 5 May 1527; in the presence chamber, the presentation of New Year gifts to the King on 1 January 1538. And each section is a sort of tableau, in which paintings, objects and documents combine to recreate the event in question. The result is a journey, in time through the reign, and in space through the palace. Its conclusions do not pretend to be definitive, but at least, in this quincentennial year, they begin the long overdue reappraisal of Henry's place both in sixteenth-century Europe and in English history as a whole.

Henry VIII was born at Greenwich on 28 June 1491, the second son of Henry VII and Elizabeth of York (II.11-12). For his first ten years he was brought up quietly with his sisters Margaret (II.17) and Mary (III.9), much of the time in the vicinity of Greenwich, until the death of his elder brother Arthur in 1502 brought him to prominence as heir apparent. On 22 April 1509 Henry VII, who had held his shaky throne by guile and widespread intimidation, died. For the young Henry, who seems never to have been close to his father, his accession was the opportunity to achieve his dreams of greatness; for his subjects, including Thomas More, it seemed the beginning of a new age (II.21).

In the first two sections we try to put both Greenwich and its new master on the map. Greenwich was strategically sited on the southern bank of the Thames: it was five miles down stream from London, while directly to the south, beyond the steep rise to Blackheath, lay the London to Dover road. The site was beautiful as well: the palace's official name was 'Placentia' or 'Pleasure' and it was surrounded with excellent hunting and hawking country. But it owed its sudden prominence to the fire in 1512 which devasted the palace of Westminster. The great hall and other buildings round Palace Yard, where the law courts sat and public business was transacted, were untouched, but the King's lodgings were burned out. They were never rebuilt. Instead, for the next twenty years Henry principally based himself at Greenwich. On the rare occasions that his presence was necessary, he came to Westminster by boat; ministers and ambassadors made the return journey to Greenwich more frequently, and messengers and courtiers travelled up and down all the time. All this we trace in Section I, thanks to the panorama of London from Westminster to Greenwich, drawn by Wyngaerde towards the end of Henry VIII's reign (I.1-3).

We first meet the King himself in Section II: The Friars' Church. Here in the church of the palace friary Henry was christened and, on 11 June 1509, married his first wife Catherine of Aragon. The King was as much at a crossroads as his palace. His formal education was good and he knew reforming scholars like Erasmus (II.19-20) and Thomas More. But he was also a sportsman and a jouster who longed to re-enact the warlike deeds of his ancestor Henry V. It is tempting to think of these contrasting traits as new and old; instead they were to remain as complementary aspects of upper-class culture for over a century. The Friars' Church, as their austere pattern of living demanded, would have been very plain. But here the ecclesiastical setting is used to display two important and rather neglected art forms which correspond to the 'old' and 'new' aspects of early sixteenth-century culture: heraldic stained glass and Renaissance portrait sculpture. Both were the work of foreign craftsmen: the glaziers were Flemish and the sculptors Italian. Glazing survived the Reformation; sculpture, more narrowly ecclesiastical in character and directly dependent on contacts with Italy, died.

The most important Italian sculptor was Pietro Torrigiano. He may have been introduced to England by Baldesar Castiglione on his visit in 1506 to receive the Garter on behalf of his master, Duke Guidobaldo of Urbino. The visit shows that cultural exchange between England and Italy was not one-sided. Castiglione brought Raphael's *St George and the Dragon* and perhaps Venetian glass (II.14); he took away not only the Garter for his master but the royal livery chain for himself. And both master and man joined a long stream of Italian princes and nobles who had been proud to wear the livery of the English kings. The first years of Henry VIII enhanced England's chivalric status in Europe still further. In 1513 Henry won a crushing victory against the Scots and a showy one against the French; scarcely less important was the mock war of the jousts. The English Court put on a series of dazzling tournaments, of which the King was the undisputed star. Typical were the jousts of 7 July 1517 which form the subject of Section III. The jousts took place in the tiltyard at Greenwich, which, with its viewing galleries and flanking octagonal towers, had been built for such spectacles in 1515. The occasion for the jousts was the presence of many foreign ambassadors at Henry's court, and the audience was suitably appreciative: 'In short', the papal nuncio concluded his letter about the jousts, 'the wealth and civilization of the world are here; and those who call the English barbarians appear to me to render themselves such. I here perceive very elegant manners, extreme decorum, and very great politeness; and amongst other things there is this most invincible King.' (*CSP Ven* II (1509-19), p.400) The letter, addressed to Isabella d'Este, marchioness of Mantua, shows why (apart from the fun of the thing) such money and effort was lavished on these ephemera.

The context of international relations is also important. Henry VIII had come to the throne determined to renew the Hundred Years War against France, and he had married Catherine of Aragon (V.46) as much to gain Spain as an ally as to get a wife. But the Spanish alliance proved unreliable and in 1514 England and France made a separate peace. The situation was destabilized once more by the accession of the ambitious Francis I of France in 1515 (V.32), and the coming of Charles of Burgundy into his vast inheritance of Spain and the Empire (V.1). In terms of these two conglomerations of power Henry VIII was outclassed: France was three times the size of England and Wales (177,000 square miles against 55,000) and had over five times the population (15 million against 2.75 million) and with Charles V's empire the disproportion was even greater. Yet Henry VIII managed a sort of equality. In his 1523 speech Cromwell referred to Henry, Francis and Charles as the 'three governors of Christendom'; Francis Bacon, more sonorously, called them 'that triumvirate of kings'. How was the bluff, for bluff it was, effected? The answer lies in gesture: by behaving and spending like a great power Henry was accepted as one. For this purpose peace, provided it was grandiose enough, could be as effective as war (and was far cheaper). In 1518 and 1527 England and France signed the treaties of London and Westminster. Essentially, the treaties were bilateral arrangements between the two countries. But they were also broadened, at least in intention, into pan-European security pacts. They were given appropriately grandiose names: in 1518, the Universal and Perpetual Peace; in 1527, the Eternal Peace. And they were followed by unprecedentedly lavish celebrations: the Field of Cloth of Gold in 1520 and the Greenwich reception of 1527. Section IV briefly presents the Cloth of Gold in its proper context as an extended joust; Section V documents the Greenwich reception in detail.

The reception was held in two specially-constructed 'houses' - the one a banqueting house, the other a disguising house or theatre - which were added at either end of the tiltyard gallery at Greenwich. The houses were plain shells of buildings, designed to take a theatrical interior decor of hangings and painted and modelled sets and flats. In 1527 the most spectacular effects were devised by the King's astronomer, Nicolaus Kratzer and executed by Hans Holbein as his first English commission (V.10-18) In this setting appropriate gifts - armour, miniatures, and the Orders of the Garter and the St Michael (Section VI) were exchanged. As in 1517, international reaction was very favourable and the Venetian envoy was particularly struck 'with the order, regularity and silence' observed by the spectators, 'never having witnessed the like anywhere [else]' (*CSP Ven*, IV (1527-33), p.59). But that was about the only specifically English contribution to the spectacle: otherwise the craftsmen and artists who had created it were German, with a handful of Italians, while the conception of the theatre and even the details of its decoration were copied from the reception given to the English embassy at the Bastille in 1518. Indeed in these years England became almost a cultural colony of France. The way was led by Henry, who slavishly imitated his rival Francis I of France in changing the place of the royal signature on autograph letters and in displaying the royal arms encircled with the Garter collar rather than the Garter itself (V.35). Henry's cook came from France; so did the fashion for beards and the style of most of the clothes that he and his Queens wore. He even wrote his love letters to Anne Boleyn, herself brought up in two French-speaking courts, in French. But perhaps the most important borrowing was the institution of the post of gentleman of the Privy Chamber in 1518. The post was a direct imitation of Francis I's *gentilshommes de la chambre,* several of whom had come with the French embassy to London. Thereafter, holders of the two posts were frequently exchanged as ambassadors and provided a channel of cultural interchange between the two countries (VII.25).

Finally, in the last three sections we move to the interior of the palace and internal politics. Section VII deals with the christening procession of Elizabeth, daughter of Henry VIII and Anne Boleyn on 10 September 1533, and shows how the event represented a family triumph for the Boleyns and their Howard cousins. In Section VIII we see how a royal progress took new ideas in religion and culture from the centre to the localities; while Section IX shows that New Year's Day (1538 is the one we have chosen) bound the King and his Court in mutual exchange of gifts - largely of gold. The presentation of gifts took place in the presence chamber, the most formal of the royal apartments, where stood the elite guard of gentlemen pensioners (Section X). Beyond the presence chamber was the privy chamber. This was the first of the privy lodgings and here only the gentlemen of the Privy Chamber and the members of the Privy Council were permitted to enter. At the heart of the royal lodgings was the bedchamber (Section XI). Here in January 1540 took place the most humiliating of the 'sundry troubles of mind which had happened to him by marriages' - Henry's failure to consummate his marriage with Anne of Cleves.

The King's marital saga had now become a European byword. Breaking his first marriage to Catherine of Aragon led directly to the Reformation, of which Anne Boleyn, Henry's second wife, was both the symbol and the patroness (VII.3-13). But she failed to produce a son and was swept aside in favour of Jane Seymour. Jane gave Henry his longed-for heir but died immediately afterwards. This left the way clear for Thomas Cromwell (IX.3), Henry's minister, to try to cement his hold on power by marrying the King to a German princess. The Germans had begun the Reformation (which Cromwell strongly favoured) and they were Europe's most skilled metalworkers and instrument-makers. But their women and female fashions were regarded as outlandishly ugly. Hence the debacle of the Cleves marriage which also destroyed Cromwell.

Cromwell was a man of wide culture, who shared his table and conversation with Holbein, the King's painter, Kratzer, the royal astronomer, Butts, the King's physician (XI.4), and goldsmiths, merchants and educated courtiers. If anything, Henry's interests were even wider: the privy lodgings were hung with pictures and maps, and drawings and plans were heaped in cupboards, alongside scientific instruments and sporting equipment. In part, this was another form of magnificence (combined with a magpie acquisitiveness which was more peculiar to Henry). But there were important long-term consequences. Henry's fascination with maps and patronage of their makers led directly to the great Elizabethan enterprise of mapping England county by county (the first country for which this was done); his technical interest in guns and determination that they should be made in England laid the foundations of a munitions industry that rendered England a net exporter of ordnance by the end of the century; his requirement that his ships should be big and heavily armed determined the future lines of English naval architecture, while the number of his ships led to the creation of a Navy Board, giving England, unlike her rivals, the rudiments of a permanent naval administration (Section XII). Elizabethan England, in short, did no more than hatch a few of the eggs that Henry VIII had laid. This is true even in literature. In 1532 the first complete *Works* of Geoffrey Chaucer was printed. The Preface, written by Sir Brian Tuke, advanced a bold claim for English as a great European language, and for Chaucer as its supreme poet. Tuke wrote these words as he 'was tarrying for the tide at Greewich' (IX.6). It was a tide which was to take England from a European to a world destiny. Now, five hundred years after Henry VIII, we are - save for our language - back where we started: a little country in a corner of Europe.

I Greenwich and the River

GREENWICH was at the crossroads between England and Europe. To the north, the river Thames provided rapid communication between the palace and the capital. To the south, on the other side of the park, the Dover road passed by Shooter's Hill. All Henry VIII's journeys to the continent, whether for war or peace, began here. From east and west, England's trade passed on the Thames and in front of the windows of the Greenwich library (below, p. 155). Finally, to the west of Greenwich was Deptford, the base for Henry's expanded and remodelled navy.

Early Tudor London
BY ROSEMARY WEINSTEIN

The 'long view' or panorama of London attributed to Anthonis van den Wyngaerde, an Antwerp artist, is famous as the earliest detailed topographical study of London. Dated on internal evidence to 1539-44,[1] the panorama comprises fourteen pen-and-ink sketches, which appear to have been done on the spot - probably in Southwark - and bring the City vividly to life. The panorama stretches from Westminster, the seat of royal administration, to Greenwich, the main royal palace for the first twenty years of Henry VIII's reign, and centres on the river Thames, the principal means of transport. Some two decades previously, Henry VIII's cousin, the young earl of Devon, was attending on the King at Greenwich as one of his gentlemen of the Privy Chamber. His accounts for 1519 survive and detail his journeys up and down the river from his apartments at Greenwich[2]. We will follow him against the backdrop of Wyngaerde's panorama.

Most people travelled on the river in one of the innumerable wherries or 'pair-oared row boats', which plied for hire from the river stairs or landing stages. These were to be found at every substantial property as well as by most streets giving on to the river. The wherries were

pleasant craft, seating two side by side, with cushions and awnings.[3] But Devon hired a boat privately, naming a few individual boatmen such as William Griffiths, William Yerde and William Turks.

About a mile to the west of Greenwich, the earl of Devon would have passed the ships being built in the bend of the river at the King's newly established (1513) dockyard at Deptford. Deptford was also the base for the mariners known in the medieval period as the Guild or Brotherhood of the Most Glorious Trinity and of St Clement. Granted a charter in 1514, and known as Trinity House since 1547, the mariners controlled pilotage up the Thames to London Bridge and charted the dangerous waters at the mouth of the river. Further west again on the port side lay the Cluniac abbey of Bermondsey, dominating the countryside with its huge estates scattered throughout the county. At the dissolution the abbey was bought by Sir Thomas Pope (XI.26). Pope started to convert the abbey into a mansion house in 1543, the cloister becoming the main courtyard. To starboard, the great loop of the Isle of Dogs fell behind as the earl approached the dark red gravel shore of Ratcliffe [Redcliffe] to dine with Lord Darcy. All the way along the river, from here to London, were signs of a growing maritime industry: Limehouse with its ships, wharves and limekilns, past the mills at Wapping and the gibbet for hanging pirates and sea rovers at low water. Here at Wapping the King's ships were refitted and provisioned. A mile on again, closer to London, the earl passed St Katharine's, with its church, hospital and surrounding houses, its mills and dock. Protected by the patronage of successive queens, St Katharine's avoided closure at the dissolution and remained independent until it was obliterated by the dock of that name in 1825. St Katharine's marked the beginning on the eastern side of the ring of religious liberties - protected and privileged places - around London. Now, white in the sun, loomed the huge bulk of the Tower, dominating London on the eastern side. South of the Tower Wyngaerde shows the open quayside with cannon and cranes flanking Traitor's Gate, the chief riverside entrance. The earl of Devon himself probably passed through it following his arrest for treason in 1538.

From the Tower the earl of Devon was rowed towards London Bridge, past a mile of wharves, where merchants from Antwerp, Hamburg, Bordeaux, Venice and the exotic Levant

View of London (circa AD 1550) by Antony Van den Wyngaerde.

unloaded their metalware, pitch and timber, pottery and glassware, wines, spices, carpets and silk. England's cloth trade was flourishing and merchants filled their holds with woollen cloth, and to a lesser extent, tin, corn, coal and salt. These quays and moorings which stretched from the Tower to Baynard's Castle were known as the Port of London. Here, at the Custom House, Billingsgate and Botolph Wharf (next to Lion Quay where the earl alighted), and with Queenhithe to the west of the bridge, barges and ships could be unloaded. Wyngaerde shows two large vessels anchored at Billingsgate. Larger vessels needed deeper water and moored out in the river, discharging their cargoes into small boats and lighters for bringing cargoes ashore. Ships grew ever larger and more numerous, so moorings extended eastwards downstream. Billingsgate also seems to have been accessible to non-commercial traffic. From here Cardinal Wolsey embarked for his customary Sunday visit to the Court at Greenwich,[4] after alighting upstream at Three Cranes Stairs to avoid the perils of shooting the rapids under London Bridge, regarded as especially dangerous at the 'half ebb'. The earl alighted at Lion Quay (so named after a former owner) in the shadow of London Bridge, on which houses stretched from end to end. The 'church of considerable size' on the bridge, singled out by an impressed Italian visitor Andreas Franciscius in 1497, was in fact the tall chapel dedicated to St Thomas Becket, the much venerated martyr saint.[5] Here, however, Wyngaerde records a sign of the changing times: the dedication to Becket has been altered to that of St Thomas the Apostle, by the King's command.[6] A boat trip over to Southwark cost the earl 1d, and must have been preferable to attempting to cross London Bridge, thick with traffic. In Southwark he dined with Charles Brandon, duke of Suffolk, and must have admired the new residence the duke was building for his bride, the King's widowed sister, Mary (III.9). Wyngaerde shows Suffolk Place as a sumptuous new house with its courtyards, turrets, onion domes and terracotta mouldings in the new Renaissance fashion, an amazing addition to what is now Southwark High Street. By 1536 Suffolk Place was in the King's hands, and a mint was established there. A near neighbour, the bishop of Winchester, was also host to the earl in 1519. Wyngaerde records his palace on Bankside, conveniently placed for visits to both City and Court, especially if the incumbent was also the current chancellor,

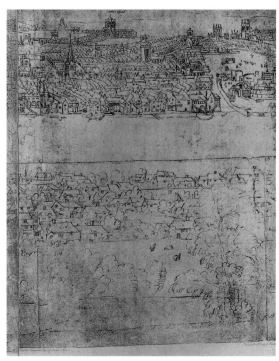

like several of his predecessors. The gabled western wall and great rose window of the bishop's hall, together with the priory church of St Mary Overy ('over the water') - now Southwark Cathedral - are the only surviving structures of this monastic house, although the notoriety of the bishop's prison, the Clink, gave a lasting name to the surrounding liberty and, later, to the district. The hospital, dedicated to St Thomas Becket, had earlier transferred to the east side of the High Street, after a fire in 1212 had destroyed the priory, and developed separately. The care extended to the sick at St Thomas's hospital perhaps offset some of the diseases promoted by the Bankside 'stews', originally public bathhouses licensed by the bishops of Winchester. Early Tudor London was in the grip of syphilis, an unwelcome introduction from the new world, and Henry VII closed the 'stews' in 1506. Soon reopening, they flourished for another forty years until Henry VIII issued another such proclamation.

The view from Bankside was the best in London, and the rooftop of a building there was taken by Wyngaerde as his vantage point. From St Mary Overy the earl was rowed on to Cardinal Wolsey's house, York Place, Westminster. Before exploring further upstream, however, we should investigate the activities of the north bank due opposite, where the earl also visited. Boat hire from Greenwich to Paul's Wharf cost the earl 12d. This was the most frequent of all his specified destinations, and was especially convenient for visits to the west end of Cheapside and, of course, to St Paul's itself. The previous year (1518) no doubt saw its use by numerous important visitors, on the occasion of the Universal Peace with France, when Wolsey celebrated mass before Henry VIII.[7] At other times the earl made do with humbler service from one of the cathedral's many priests.

An adjacent landing-place also used by the earl was Broken Wharf, so called from the decayed state of the structure following a forty-year dispute between two former owners. It was known as the duke of Norfolk's from 1477 when it came into the possession of that family, who apparently also owned an adjacent stone building called Bygots House. Recent archaeological excavations at neighbouring Trig Lane[8] reveal that these decayed structures were regularly replaced with new, extended ones, encroaching into the Thames. After 1500 the drawbridge on London Bridge no longer worked, and the largest vessels could not get upstream. From then on

I.1 Facsimile: Panorama of London by Anthonis van den Wyngaerde

This panorama is the first detailed topographical view of London. It was drawn in 1539-44 by the Flemish artist Wyngaerde from a vantage point in Bankside, Southwark. Here the meander of the river gave a view from Westminster in the west to Greenwich in the east to show the two royal palaces that were the twin poles of early sixteenth-century government. Little is known about Wyngaerde; while the panorama, made from fourteen sheets of paper glued together, has now been broken up into its separate sheets for conservation reasons. But this facsimile, made in 1882 by the accurate collotype process, preserves something of the original appearance of the panorama. D.S.

Paper mounted on linen, 680 x 3000
London Topographical Society, 1882

Queenhithe developed as the port for down-river trade. Corn and foreign fish were its main commodities, the corn being stored there in granaries and the fish sold at Old Fish Street market nearby. The waterfront was one of the wealthiest areas in London. Each ward had its own characteristics: wool and fishmongers at Billingsgate and Bridge wards, international trade with the Hanseatic merchants from the Steelyard at Dowgate (VII.15); Vintry the heart of the wine trade, and the corn market at Queenhithe. Coal from Newcastle was unloaded at Sea Coal Lane near the Fleet river and many traders practised along the waterfront, including dyers, coopers and brewers. Indeed, the whole waterfront was akin to an industrial zone.[9] Other waterside landmarks were the Three Cranes in the Vintry, the distinctive timber cranes for unloading wine barrels. Here the earl disembarked to dine with the earl of Worcester, the Lord Chamberlain, at nearby Worcester House.

Henry VII began the transformation of Tudor London with the rebuilding of his house, the so-called Baynard's Castle, on the river between Blackfriars and St Paul's Wharf in 1496-1501. Archaeological excavations in 1972 revealed a large late-medieval building, the south frontage of which had been built about 1500, producing the gloomy though impressive façade shown by Wyngaerde.[10] Journeying onwards towards Westminster, the earl passed the extensive royal building (1515-22) at Bridewell, on the western side of the Fleet. Tantalizingly, Wyngaerde leaves a space here for later inclusion of a detailed sketch. By 1519 the earl would have noticed work on the southern wing leading to the river and its water approach, by means of which building materials were transferred to the middle of the site. Excavations reveal an outer courtyard, built on the eastern side of the inner principal court with its royal apartments. A bridge over the Fleet provided access to this outer courtyard. This was probably the last building phase, between 1519-21, at reduced expenditure.[11] In use as a royal residence for only seven years, Bridewell proved too small and smelly for prolonged royal usage. By 1530 Henry was owner of Wolsey's York Place, as well as Hampton Court, and so royal attention was diverted from the City. Up river from Bridewell the river view broadened out. Here citizens boated for pleasure as in Venice, passing the stately ecclesiastical inns on the north bank, and green meadows on the south as far as Lambeth Palace, chief residence of archbishops of Canterbury. The palace lay conveniently close for the archbishop's attendance at Court across the water at Westminster. Archbishop Morton provided an improved entrance, by way of a traditional (albeit five-storey) gatehouse, built about 1495.

I.2 Panorama of London by Anthonis van den Wyngaerde: sheet (1), Westminster

This sheet shows the Palace of Westminster. After the fire of 1512 the palace ceased to be the King's principal residence but remained the administrative headquarters of royal government. Projecting into the Thames, with the King's beasts on posts, is the landing-stage or stair; behind is Palace Yard, with the conduit-head in the middle and the clock tower to the right. Opposite, in the south-east corner, was Star Chamber, then came the Exchequer, Westminster Hall, where the law courts sat, and, beyond the Hall, the White or Parliament Chamber and the vast bulk of the Abbey. To the far south are the pinnacles of St Stephen's Chapel. D.S.

Pen and chalk on paper, 242 x 435

5/1, Ashmolean Museum, Oxford

HKW III, pp. 286-92

I.3 Panorama of London by Anthonis van den Wyngaerde: sheet (13), Greenwich

This sheet shows Greenwich in the distance, surrounded by largely open country. On the north bank of the Thames is the eastern suburb of the City around St Katharine's, then Wapping, Limehouse and Ratcliffe and the great loop of the Isle of Dogs. On the south bank, Bermondsey, Deptford (invisible because of the curve of the river) and the town and palace of Greenwich. Romance and distance combine to produce a very inaccurate view of the palace: Wyngaerde exaggerates the height of the tiltyard towers, and he turns the projecting waterstair wing of the palace into a gigantic Piranesi-like arch. But at least this highlights the importance of the palace's river access. D.S.

Pen and chalk on paper, 232 x 416

5/13, Ashmolean Museum, Oxford

I.4 Household Accounts of the Earl of Devon, 1519

The household accounts of Henry Courtenay, earl of Devon for the first quarter of 1519 give a vivid picture of both winter court life at Greenwich - with time

spent jousting and throwing snowballs outside, and playing tennis and shuffle-board inside - and the ease of communication to London by river. On one day-trip, for example, the earl went from Greenwich to Westminster and back again, calling at the Savoy, Worcester House, Winchester House and York Place. The earl, Henry VIII's first cousin and a member of both the Privy Chamber and the Council, remained in high favour until his die-hard support for Catherine of Aragon and Princess Mary led to his execution in 1539. The papers of suspect traitors were seized, which is why these accounts have been preserved. D.S.

MS on paper, 320 x 510

E36/218, Public Record Office

LP III i, 152

Detailed description of the Strand waterfront as seen by the earl in 1519 is very difficult since Wyngaerde's view records the new features of the 1530s and 40s, when several of these properties had passed into the hands of the nobility. In recording this stretch of the river, Wyngaerde is less accurate than elsewhere, with some buildings apparently missing, such as Norwich House, (swapped for Suffolk Place by the duke of Suffolk in 1536) and Durham House, home of Edward VI, the Princess Elizabeth and Lady Jane Grey between 1536 and 1553. Quite recognizable, however, are the monastic buildings at Whitefriars, and next, the round Templars' church, the new abode of London's lawyers. The earl then headed for the Savoy, the largest building on the waterfront, and once the grandest private home in England. Burnt down by Wat Tyler's mob in 1381, the Savoy remained semi-derelict for more than a hundred years. Henry VII showed interest in it, leaving money for a hospital. Perhaps the earl's visit was simply to see its chapel, completed in 1517, and one of London's sights. Here he duly received confession on one of his two trips up from Greenwich. The chapel was a 'royal peculiar' and did not face east as normal. Fortunately a rebuilt version of it survives today.

And so to Westminster, the jewel in the crown, except that in 1519 it was probably rather derelict. After the fire of 1512, which burnt out the palace, the main secular building programme was that at Wolsey's York Place, on the east side of King Street by the Thames, which the cardinal had acquired in 1514. To enlarge his new home Wolsey at first purchased 'Scotland', or land to the north, once said to have been owned by Scottish kings; and then in 1519-20 the tenements due south. Here to the south he constructed a long gallery and an orchard. The earl's visits were probably too early in 1519 to witness any of these developments and Wyngaerde leaves this area blank in front of Charing Cross and left of the tall chapel with large windows of St Mary Rouncevall, to the right. Presumably, as with Bridewell, Wyngaerde intended to add here a scaled-down version of his later detailed sketch of the palace of Whitehall, which Henry had built on the site of Wolsey's residence.

The earl had reached the furthest point in his journeys, and in his panoramic view, Wyngaerde recorded the penultimate moments of the great medieval city. Within a few years travellers in the earl's wake would describe the devastated scene. Churches and monuments had been demolished and the vast palace of Whitehall built. Both in building and destruction, Henry VIII did more to change the face of London than any previous monarch.

Greenwich Palace

BY SIMON THURLEY

Greenwich Palace was one of the English crown's principal residences throughout the Tudor and early Stuart period. It was Henry VII's third most visited palace after Westminster and Richmond, and during the first part of Henry VIII's reign it became the most frequently visited palace in the land. After the construction of the palace of Whitehall in the 1530s its popularity was partially superseded, but Greenwich remained the most popular country retreat under the Tudors and a favourite of the early Stuart queens.

Excavation has shown that the earliest house on the site begun by Humphrey, duke of Gloucester, and subsequently extended by the Yorkists, was almost completely demolished by Henry VII,[1] who built the new front towards the river[2] and the courtyard ranges behind it. The earliest reference in the king's Chamber accounts is in February 1498[3] and it subsequently becomes clear that work was underway on a major new scheme. In November 1502 there is a part payment (not the first) to the king's mason, Robert Vertue, for executing the work on a new 'plat' (or plan) of the queen's design.[4] Payments totalling more than £1,330 over the next six years include references to the garden walls, the new orchard, the gallery, the privy kitchen and the tower. It seems that works were complete by the end of 1504 as payments that year indicate that the house was being painted.[5]

Evidence about the river range, which contained the royal lodgings, comes from the accounts of the 1530s and so cannot give more than an outline of the building of Henry VII's time. The lodgings along the waterfront were ranged between the chapel in the east[6] and the privy

Figure 1: The river front of Greenwich Palace, by an unknown early 17th-century painter. (The National Trust)

I.5 'My Lord Goes by Water to Greenwich', Illustration from George Cavendish's Life of Cardinal Wolsey

George Cavendish's *Life* of his old master, long despised by scholars as 'the classic example of history as it appears to a gentleman-usher', is now valued as a uniquely well-informed account of the geographical and material realities of power. Central to these was the separation between Wolsey, who lived at York Place, next to the administrative seat of government in the palace of Westminster, and Henry VIII, who was based at Greenwich. Most Sundays in term-time, as Cavendish explains, Wolsey came to Court at Greenwich: going by water to the City, riding in state through the City, and then by boat again to Greenwich. The depiction of the scene appears in an illustrated manuscript copy of the *Life*, written by the antiquarian and bibliophile Dr Stephen Batman and initialled and dated 1 September 1578. D.S.

Illustrated MS on paper, 280 x 330
Douce MS 363, Bodleian Library, Oxford; D.N.B.

I.6 Lead Oak Leaf and Lead Tudor Rose, Excavated from Greenwich Palace.

This lead leaf and Tudor rose were found in 1970-1 excavations of Greenwich Palace near the site of the King's privy chamber. In 1535 and again in 1537 the building accounts describe the redecoration of the privy chamber with a ceiling made of a fret of wooden battens, with gilded lead leaves at the intersections. The leaf is probably a survivor from the decorative scheme (below, p. 24). D.S.

Cast lead; leaf 80-100 lgth, 50 wdth; rose 60 lgth, 15 ht
Nottingham University Museum, English Heritage

kitchen in the west.[7] The privy kitchen was connected to the inner court by an entry (passage),[8] which Wyngaerde shows as a single-storey building (Figure 4). East of the privy kitchen was a short length of two-storey building, which ended in a five-storey tower. This tower was the chief feature of the range.[9] Excavation, and a painting now at Kingston Lacy, have made it possible to reconstruct the original appearance of the tower (Figure 1).[10]

Accounts of the 1530s mention the 'long roof from the east end of the chapel unto the King's privy chamber',[11] indicating that the room immediately east of the tower was the King's privy chamber. East of this room was the presence chamber, and a short gallery connected this to the great or watching chamber.[12] A stair connected the watching chamber to the great hall.[13] The position of the hall is known because the seventeenth-century undercroft built beneath it survives beneath the present Queen Anne's Building.[14] This would indicate that the great chamber was, in fact, in the east range of the inner court and that it joined the presence chamber at right angles.[15] There seems to have been a gallery separating the holyday closets at the west end of the chapel from the presence and guard chambers.[16] Details of the Queen's side are not clear.

The great tower or donjon, towards the west end of the river range, probably contained the king's bedroom at first-floor level,[17] while in the turrets were stairs which led up to further rooms at second- and third-floor levels. These rooms were presumably the King's most private chambers, possibly including his library and study.

The style of the new works at Greenwich bears a great affinity to contemporary English courtier houses, like Tattershall Castle (Lincs.)[18] or the bishop of Lincoln's house at Buckden (Cambs.).[19] In both there is a donjon with privy lodgings behind the inner chamber. But the real inspiration are probably the Burgundian ducal palaces like Princenhof and Ghent, to which the reconstructed elevation of the river range can be closely compared. There was, of course,

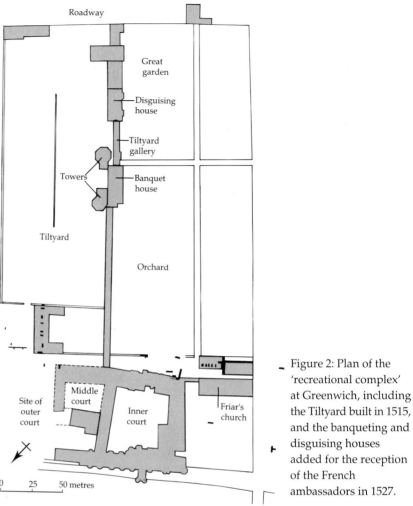

Figure 2: Plan of the 'recreational complex' at Greenwich, including the Tiltyard built in 1515, and the banqueting and disguising houses added for the reception of the French ambassadors in 1527.

nothing new about the donjon in medieval English or French architecture. A keep, or donjon, was a fundamental element of castle design from earliest times and remained an important part of the English castle right through to the fifteenth century, as at Raglan Castle, Gwent, for example.[20] But at Raglan, as in earlier houses, the donjon was separated from the rest of the castle and retained its defensive function. In the Burgundian model, however, developed in an urban context, the donjon is part of a *maison forte*, like the Italian *palazzo*:[21] structurally it is one with the rest of the house. Greenwich was the first royal palace to adopt this non-defensive urban form rather than the traditional moated castellar arrangement.

Henry VIII's accession to the throne did not immediately herald a new age of building. The young King's first works were small-scale compared with his building activities after 1530. There are two distinct groups of additions at Greenwich in the early years. The first group were connected with Henry's recreational requirements; the second with alterations to Henry VII's riverside range. Henry was a great horseman and jouster, and building work was undertaken to facilitate these interests. This included the construction of stables, and a new tiltyard with viewing towers and gallery (below, p. 165). The towers and gallery provided the maximum space for viewing tournaments and could also be utilized for other sorts of entertainment. The most famous of these was in 1527, when Henry twice entertained the French ambassadors at Greenwich, and the complex was extended by the addition of two new halls (below, p. 65).

The remainder of the building work in the early part of the reign was related to Henry VII's river range. First there was a major alteration to the chapel. It is unclear exactly what was undertaken, but the implication is that the chapel was rebuilt in these years.[22] The other addition mentioned in the Chamber accounts is a library (below, p. 155).[23] This is likely to have been in the 'two lodgings there over the gallery into the Thames' which are also mentioned with the chapel.[24] We learn from later accounts that these lodgings, containing a library or closet, were those which protruded over the river on the north side of the donjon.[25] This structure was shown in excavation to post-date the original range.[26] and the way it awkwardly abuts one turret of the donjon (Figures 1 and 3) bears this out.

Few other major additions were undertaken in Henry's reign, but voluminous accounts of the 1530s allow us to undertake a tentative reconstruction of the plan of Henry's house (Figure 3). The King's outward rooms remained much as Henry VII had left them. The King's privy chamber, on the first floor of the donjon, is described in the accounts. It was served by two vice stairs. One, described as the back or privy stair, 'coming forth from the king's privy chamber into the conduit court', was an addition of Henry VIII's.[27] The other stair led down from the privy chamber to the ground-floor gallery, which ran along the north front of the range and the donjon:[28] 'the door at the stair foot coming from the king's privy chamber into the gallery by Mr Norris's chamber door'.[29] Both of these stairs probably also led up to the donjon's upper rooms (Figure 3). Bay windows looked out over the Thames and into the conduit court.[30]

West of the privy chamber, in the 1530s, was the bedchamber.[31] To the north of the King's bedchamber, approached by a short gallery, was the room built over the waterside in 1519; it was called, in the 1530s, St John's chamber.[32] In Henry VIII's Inventory (below, p. 167), it is called the 'closet over the waterstair'.[33] This room was part of the King's secret lodgings and was used to store many personal and valuable items. Above this room was the library, containing, in 1547, 329 books (below, p. 155). Somewhere near these two rooms, was 'the lower study being a bayne'.[34] Between the King's bedchamber and raying chamber, which lay further to the east, was the King's study.[35] Then, a gallery connected the raying chamber with the Queen's chambers.[36] The exact arrangement of these rooms cannot now be deduced, but it seems as if the Queen's chambers must have been in the west range.

In 1534 plasterers were working on the 'stair going forth the said [great] hall into the King's and Queen's chambers',[37] indicating that the Queen's great chamber, like the King's, could be approached from the hall. Between the conduit court and the middle court was an 'entry' and over this was the Queen's great chamber (Figure 3).[38] The rest of the Queen's lodgings seem to have been ranged along the south side of the conduit court, for spiral stairs are mentioned leading down from her rooms into the conduit court on the north, and into the garden on the south.[39]

There are problems connected with the interpretation of the west range of the conduit court. No satisfactory explanation can be given as to why the range tapers to the south, and excavation has failed to provide any clue. One factor which may help to explain the form of the range is the location of the friars' church. The House of Observant Friars at Greenwich was founded by Edward IV, and presumably the church shown by Wyngaerde to the west of the palace was the building erected by them after 1482.[40] When Henry VII levelled the existing buildings on the site, the friars' church remained as the sole fixed point. He may have wished to connect his lodgings to the church by a gallery, as he did at Richmond Palace. This would have necessitated a gallery running from the west corner of the north range to the east end of the church, that is, along the west side of the conduit court. Accounts of 1536 mention just such a gallery.[41] It was shown above that the King's raying chamber led to the Queen's rooms, principally the Queen's bedchamber, which was separated from the King's bedchamber by a short gallery.[42] Beyond the Queen's rooms was a gallery running the whole length of the range to join the western corner of the south range.[43]

This whole arrangement changed in 1543-4. The King had suppressed the friary in 1534,[44] and in 1543 he began to convert the redundant friary church into a new armoury mill, and the garden to its south to a gravelled yard.[45] In the same phase, lodgings were set up for the young Prince Edward. These were 'on the west side ... to the Friars' church ward'[46] - that is, in the west range, but the prince's bedchamber was next to the King's and overlooked the waterside.[47] The King, meanwhile, had a new second bedchamber 'toward the garden',[48] in other words, on the Queen's side.

No view or drawing of the internal decoration of the Tudor palace of Greenwich survives, yet it is possible to visualize something of the palace's interior from the repair accounts and from surviving parallel examples. The accounts relating to the redecoration of the King's privy chamber in early 1537 illustrate the type of internal decoration in the more important rooms. The shell of the privy chamber, and its first decorative scheme, were set up by Henry VII but no information about them survives. The first we learn of it is in 1537, when Richard Ridge, the King's joiner, made battens for its ceiling. Ridge was the man who had undertaken the bulk of the carving on the great hall roof at Hampton Court with its 'antique' (i.e. grotesque) decorations. The new ceiling at Greenwich was to be 'after the antique fashion' as was the 'jowpy' or cornice.[49] Details of the ceiling indicate that it was made up of a geometrical pattern of battens, with gilded balls and leaves at their junctions. Lead leaves found in the excavations confirm this (I.6). The ceiling must have been very like the contemporary ceiling in the holyday closet at Hampton Court. While the new ceiling was being erected the chimney piece was protected by canvas and accounts indicate that over the chimney was a roundel containing a bust.[50] This may have been similar to the roundels supplied to Wolsey at Hampton Court in the 1520s and still set in the gatehouse in Clock Court. Certainly the fact that the roundel was protected would suggest that it predated the 1537 scheme.[51] The floors were matted wall-to-wall, and there was a fitted settle and stools. Other furniture included chests, and at New Year a sideboard to display the King's gifts (below, p. 126). The accounts tell of curtains, and curtain rods, probably for the windows in addition to the shutters.[52]

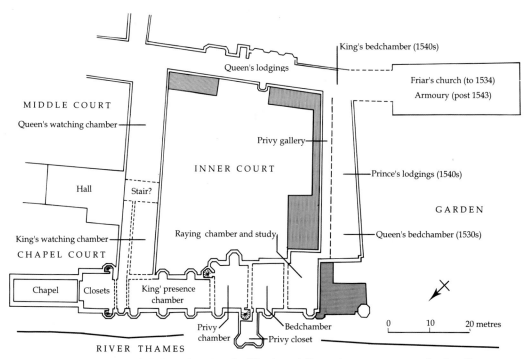

Figure 3: Plan of Greenwich Palace showing the King's and Queen's apartments on the first floor.

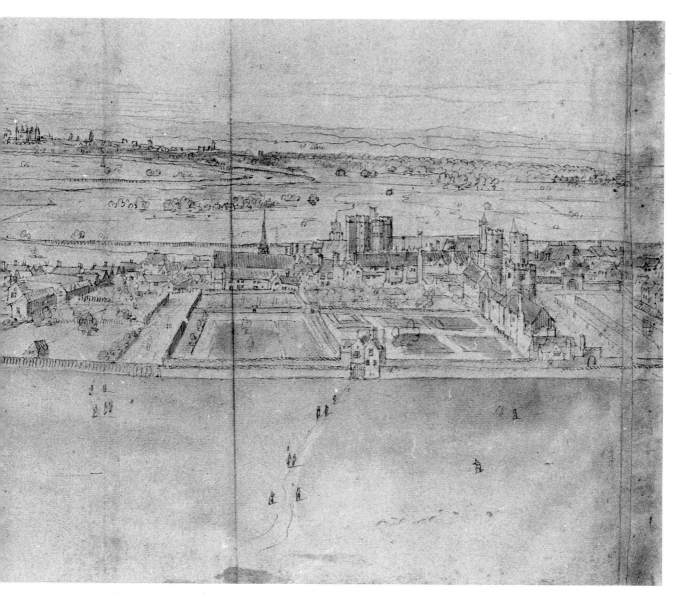

Figure 4: Wyngaerde's view of Greenwich Palace, showing the 'recreational complex'. (Ashmolean Museum)

Under Elizabeth, Greenwich was the most favoured out-of-town palace, although there were no major additions to it. Under James I there began a shift in the use of the building. In 1607-9 new lodgings were built for the queen. These were housed in the two-storey building seen on the garden front in Hollar's engraving. Soon after these new lodgings were completed James assigned Greenwich to his wife for life. This gift led directly to the start of work on a new part of the palace, the building known today as the Queen's House. It was the accession of Charles II which sounded the death-knell of the Tudor palace. He resolved to replace the entire building with a new palace which was to lie on the site of the old between the Queen's House and the Thames. In 1662 work began on the demolition of the Tudor buildings and on the construction of the surviving King Charles block, the only part of his grandiose scheme to be built. The Tudor hall and chapel outlived the Tudor royal lodgings, the hall till 1866 and the chapel until the end of the century, but today only James I's undercroft and a few stones of the palace's service buildings remain.

II The Friars' Church: Christening and Marriage

HENRY VIII WAS BORN at Greenwich Palace on 28 June 1491, and christened in the Church of the Observant Friars there by Richard Fox, later bishop of Winchester. Eighteen years later almost to the day, on 11 June 1509, Henry married Catherine of Aragon in the same church.

The Observant Friary at Greenwich had been founded by Edward IV in 1478, and was part of a pattern by which most of the major royal residences became palace-monasteries: the old palace of Westminster lay next to the great Benedictine Abbey; the newer palaces, like Richmond and Greenwich itself, were linked to the more extreme mendicant Orders fashionable in the later middle ages, in particular the Observant Friars.

Henry spent much of his boyhood in Greenwich or its vicinity, and it was at nearby Eltham that in 1499 he was introduced to Erasmus (II.19-20) by Thomas More. Years later Erasmus recalled the event: 'I was staying at Lord Mountjoy's country house when Thomas More came to see me and took me out with him for a walk as far as the next village, where all the king's children, except Arthur, who was then the eldest son, were being educated. When we came into the hall, the attendants ... were all assembled. In the midst stood Prince Henry, now nine years old, and having already something of royalty in his demeanour in which there was a certain dignity combined with singular courtesy. On his right was Margaret (II.17), about eleven years of age, afterwards married to James, king of Scots; and on his left played Mary, a child of four' (III.9). More, an adept courtier though an avowed hater of courts (II.21), had brought a writing to present to the prince; Erasmus, who had failed so to prepare himself, was covered in embarrassment, the more so when Henry sent 'to challenge something from my pen' while they were at dinner. The result was a poem, dedicated to Henry, in which Britain speaks the praise of Henry VII and his children. Seven years later, Erasmus again wrote to Henry, now prince of Wales, to condole with him on the death of his brother-in-law, Philip of Burgundy. Henry replied with a friendly letter, inviting the great scholar to continue the correspondence.

In other words, Henry, like his father, was well aware of the international prestige value of patronage. Patronizing a scholar, even one as distinguished as Erasmus, was cheap; more serious was the expenditure on building projects, like Henry VII's Chapel at Westminster, his tomb, Henry VIII's own tomb, and finally his palaces and fortifications. In most of these the basic structure was traditional in style and was the work of native craftsmen. But the decorative features were often exotic, in both conception and workmanship. Two principal groups of foreigners were involved: Flemings, who made the glass, and Italians, who fashioned the sculpture. Henry's frequent remarriages, on the one hand, and the desire of his leading subjects to express their loyalty by the use of the royal arms, on the other, made the early sixteenth century 'the great age of English heraldic glass' (II.1-8).

To begin with, prestige projects like Henry VIII's tomb promised an equally notable age of sculpture. Contacts with Italy, both through the papacy and through Italian princelings, who were eager for the Garter, were close and it was to receive the Garter on behalf of the duke of Urbino that Castiglione came to England in 1506 (II.14). He may have brought the sculptor Torrigiano; at all events Torrigiano had arrived by 1511 and was contracted to produce the tombs of Henry VIII's grandmother and his parents (II.11-12). The prominence of portraiture (II.10-11) in his English output suggests that this was one area of Renaissance achievement that the English were well able to grasp. But Torrigiano left England in 1522 and in the 1530s the Reformation cut off direct contact with Italy.

II.11 Henry VII, by Torrigiano (Electrotype), 1512-18

Torrigiano follows the usual portrait-type of Henry VII (cf. II.16), but refashions the features into a model of lofty austerity. The artist worked on the tomb - 'the finest Renaissance tomb north of the Alps' - of the king and his queen Elizabeth of York (II.12) between 1512 and 1518. In the latter year he returned to Italy to recruit more skilled Italian craftsmen, and these probably assisted him in the construction of the elegant altar which stands before the tomb.

The altar was demolished in 1644 and reconstructed in 1932-5. After the deaths of his eldest son, Prince Arthur, in 1502 and his wife the following year, Henry VII exercised a jealous supervision over the upbringing of his younger son, the future Henry VIII, on whom depended the whole future of the Tudor dynasty. D.S.

Electrotype, 864 ht
290, National Portrait Gallery
A. P. Darr, 'The Sculptures of Torrigiano: the Westminster Abbey Tombs', *Connoisseur* 200 (1979), pp. 177-84

Stained Glass in Henry VIII's Palaces

BY HILARY WAYMENT

In the great houses of later medieval and early Renaissance England 'imagery' or figural glass was normally confined to the chapel, while only heraldic pieces were to be seen elsewhere. Unfortunately the records of the period are sporadic, and actual examples of 'imagery' from domestic chapels even rarer. We know, however, that Wolsey, at Hampton Court c.1526-8, in addition to the hundreds of heraldic shields, badges and mottoes with which he filled the windows of the palace, set up in the east window of the chapel a Crucifixion and other Passion scenes, accompanied by his own and his sovereign's figures, together with those of their patron saints.[1] After Wolsey's fall, Henry replaced many of the figures in the chapel, and much of the heraldry throughout the palace, to mark the change of ownership and also his own change of queens; the Commonwealth obliterated everything. However, at Hengrave Hall, Suffolk, built in 1525-40 by the merchant adventurer Sir Thomas Kytson,[2] there survives a glazing scheme which was no doubt typical of many of Henry's own houses. Kytson engaged a local glazier, Robert Wright, to put up shields of arms in the windows of the hall and the internal galleries, while filling the great south-east window of the chapel with twenty-one scenes telling the history of the world from the Creation to the Last Judgment; these were painted apparently in the Troyes region of France about 1525-7.

There are few accounts of royal activity of this kind. At Leeds Castle in 1536 Galyon Hone, the King's glazier, reset twenty-seven feet of 'old glass with image work' in the chapel;[3] and it is probable that the chapels of many of the royal houses had been glazed with figural work before 1532, when James Needham's full accounts of the royal works begin.[4] Before this we have only occasional glimpses of such activity. We know, for instance, that the Savoy Hospital was glazed between 1513 and 1520, by Barnard Flower, Hone's predecessor as King's glazier, and Richard Bonde, with four figural windows, including a Doom or Last Judgment in one window, and in

II.1 Shield of Thomas Cranmer, Archbishop of Canterbury

The shield is enclosed by scrolling foliage with a clasp at each side. The heraldic self-consciousness of the arms shows an unexpected side of Archbishop Cranmer. The original canting (or punning) arms of the Cranmer family were argent a chevron between three cranes azure, but Thomas Cranmer changed the birds to pelicans vulning (wounding) themselves sable, since, as he said prophetically, he was ready to shed his blood for his little ones. He also added the three cinquefoils argent. The quartered coat of Newmarch, argent five fusils in fess gules on each an escallop or derives from his great-grandfather. The crescent gules indicates a second son. Not only the cinquefoils and the escallops but the whole field of the Newmarch quarterings are abraded from the flashed glass. H.W.

English, c.1535
Stained glass, 310 x 250
2311-1900, Victoria and Albert Museum

28

II.2 Garter Shield of George Neville, 5th Baron Abergavenny

Lord Abergavenny had one of the most illustrious Tudor lineages and his arms quarter Neville, Warenne, Clare and Despencer, themselves quartered, and Beauchamp, all within a Garter inscribed with the motto of the Order. In the quarterings of Clare, Despencer and Beauchamp the ruby glass is laboriously abraded to produce argent or (if subsequently stained) or, but in the repair of the first Clare quartering separate pieces of plain and ruby glass are leaded in. The glass was in Horace Walpole's collection at Strawberry Hill. H.W.

English, early 16th cent.

Stained glass, 410 x 330

6917-1860, Victoria and Albert Museum

'Catalogue of the Sale of Horace Walpole's Collection of stained glass... Saturday the 21st day of May, 1842', *Journal of the British Society of Master Glass Painters* 7 (1938), pp.131-2, nos. 47-9

II.3 Garter Shield of a Howard, Duke of Norfolk

The shield quarters Brotherton, Howard, Warenne and Mowbray. It is encircled by the Garter with the motto of the Order, and ensigned with an intruded and inappropriate crown, added after 1920. The shield probably dates from 1520-5, as the late-gothic script suggests, and may belong either to Thomas Howard, 2nd duke, the victor of Flodden, or to his son of the same name, the 3rd duke. The Flodden augmentation in the second quarter, given for killing and defeating James IV of Scotland, is described in the royal award as 'a demi-lion pierced in the mouth by an arrow, depicted in the colours which ... James, late king of Scots, bore.' The ruby glass has been abraded on the back in the Brotherton and Mowbray quarters, but on the front in the Howard quarter. H.W.

English, c.1520-5

Stained glass, 530 x 330

C.798-1920, C.499-1915, Victoria and Albert Museum

another 'the Crucifixion, Mary and John, the King's Arms and the Orate'.[5] Again, we can get some idea of the splendour which might be contributed by continental glaziers in the magnificent figures of Henry VIII, Catherine of Aragon, Margaret Queen of Scots, and their patron saints, which now grace the east window of The Vyne, Hampshire, though they were probably painted, c.1522, for the Chapel of the Holy Ghost in Basingstoke a few miles away. The architectural settings, in the purest Italianate idiom, were probably designed by the young Pieter Coecke under the supervision of Bernard van Orley.[6] The King had passed through Basingstoke during his summer progress in 1516, with his sister Margaret in the company, and both of them may have contributed to the cost of the glass which Lord Sandys commissioned six years later. Equally, the inclusion of their figures may have been no more than a gesture of loyalty.

From Henry's own houses only one figural window survives, namely the Crucifixion, with the figures of the King, his first Queen and their patron saints, which is now in the east window of St Margaret's Church, Westminster; this was probably given by Henry to Waltham Abbey, where there were royal 'lodgings', in the 1520s, and transferred to his palace at New Hall, Boreham, with modifications and additions, after the dissolution of the monastery in 1540. This is the work of Dutch glaziers, who no doubt lived in Southwark or Westminster; the tracery angels added c.1540 are probably Dutch work also.[7] The window was repainted and refired by William Price the Younger in the middle of the eighteenth century, on its transfer from yet another house, Copt Hall, Essex, to Westminster. The early Renaissance style of this unique window is thus overlaid by the baroque, and obfuscated in the process.

Of heraldic glass, by contrast, a great wealth survives from Henry's reign, though not much of it *in situ*. It is doubtful, indeed, whether a single shield of arms, badge, motto or scroll remains in its place in any of his palaces, though a few of his subjects' houses, such as Sutton Place, Surrey,[8] or Ightham Mote in Kent,[9] still retain their original heraldry. Owners of palaces and great houses took a pride in decorating the windows not only of their halls and chapels, but often also of their private rooms, galleries and staircases with their shields of arms and

II.4   Tudor Royal Arms

On a shaped shield encircled by a wreath bearing eight red and two white roses France modern and England quarterly, ensigned by a closed crown of England. The lions and fleurs-de-lis are on separate pieces of white glass painted, stained and leaded in, the fleurs-de-lis being inserted in the blue.
Minor repairs to the second lion in the 3rd quarter, and to the white rose on the right. This fine royal coat of arms came from the house built at Cowick, after the dissolution of the monastery, by John Russell, 1st earl of Bedford (IX.4).   H.W.

English, c.1540
Stained glass, 440 x 360
C.452-1919,Victoria and Albert Museum
C. Woodforde, *English Stained and Painted Glass* (Oxford,1954), p. 33 and pl. 46

II.5   Arms of Henry VIII and Jane Seymour

On a jousting shield France modern and England quarterly impaling quarterly of six 1. Seymour augmentation 2. Seymour 3. Beauchamp of Hache 4. Esturmy 5. MacWilliam 6. Coker, the whole encircled by a green wreath bearing five red and two white roses, and clasped at the foot by a lion mask. The crown (c.1540) above was originally, in all probability, separate from the wreathed medallion. The fleurs-de-lis of France are painted and stained on pale blue glass, and the lions of England abraded out of flashed ruby and then painted and stained. The tinctures of the six Seymour quarterings have been most conscientiously rendered by the same techniques.   H.W.

English, c.1536
Stained glass, 430 x 280
C.455-1919, Victoria and Albert Museum

badges. These would often be set on a background of 'scriptures' or mottoes set diagonally across the window, as at Ockwells Manor, Berkshire (c.1460),[10] or in the restored bay of Wolsey's hall at Christ Church, Oxford (1528).[11] When Henry rebuilt Hunsdon Hall in Essex, c.1525-34, Galyon Hone was paid the large sum of £91 'for divers and sundry windows as well in all the King's new lodgings, gallery and closets, as in all the windows in the ground chambers under the same and with the making of the King's arms, posies, badges and bends set and glased in the said windows'.[12] This is typical of all the houses that Henry built, confiscated or gained by exchange. Moreover he was constantly bringing the heraldry up to date. At Greenwich, as in many other places, Catherine of Aragon's arms and badges were replaced in 1533 by Anne Boleyn's, and Anne's, three years later, by Jane Seymour's.[13] Again, at Rochester in 1540, the year of Henry's marriage to Catherine Howard, arms, badges and 'scriptures' were set up, but in 1542 Catherine's were destroyed. Examples have come down to us, nevertheless, of the shields of all his six queens, including Anne of Cleves.[14] For Henry's subjects loyally set up his arms and badges in their houses, and those of his queens, beside their own.

Henry VIII's reign was indeed the great age of English heraldic glass. Shields of arms were still relatively uncomplicated, and were not yet overloaded by the multiple quarterings which became so popular towards the end of the century.[15] Glaziers still used 'potmetal' (that is, glass through-coloured in the melting pot), which was often handled with astonishing virtuosity. Pieces of one colour would be 'inserted' in the ground of another, as for example painted and stained fleurs-de-lis in an azure field; flashed ruby or blue glass might be abraded to show the white glass below, which was then painted and stained in its turn. If charges were too minute, however, or changes of tincture too frequent, some simplification of form or colour might be introduced, to avoid excessive leading; the enamels which were in general use by the end of the century, and tended to reduce the brilliance of the glass (as at Montacute, for instance)[16] had not yet taken the place of potmetals. The shields themselves sometimes retained the heater shape which was normal in the previous century. More often they were notched in the dexter chief like a jousting shield, or waisted and set between scrollings of alternating colours above and below, or even more capriciously shaped.

Shields and badges might when appropriate carry mottos or initials, be set within a Garter (II.2, 3), or be ensigned with a crown or coronet (II.4, 5, 7). Occasionally they were flanked by supporters. More often than not they would be enclosed within a wreath budded with red or white roses (II.4, 5), or gripped by clasps (II.1) which were decorated with lion masks, dolphins, profile heads, cupids or grotesques half human, half vegetal (II.6): in a word with all the fantasy of the Renaissance. The most striking and elaborate specimens are probably those from Wroxton Abbey, Oxfordshire, which are now in the Philadelphia Museum of Art;[17] but the examples of heraldic stained glass in the present exhibition, whether royal or not, are excellent examples of their kind.

II.6 Shaped Shield with the Badge of Prince Edward, later Edward VI

Party per pale azure and purpure three ostrich feathers argent threading a coronet or and a scroll inscribed 'HIC.DEIN', with the letters 'E' and 'P' on either side at the waist, within a grotesque border round which run bearded men whose bodies end in scrolls. The awkward rendering of the Renaissance motif and the misspelling of the motto *Ich dien* point to a native glazier unable fully to assimilate the continental idiom. This glass also comes from Russell's house at Cowick (II.4). H.W.

English, 1537-47

Stained glass, 410 x 360

C.453-1919, Victoria and Albert Museum

Anne Payne and R. Marks, *British Heraldry*, Exhibition catalogue: British Museum (1978), no. 69 p. 41

II.7   Roundel with the Royal Arms of England

A shaped shield France modern and England quarterly, within a Garter with the motto 'HONI.SOIT.QUE.MAL.Y.PENSE', ensigned with a closed crown of England and supported by a rampant lion crowned and a dragon. The tinctures, whether gules or azure, are rendered in yellow stain, which is also used for the crown, the lion and the decoration of the Garter. The ground at the foot of the roundel is rendered by a wash. The arms are Henry VIII's, c.1540. H.W.

English, c.1540
Glass, painted and stained, 180 dia.
56/6-24/1, British Museum

II.8   Roundel with the Badge of Prince Edward, later Edward VI

Three ostrich feathers passing through a stained open crown of England and threading a twisted scroll inscribed ICH DIEN, all within a stained border c.25 cm wide and rayed like a sun in splendour. The field within the border and the extremities of the scroll and feathers overriding it are covered with a light wash which is picked out with the stick to render highlights. The pearled crosses in the crown are similar to those in the crowns of (II.4, 5). H.W.

English, 1537-47
Glass, paint and brassy stain, 170 dia.
56/6-24/2, British Museum

Torrigiano and Italian Renaissance Sculpture in England

The Florentine sculptor, Pietro Torrigiano (1472-1528), has a double claim to fame: he broke Michelangelo's nose and was also the first Italian to practise the Renaissance style in England. He was involved in three major commissions: the tomb for Lady Margaret Beaufort at Westminster Abbey; the tomb for Henry VII and Elizabeth of York, also at Westminster (II.11, 12), and finally a tomb for Henry VIII himself. Henry VII's monument has been called 'the finest Renaissance tomb north of the Alps'; Henry VIII was determined to outdo it. His tomb was to be of black and white marble, and a quarter larger than his father's. By 1521 the project had inflated to megalomaniac vastness: 142 life-size gilt bronze figures would stand round a triumphal arch crowned by an equestrian statue of the King. A year or so later Torrigiano seems to have left England under a cloud and the project was abandoned. In 1529, Henry VIII took over the incomplete tomb of his fallen minister, Cardinal Wolsey, at Windsor. But work progressed only intermittently and it was still unfinished at Henry's own death. And what had been built was dismantled by the Commonwealth in the mid-seventeenth century. Only the sarcophagus, re-used for Lord Nelson's monument at St Paul's, remains.

As well as his royal commissions, Torrigiano also designed tombs for Dr John Yonge (II.9) and Dean Colet (II.13). All incorporate effigies which are remarkable likenesses. There were sculptures from the life as well, in terracotta or bronze (II.10). The result is a gallery of realistic portraits before Holbein. And the two traditions connect in Holbein's brilliant drawing of Torrigiano's bust of Colet.

II.9 Tomb of Dr John Yonge (1467-1516), probably by Torrigiano and Assistants

Dr John Yonge, the master of the Rolls, may have come into contact with Torrigiano, then in Brussels, on diplomatic missions in 1508 and 1511. Yonge's will prescribes the place of his burial in the Rolls Chapel and that a tomb was to be erected over his remains. Though the chubby winged seraphim are of poorer quality than the rest, the head of Christ and the figure of Yonge are sufficiently close to Torrigiano's documented work to be by his hand. In concept, however, the tomb is unlike anything else by him that survives. It is fashioned in the pure Florentine style and consists of a wall sarcophagus of stone, recessed under a round-headed arch. There are no English precedents for this type of tomb; similarly, there is even less of the gothic in the terracotta figure of Yonge than in the effigies of Henry VII and Elizabeth of York (II.11, 12). Torrigiano's altar for Henry VII's chapel at Westminster (begun 1517; destroyed in the 1640s) was also in this Florentine Renaissance style. E.C.

Pietro Torrigiano and assistants, attrib., c.1516
Marble and terracotta, painted and gilded
Public Record Office
A. Higgins, 'On the work of Florentine Sculptors in England in the early part of the sixteenth century ...', *Archaeological Journal* 56 (1894), pp. 150-52; A. P. Darr, 'Pietro Torrigiano and his Sculptures for the Henry VII Chapel, Westminster Abbey' (New York University Ph. D. thesis, 1980), pp. 422-3

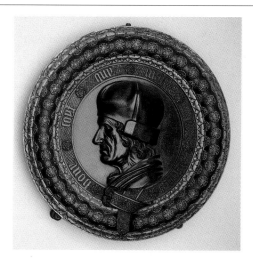

II.10 Roundel of Sir Thomas Lovell (c.1450-1524)

Sir Thomas Lovell, a shrewd professional lawyer, early threw in his lot with Henry VII and became, as treasurer of the Household and knight of the Garter, one of his most intimate servants. Henry VIII's accession in 1509 only reinforced his position. In 1516

there were tensions with Wolsey, but he did not resign the treasurership till 1522 (when he was at least seventy). He died two years later. Formerly above the entrance archway of the gatehouse to Lovell's estate at East Harling, Norfolk, the relief portrait is in bronze with a very high (English-style) copper content. It is framed by a wooden roundel with Tudor roses and a bronze Garter with the motto in gothic lettering similar to that on Torrigiano's medal of Federico da Montefeltro. The attribution to Torrigiano is based purely on style, especially similarities with the Henry VII effigy and bust. E.C.

Pietro Torrigiano, attrib., c.1516
Bronze, 673 dia.
Cloister Museum, Westminster Abbey.
T. A. Cook, 'The Bronze Medallion in Henry VII's Chapel in Westminster', *Monthly Review* (August 1903), pp. 89-97; Darr, op. cit., p. 424 and works cited on p. 447

II.11 Henry VII, by Torrigiano (Electrotype), 1512-18: See page 27

II.12 Elizabeth of York (1466-1503), by Torrigiano (Electrotype), 1512-18

Torrigiano could have modelled this posthumous image either on Queen Elizabeth's funeral effigy, the head of which still survives at Westminster, or on the painted portrait type which Holbein followed in the privy chamber mural. Henry Tudor promised to marry Elizabeth, eldest daughter of Edward IV, while still in exile in Brittany. But he delayed fulfilling his promise until after his own coronation as king. This was to make clear that he held the crown in his own right, not that of his wife. There is an affecting report of Henry and Elizabeth's grief after the death of their eldest son Prince Arthur in 1502, and their mutually comforting each other. Elizabeth herself died the following year. Her privy purse expenses for 1502-3 show that her nephew, the future earl of Devon (above, p.14), was brought up at her expense. D.S.

Electrotype, 864 ht
291, National Portrait Gallery

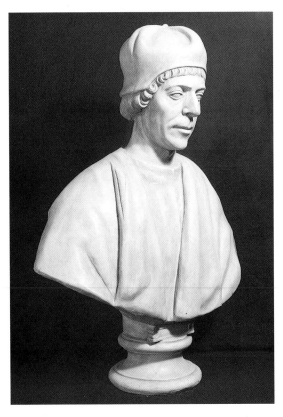

II.13 John Colet (?1466-1519), by Torrigiano

Son of a wealthy mercer and twice mayor of London, Colet went to Oxford, then studied in Italy and returned to give a revolutionary series of lectures at Oxford on Paul's Epistles. As dean of St Paul's he was an outspoken critic of both clerical abuses and Henry VIII's warmongering. In 1509 he established St Paul's School as a lay foundation, where boys were to learn good religion in good Latin. He built himself a simple tomb in St Paul's, but after his death in 1518 his own 'little monument' was replaced by an elaborate tomb, with a portrait bust by Torrigiano set in a shell niche. The tomb was lost in the Great Fire, but an old cast of the head, from which this cast in turn is taken, survived at St Paul's School. Holbein also executed a posthumous portrait drawing, based on the bust, perhaps for Thomas More. D.S.

Plaster cast, 838 ht
4823, National Portrait Gallery
F. Grossmann, 'Holbein, Torrigiano and the Portraits of Dean Colet', *Journal of the Warburg and Courtauld Institutes* 13 (1950), pp. 202-36

Italian Influence

In general, the Italian influence ran strong in these early years of the sixteenth century: many Englishmen, like Colet (II.13) studied in Italy and relations with both the papacy and Italian princely courts were close. The manuscript (II.15) is a souvenir of study in Italy; (II.14) may be a gift brought by Castiglione on his mission to England in 1506.

II.14   Lattimo Vase of Henry VII

Made of opaque-white glass (lattimo) and decorated in two stages with fired gold-leaf and enamel colours. The production of lattimo was unique to Venice in this period but, as this form is neither Venetian nor, indeed, Italian, it was probably a special order and intended for north-west Europe, where painted pottery versions ('galley-ware') were highly fashionable in the late fifteenth century, especially in the Netherlands and in England. Furthermore, the two roundels on this vase depict Henry VII (wearing the 'closed' crown) and his personal badge (the portcullis and chains in a 'glory'). The vase may therefore have been part of the gift brought by Castiglione to London in 1506 when he came to receive the Order of the Garter as proxy for his master the duke of Urbino. H.T.

Venice, c.1500

Glass, 198 ht

1979.41.1, British Museum

H. Tait, *The Golden Age of Venetian Glass* (1979), pp. 95, 120-22

II.15   Pandolfo Collenuccio, Apologues; Lucian, Dialogues

The finest Italian illuminated manuscript surviving from Henry VIII's library was commissioned as a gift to him by one Geoffrey Chamber, who ordered it while travelling in Italy. It was apparently made between 1509 and 1517. The volume contains two fashionable satirical works: one by Lucian himself, the other by a fifteenth-century imitator. The scribe has been identified as the great Ludovico degli Arrighi, author of the first and finest published writing book, *La Operina* (Rome, 1522), and the illuminator as Attavante degli Attavanti, the most fashionable Florentine bookpainter of the day. J.M.B.

Illuminated MS on vellum, 205 x 135

Royal MS 12 C VIII, British Library

Mark Evans, 'Pandolfo Collenuccio, *Apologues;* Lucian, *Dialogues*',

in Thomas Kren, ed., *Renaissance Painting in*

Manuscripts: Treasures from the British Library (New York, 1984),

pp. 132-5

Henry VIII: Family, Upbringing and Accession

Henry, Henry VII's second son, was brought up with his sisters apart from his elder brother Arthur, prince of Wales. He received the sort of wide education advocated by theorists like Castiglione and Elyot (Figure 10), in which academic skills were combined with gentlemanly attainments, such as music and jousting. This made Henry equally at home with Erasmus and More (II.19-21) or Lord Berners, Froissart's translator (II.23). The 'two cultures' in the young prince fused in his determination to usher in a Golden Age, when, not yet eighteen, he succeeded his father on 22 April 1509.

II.16 Henry VII (1457-1509)

This later Tudor portrait-type of Henry VII is derived from Holbein's posthumous representation of the king in the Whitehall privy chamber painting.
It supplies pose, and almost every detail of dress and jewellery. All portrait-types of the king agree on his long, finely-featured face and his hair, also worn long (II.11). But the air of languour is peculiar to the images derived from Hobein. No doubt Holbein was prepared to sacrifice accurate characterization of Henry VII for the sake of contrast with the vibrantly powerful image of Henry VIII. D.S.

Unknown artist, later 16th cent.
Oil on panel, 610 x 510
BHC2762, National Maritime Museum
Strong, *NPG* I, p. 151

II.17 Book of Hours, inscribed by Henry VII and Margaret Tudor

This Book of Hours, written and illuminated in Flanders for the English market, was given by Henry VII to his eldest daughter Margaret, who married James IV of Scotland in 1503. The king inscribed the volume in two places. The longer of the two messages reads: 'Pray for your loving father that gave you this book and I give you at all times God's blessing and mine. Henry R.' The use of prayer books as family autograph albums was common enough; Henry VII's obsessive piety was more unusual. No similar evidence survives about the king's relationship with his son, the future Henry VIII. D.S.

Illuminated MS on vellum, 205 x 140

Chatsworth Collection

Treasures from Chatsworth, Exhibition catalogue (1979-80), no. 132

II.18 Drawing of Henry VIII as an Infant

The portrait comes from a collection of fifty-one drawings in red and black chalk. According to Rouard this manuscript could be 'a direct and contemporary' copy of a fuller original. The original, dating from 1515-24, was an album of mottoes, sayings and lampoons which Francis I dictated to Catherine de Boisy, wife of Artus de Boisy, Great Master of France. The portrait, inscribed 'Roy Henry Dangleterre', shows a young child (probably about three or four years old), wearing a cap with a feather. The artist is unknown. Rouard speculates that the original could have been brought to France by Mary Tudor, sister of Henry VIII, when she married Louis XII of France in 1514. X.L.

Chalks on paper, 284 x 191

Res. MS 20, Albanes 442 olim 967, Bibliothèque de Méjanes, Aix-en-Provence

Rouard, *François 1er chez Mme de Boisy* (Paris, 1863)

II.19 Erasmus (?1469-1536), after Holbein

This is an old copy of the portrait of Erasmus, painted in 1523, and almost certainly sent to Archbishop Warham (VII.2). With the furred robe and elaborate pilaster, the portrait represents Erasmus as the prince of scholars and correspondent of princes. The friendship between artist and sitter established by this painting opened the way to Holbein's English visits. Erasmus himself had first visited England in 1499, when, in company with Thomas More, he met the young Prince Henry at Eltham, near Greenwich; he returned in 1506, and again in 1509, after the accession of Henry VIII seemed to offer a land of milk and honey. The promise did not materialize and Erasmus spent 1511-14 at Cambridge instead. But Erasmus's friendship with More endured and he long professed admiration (from a distance) for Henry VIII's Court. D.S.

Artist unknown, after Holbein

Oil on panel, 753 x 533

J. Chichester Constable

Rowlands, no.13

II.20 Medal of Erasmus, by Quentin Matsys

The medal is dated and inscribed (in Greek) 'His writings give a better picture', and (in Latin) 'His portrait taken from the life'. On the reverse is Erasmus's 'Terminus' device, with the inscription 'I yield to none'. Erasmus's friendship with More expressed itself in a joint fondness for Lucian's satires. Erasmus wrote the *Encomium Morae*, which is a punning title meaning 'The Praise of Folly (or More)',

in More's house in 1509; while More's *Utopia* (1516) is a more sober reply. Both works dealt with the relationship between learning and the real world, especially politics - with which Erasmus, unlike More, successfully avoided contact. D.S.

Lead, 105 dia

4613-1858, Victoria and Albert Museum

More: NPG, no. 87

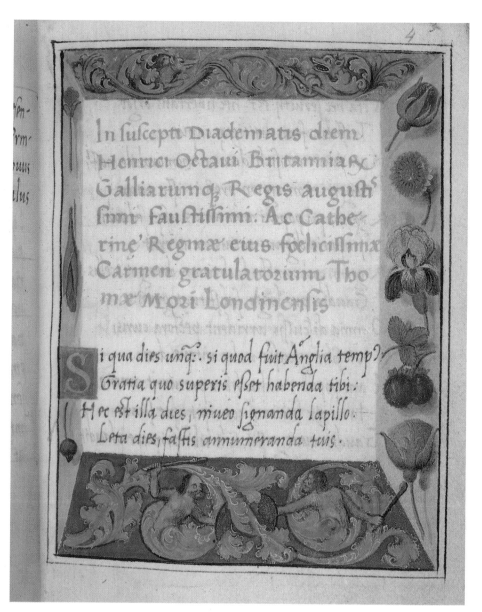

II.21 Presentation Copy of More's Epigrams on the Coronation of Henry VIII, c.1509

Thomas More composed a substantial body of Latin verse, among which are five poems, written in ecstatic style, to celebrate the coronation of Henry VIII and Catherine of Aragon on 24 June 1509. This modest copy of the poems, which the author apparently commissioned for presentation to the royal couple,

is written out in an elegant italic script and decorated in the undistinguished Flemish style current in English Court circles. Ornament in the manuscript incorporates the Tudor rose, the pomegranate of Granada, the fleur-de-lis and the portcullis badge. J.M.B.

Illuminated MS on vellum, 170 x 265

Cotton MS Titus D IV, British Library

More: NPG, no. 37

II.22 Pilgrim's Bottle

Made of buff earthenware, with a mottled green glaze, the two circular sides are decorated with stamped ornament in relief. On one side, the arms of England over a Tudor rose within the Garter, with a crown and dragon and greyhound supporters, the whole enclosed in a square formed by four sections of the inscription: DNE SALVVM FAC REGEM REGINAM ET REGNUM (God save the king, queen and kingdom). On the other side, four circular applied medallions: a heart and the legend, LEAL (loyal); the sacred monogram, 'IHS'; two rosettes or daisies, one very

damaged. The inscription and arms could apply to either Henry VIII (before c.1525) or Henry VII; the daisy was the badge of both Henry VII's mother, Lady Margaret Beaufort, and his daughter, Margaret Tudor. The bottle, purchased by the British Museum in 1856, was stated to have been dug up in London in its present damaged condition. H.T.

English or perhaps northern French, c.1500-1550
Glazed earthenware, 152 ht, 170 dia. with loops
56.7-1.1596, British Museum
Bernard Rackham, 'Early Tudor Pottery', *Transactions of the English Ceramic Circle* 2 (1938), p. 18, pl. Va.

II.23 John Bourchier, Lord Berners (1467-1533)

Lord Berners represents the other, chivalric side of Henrician culture. After a distinguished career as a soldier, he became deputy or governor of Calais in 1520. There he spent much of his time making translations from French into English: the first volume of Froissart's *Chronicle* was published in 1523, with a preface linking it to the renewal of war with France that year; then followed the romance *Huon of Bordeaux*, *The Castle of Love*, done at the request of Elizabeth, wife of Sir Nicholas Carew (V.6), and *The Golden Book of Marcus Aurelius*. The last was a 'mirror for princes'; the others glorified war and courtly love. They were deeply disapproved of by Erasmus and More, but, despite Henry VIII's appetite for learning, appealed to both King and Court. D.S.

Unknown Flemish artist, 1520-26
Oil on panel, 495 x 394
4953, National Portrait Gallery; *DNB*

III The Tiltyard: the Jousts of July 1517

ON 7 JULY 1517 Henry VIII held a great joust at Greenwich for the 'solace' of the ambassadors at his Court. One of the ambassadors, the papal nuncio, gave an account of the scene. The jousts were held in the newly built 'tiltyard made expressly for such exhibitions ... enclosed with a wall and having stands for the spectators'. First to enter was Sir Edward Guildford, the master of the Armouries. He acted as marshal of the jousts and was attended by twenty-four trumpeters. Then came forty mounted spears, with gold chains of 'H' and 'K' and silver horse-trappings 'on which were chiseled all the royal emblems'. Next entered the King, at the head of the band of fourteen challengers, and the duke of Suffolk with the same number of answerers. Pressure of time forced the number of courses run by each knight to be limited to six. Henry and Suffolk ran against each other like 'Hector and Achilles'; while Hall reports Guildford as reckoning that 506 spears were broken in all (III.6). The jousts were also notable for a solo performance by Sir Nicholas Carew (V.6) After the jousts, in which he had taken part as one of the King's aides, were over, he re-emerged and a huge lance 'nine inches in diameter and twelve feet in length was brought in by three men and placed in his lance rest with three forked poles'. Carew then carried 'the great burden' three-quarters of the length of the lists 'to the extreme admiration and astonishment of everybody'. It was a case of practice makes perfect, for there was a 'place of the King in Greenwich that Mr Carew keepeth for a tilt to run at and for a shed to arm in'.

These jousts, and there were many other such, were a piece of martial theatre, calculated to impress an international audience and evidently succeeding. The nuncio knew that the tiltyard had been purpose-built. Work had started in 1515 and the same year Henry had organized the 'Almain armoury', also at Greenwich, which henceforward made almost all his armour (below, p. 42). Within a few years its reputation was international too, and in 1527 the King offered the visiting French ambassador a suit like his own, 'which are said to be the safest and the easiest that are made'.

But the entertainment of 1517 was not over. After Carew had concluded his stunt, another procession formed up and rode round the lists to the palace, where the King gave a splendid banquet. The nuncio commented on the vast cupboard, loaded with gold and silver gilt plate, none of which was touched during the meal (below, p. 131); he also noted appreciatively that 'each man paired with a lady' and the seating plan showing the arrangement has survived (III.5). The seating plan performed a delicate diplomatic balancing act between the Empire, whose chief ambassador was seated next to Henry's sister Mary, and France, whose ambassador was placed next to the duchess of Norfolk. Henry VIII had come to the throne determined to renew the Hundred Years War with France. But the international scene had changed greatly since the days of England's greatness under Edward III and Henry V. France was newly consolidated, as was Spain. And Spain was linked by marriage to Burgundy and the Habsburgs. Henry VII had tied England to Spain with the marriage of Prince Arthur to Catherine of Aragon and Henry VIII had reaffirmed the tie when, as one of his first acts as King, he married his brother's widow. But when Henry actually invaded France in 1513, Spain and the Habsburgs proved unreliable allies. England reacted by making a separate peace with France. Things were destabilized once more by first, the accession of the expansionist Francis I of France in 1515, and second, the coming of Charles of Burgundy into his inheritance of Spain. Francis decided to help Charles make good his claim, hoping no doubt to embroil him in a Spanish civil war; Henry also offered help and cash, trusting to make Charles a counterbalance to Francis. Such were the thoughts going through the diners' heads in 1517.

III.7 Challenge for Taking a Castle at Greenwich, Christmas 1524

This is the challenge for the Christmas entertainment at Court in 1524. A captain and fifteen gentlemen offered to defend Castle Loyal and its four attendant ladies against all comers in four forms of combat (the choice to be indicated by touching the appropriate shield): the tilt (on horseback with lances); the tourney (on horseback with swords); the barriers (on foot with swords) and a general assault on the castle. The King threw himself into the game, and the castle, 20 feet square and 50 feet high, was built in the tiltyard, according to the King's device. 'But the carpenters were so dull that they understood not his intent and wrought all thing contrary.' The assault was therefore abandoned and replaced with a simple tournament. The sketches show (from left to right) the challenge, the tourney and the barriers. D.S.

Elizabethan copy
MS on paper, 385 x 265
MS M 6, fos. 57v-58, College of Arms
E. Hall, [*The Chronicle*] (1550), fo.133v

Henry VIII and the Founding of the Greenwich Armouries

BY KAREN WATTS

When Henry VIII came to the throne in 1509, there were no native English armourers skilled enough to produce the fine quality armours which he and his Court required. For a king so passionately fond of the tournament and so interested in armour design, this was not something to be tolerated long.

It is true that there had been an Armourers' Company in London since the early fourteenth century but no piece of their production has been identified,[1] and it seems evident that they were unable to make either the quality or quantity required. From the late middle ages, therefore, those Englishmen wealthy enough to afford it sent abroad for their armour. The best continental centres were patronized: Flanders, northern Italy, especially Milan, and southern Germany, especially Augsburg and Nuremberg. These overseas suppliers created a difficulty; a suit of armour, like a suit of clothes, is best made to measure. As Henry VIII and his Court could hardly cross the Channel, let alone the Alps, to be measured, they were obliged instead to send their doublets and hose as a guide to shape and size.

The way forward had already been indicated by the Emperor Maximilian I, who had established a court workshop at Innsbruck in 1504 with Conrad Seusenhofer as his master armourer. In 1511 Henry VIII commissioned two armours from Seusenhofer; at the same time Seusenhofer began work on another magnificent armour for Henry, which was to be a gift from the Emperor Maximilian. Not altogether coincidentally, perhaps, it was in the same year of 1511 that Henry VIII first set about employing his own Court armourers. They were brought from Milan and Brussels.

The two Milanese armourers, Filipo de Grampis and Giovanni Angelo de Littis, were put under contract in March 1511. They agreed to work for the King for two years, together with three other craftsmen of their choice whose names are not known. In return, they were to be paid their expenses and a combined salary of £80.[2] They seem to have been based in Southwark, like many of the émigré craftsman community. Of the armourers from Brussels only the names of Peter Fevees and Jacob (alias Copyn) de Watte are recorded. A forge was set up for them in Greenwich and sums of money were laid out to equip their workshop.[3] Despite their close ties to the King, however, these craftsmen were not liveried members of the royal Household, that is, his servants. Instead, they were more independent: they invoiced the King for materials and work, and were free to work for anyone they pleased. Beyond these bare facts, little is known about these craftsmen or their backgrounds. Hardly anything more is known about the work they did for the King or others, and none of their work can be identified with certainty.

At more or less the same time, Henry VIII received a gift from the Emperor Maximilian I of a 'bard' or armour for a horse, known as the 'Burgundian Bard' (III.1).[4] This gift probably influenced the King in his subsequent choice of craftsmen. Two were involved. The bard was made by an armourer whose mark was an 'M' surmounted by a crescent. This has been identified as the mark of the armourer Martin van Royne.[5] He was probably from the Netherlands and, as the Netherlands were part of the Habsburg domains, he had most likely trained at the Habsburg court. The bard was decorated by a specialist etcher and gilder called Paul van Vrelant of Brussels. Henry must have liked the workmanship on the bard, for he soon brought over both craftsmen to work for him.

First was Vrelant. In February 1514, an indenture was drawn up between Sir Edward Guildford, the master of the Armouries, and Sir John Daunce, the treasurer of War, and 'Paule

III.1 The 'Burgundian Bard'

Known as the 'Burgundian Bard', this horse armour was probably a gift from the Emperor Maximilian I to Henry VIII on the occasion of his marriage to Catherine of Aragon in 1509. It is described in an English inventory of 1519 as 'given by the Emperor'. The bard is embossed with a trailing design of pomegranates, the badge of Catherine, and the fire-steels and raguly crosses of the Burgundian Order of the Golden Fleece, which Henry had received in 1505. The crupper (rear defence) is stamped with the armourer's mark: a letter 'M' surmounted by a crescent. This is now thought to be the mark of Martin van Royne, who later became the first master armourer of the royal workshops at Greenwich. The whole armour was engraved and gilded by Paul van Vrelant, who is first recorded working in Brussels for Philip the Fair, son of Maximilian I. By 1514 he was working for Henry. On 7 July 1517, Vrelant was present at the jousts held at Greenwich, as is shown by an entry in the account of expenses incurred on this occasion by the master of the Revels for 'two long coats of satin for Blewbery [yeoman of the Armoury] and Povll Frelande' at 16d each. K.W.

Flemish, about 1511

Steel embossed, engraved and formerly gilt, 1400 ht, 2540 lgth, 990 w

VI 6-12, Royal Armouries, HM Tower of London

H. Nickel, S.W. Pyhrr, L. Tarassuk, *The Art of Chivalry* (New York, 1982).

Claude Blair, 'The Emperor Maximilian's Gift of Armour to King Henry VIII and the Silvered and Engraved Armour at the Tower of London', *Archeologia* 99 (1965)

van Vrelant of Bruxelles in Braband Harness gilder' in which Vrelant agreed to decorate an armour for the King.[6] Vrelant was paid £40 for the work as well as his expenses for materials. Another surviving example of his work is the decoration of a magnificent armour for man and horse in the Royal Armouries. It is covered with silvered and engraved ornament, originally gilt, and includes scenes from the lives of St George and St Barbara, and the badges and devices of Henry VIII and Catherine of Aragon. The armour appears to be referred to in a tournament held at Greenwich in 1516, so could perhaps date from c.1515. It is not certain who made the suit of armour but Claude Blair suggests that it was produced at Greenwich by Henry's Milanese armourers.[7] The horse-bard, however, was probably made by Martin van Royne as it bears the 'M' surmounted by a crescent mark.

Henry VIII now had craftsmen capable of making and decorating armour to a sufficiently high standard. But these Italians and Flemings worked independently of each other: they were not formed or united in a single workshop under a master armourer and do not therefore seem

III.2 The 'Flemish Bard'

The body of the horse is protected by four elements: a peytral and crupper at the front and rear, with a flanchard at each side. An articulated crinet of shallow lames (small overlapping steel plates) joined by internal leathers and sliding rivets protects the neck and the lames are embossed to simulate vertebrae. Finally, a shaffron protects the head. Each part would be lined to prevent chafing. The whole armour is fairly heavy, about 54lbs (25kg), a weight, however, easily carried by a heavy hunter. The saddle is narrow and the stirrups low to accommodate a straight-legged riding position. The rider would be virtually standing and leaning slightly forwards to use the lance. In the early years of his reign Henry VIII acquired much arms and armour from Flanders to equip himself and his army. K.W.

Probably Flemish, c.1520

Steel, 1400 ht, 2540 lgth, 990 w

VI 21, 66, 79, 83, 90, 91, Royal Armouries, HM Tower of London

to have developed a particular style. In 1515 Henry VIII decided to enlarge his armoury and he formed the royal workshop proper. For this he brought over eleven 'Almains'. This term included Dutch craftsmen as well as Germans and they formed what became known as the 'Almain Armoury' even when, as much later, it was staffed almost entirely by Englishmen. The first master armourer of the new workshop was Martin van Royne.

The establishment of the Almain Armoury may have been triggered by another gift from Maximilian I. In 1511, as we have seen, work had begun on an armour for Henry VIII in the imperial workshops at Innsbruck. Because of financial and other difficulties, the armour was not delivered until 1514. A curious parade helmet is all that survives of it.[8] The rest was sold as scrap iron and silver after Charles I's execution in 1649. It is known from the records, however, that it was almost exactly like an armour made for the young Archduke Charles, the grandson of Maximilian.[9] This armour was decorated with fine etching and wrought silver-gilt, showing purple velvet beneath. The workmanship was evidently superior and may have influenced Henry to import new 'Almain' craftsmen, while still retaining the Flemings and Italians who continued to work individually.

Under Martin van Royne in 1515 were four hammermen, three polishers and one apprentice.[10] Whereas the Italians and Flemings were required to buy their own materials and charge these to the King, the Almains were supplied with their materials. Similarly, whereas the

Italians and Flemings had been free to work for others, the Almains were liveried servants of the King; they were only permitted to work for him and for favoured private individuals who received a warrant for the privilege. Initially, these craftsmen were employed by the royal household at Greenwich. In 1516 they were moved to Southwark, but moved back permanently to Greenwich some time before 1525. The site of the Greenwich workshop was close to the Friars' Church, near the river. The millhouse was repaired in 1519, and in 1543 the church itself (redundant since the dissolution of the friary in 1534) was converted into a new armoury mill (above, pp. 23-4).

The earliest surviving product of the Almain Armoury is an armour for Henry VIII for foot combat.[11] It shows elements that are distinctive of the Greenwich workshops. The rounded visor has a gorget which fits over, rather than under the cuirass. Moreover, the pauldrons (shoulder-defences) are built of equal-width lames connected entirely by internal leathers, rather than to each other by sliding rivets. This was a characteristic of the Greenwich workshop throughout its history. Otherwise, the armour is a remarkable piece of engineering in which each piece locks into the next and each gap (including the entire rump defence of the armour) is filled with specially designed gussets. This is an armour without a chink in it. It was, however, never completed. Certain details such as the edges, and the upstanding haute-pieces whose central rivet hole was never punched through, show this. It is first recorded in 1611, still in the workshops at Greenwich, when it is described as 'Black from the hammer'. Ian Eaves considers that the most likely explanation for its being unfinished is that this armour was the one being made for Henry for his use in the Field of Cloth of Gold. In March 1520 work stopped on the armour because Francis I changed the rules of the foot combat. Hitherto an ordinary war armour had been required with a light closed helmet and certain extra pieces. Francis felt that this requirement was vague and altered it to specify an armour incorporating a tonlet (deep skirt) and a great basinet (helmet). It was to the Italians and Flemings that Henry turned hastily to assemble an armour according to the new specifications from old pieces in stock and then decorate it homogeneously (IV.2). It was this second armour that was actually worn at the Field of Cloth of Gold.

At some time between 1521 and 1540 Martin van Royne was replaced as master armourer by Erasmus Kyrkenar. He continued to work at the armouries, being referred to as 'Old Martin'.[12] It was during this period that the magnificent armour known as the 'Genouilhac (or Turenne) Armour' was produced, as well as the large garniture-armour of Henry VIII (V.7). Kyrkenar himself had joined the staff in 1517, only two years after the inception of the workshops. He quickly became Royne's leading hammerman, before finally displacing him.

Henry's death in 1547 could easily have marked the end of the royal workshops at Greenwich.

III.3 The 'Brandon' Lance (detail)

This jousting lance is made up of four segments of wood and is hollow for most of its length. It is deeply fluted, painted with black, white and red bands, and tipped with a blunt iron head, originally heavily gilt. The attribution to Charles Brandon (III.9) goes back to the late sixteenth century. D.S.

Wood, 4036 lgth, 9 kg
VII 550, Royal Armouries, HM Tower of London

III.4 The 'Henry VIII' Lance (detail)

This jousting lance is made of horizontal wood slats. It is fluted and painted red with gold in the flutes. The gold is patterned in black, with foliage motifs and lattice work. It is one of a pair of decorated lances (the other is VII 551) which are probably to be identifed with the two lances of Henry's listed in the 1660 inventory of the Royal Armouries. D.S.

Wood, 3080 lgth
VII 634, Royal Armouries, HM Tower of London

He was followed by the boy king Edward VI and two queens, Mary and Elizabeth, who had little need for personal armours. However, all the craftsmen had been appointed for life, and so had to be kept on. In fact they continued to be fully employed, making armour for members of the Tudor Court and as diplomatic gifts. The products of the armoury for this period are recorded in the magnificent album of designs made by Jacob Halder, a master craftsman at Greenwich, and preserved in the Victoria and Albert Museum. The royal workshops maintained a high level of craftsmanship even into the seventeenth century, when standards were declining elsewhere. They were finally closed down in about 1649, when Edward Annesley is recorded as the last master workman at Greenwich.[13]

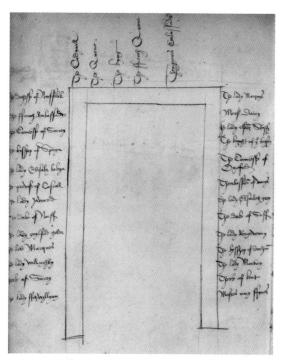

III.5 Seating Plan for the Banquet at Greenwich, 7 July 1517

The tournament was usually followed by evening entertainment. On 7 July 1517 this consisted of a great banquet for which the seating plan for the King's table survives. It takes the form of an inverted 'U'. At the top, from left to right, sit Cardinal Wolsey, the Queen, the King, the King's sister Mary and the Imperial ambassador. The fact that 'each man [was] paired with a lady' was noticed by the Italian Chieregato; he was also struck by the great cupboard of plate for display and not use (p. 131, below). The King's food was all borne in animal confections, and twenty different sorts of jellies, again sculpted into the form of animals and castles, were served. The guests sat at table for seven hours and then danced till dawn. D.S.

MS on paper, 385 x 265
MS M 8, fo. 65v, College of Arms
CSP Ven. III (1509-19), p. 398

III.6 Score Cheque for Greenwich Tournament, 19-20 May 1516

The score cheque for the tournament of May 1516 follows the usual pattern: the challengers ('the home team') are on the left; the answerers ('the away team') on the right. By each name is a parallelogram with strokes. These strokes keep the score, rather as in boxing. A mark on the upper line is a blow to the head; on the lower, to the body; if the stroke bisects the line, the lance has been broken. Strokes outside the parallelogram indicate the number of courses run. The cheques show that many of the jousters were so incompetent that neither of the riders scored a hit. Hence Henry VIII's dissatisfaction with the day's sport (below, p. 47) D.S.

MS on paper, 437 x 307
Tournament cheque 1c, College of Arms

III.7 Challenge for Taking a Castle at Greenwich, Christmas 1524: See page 41

The Early Tudor Tournament

BY STEVEN GUNN

By Henry VIII's time tournaments had been a favourite pastime of the military aristocracies of Europe for more than four centuries, but they had changed a great deal from the barely restrained private warfare of the early days. The clash of armoured knights with couched lances was still their central feature, but combat was now usually one-to-one between contestants who charged towards each other along either side of a barrier. Such jousting was a far more regulated affair than the team contests of the past when it was not always clear, for example, whether it was cheating to reinforce one's side with a small army of archers on foot.[1] Henry's tournaments involved contests other than the joust: foot combats in which knights wore special armour (IV.2) to belabour each other with two-handed swords, pikes or axes, and tourneys in which small teams fought on horseback with swords. But, in early Tudor feats of arms, the jousts were always the centrepiece.

The risks of the tournament lessened over the years, but it remained dangerous, as Henry learned at the age of sixteen in 1508 when the earl of Kent broke an arm while teaching him to joust, and as he was reminded on Shrove Tuesday 1526 when his friend Sir Francis Bryan lost an eye in a tournament in which he was taking part.[2] Henry himself had close escapes in 1524, when he forgot to fasten his visor and got a helmet full of splinters, and in 1536 when he lay unconscious for two hours after a heavy fall from his horse.[3] He gave up jousting after the second accident, as most of his courtiers did in their mid-forties. It was a sport for young men, and one that demanded considerable skill and daring, so much so that one of Henry's courtiers, Sir Nicholas Carew, chose to be remembered as a tournament star by posing for his portrait with a lance (V.6). The jouster's aim was to dismount his opponent - a rare feat - or to shatter the lance on his head or body, and it took strength, co-ordination and able horsemanship. Jousters trained by spearing at the gallop a ring suspended in mid-air, and Henry sometimes turned this running-at-the-ring into a Court occasion with fancy costumes for himself and his companions.[4]

Heralds kept score in the jousts, and some of the cheques they produced have survived (III.6). The scoring system they used is not entirely clear, but it seems that the upper line stood for the opponent's head and the lower line for his body, and a stroke through the line marked a shattered lance while a stroke which did not break the line denoted an 'attaint', or glancing blow.[5] Henry's reputation as a brilliant jouster is generally confirmed by these records, as is that of his great friend and brother-in-law Charles Brandon, duke of Suffolk (III.9); chronicles and score cheques agree that they compared well with the best jousters at the French court, though the nobles of the southern Netherlands who were the great aficionados of the late-medieval chivalrous revival rather showed them both up at the court of the Regent of the Netherlands in 1513.[6]

The cheque for 20 May 1516 at Greenwich is especially intriguing because it explains a frustrated outburst by the King at the end of the day's sport. That day Brandon rode as number two on the King's team, as he had done regularly since 1512, and scored as highly as ever. But Henry was faced with a string of incompetent opponents who failed dismally in their efforts to break lances on him and, worse still, were so wayward that he rarely landed a blow himself. Henry could not bear to be outshone, and 'promised never to joust again except it be with as good a man as himself'; from 1517 until the unnerving accident of 1524, he and Brandon led opposing teams in all the Court jousts, and the two friends' encounter was the highlight of the tournament.[7] Brandon's place as Henry's great counterpart in the lists became so fixed that the surviving lance in the Tower of London (III.3) was assumed by later generations to be his.

Henry's personal participation in the tournament was not unusual for a monarch, and even his dour and cautious father Henry VII had encouraged his courtiers to joust, had judged tournaments and awarded prizes to the winners. But royal involvement as intense as Henry's increased both the splendour and the political significance of jousting. The outfits Henry wore over his armour and even his horse trappings were made of the best materials - cloth of silver and velvet spangled with gold, silver, pearls and precious stones for the Greenwich tournament of July 1517[8] - and his closest companions in the joust wore similar glittering costumes.

Their visual identification with the King stressed the fact that he had chosen them to accompany him, and they were indeed his most favoured and influential courtiers of the moment: Brandon's rise to power at Court can be clearly charted from his place in tournaments and the increasing similarity between his outfits and the King's. The costumes were also often linked to the allegorical framework within which many jousts were set, presenting the jousters as the knights-errant of medieval romantic fiction and the tournament as the response to an heroic challenge like that issued by the defenders of the 'Castle of Loyaltie' at Greenwich in 1524 (III.7).

All this cost a good deal of money, though it was considerably cheaper than the real warfare for which it partially substituted in upholding Henry's martial honour and working off the aggression of his courtiers. But there was a political dividend from this as from all the Tudors' expenditure on magnificence. Large crowds watched Henry joust, and they must have been impressed both by the King's prowess and by the evident wealth, splendour and, by implication, power of the monarchy. The Londoner Edward Hall certainly was, for his *Chronicle,* first printed in 1548, dwelt on Henry's tournaments in awestruck detail and praised Henry and the Tudor dynasty to the skies. Foreign ambassadors were also impressed, and many of Henry's tournaments were specially arranged for diplomatic purposes, like those at Greenwich in 1517 and 1527.[9] Because England's continental rivals shared in the international courtly culture of chivalry, ambassadors themselves might promote goodwill by taking part in celebratory tournaments, as Brandon did at the marriage of Henry's sister Mary to Louis XII of France in 1514 (III.8). The greatest example of tiltyard diplomacy came at the Field of Cloth of Gold in 1520 (VI.l), where more than 150 French and English courtiers including Henry VIII and Francis I jousted, tourneyed and fought on foot on and off for twelve days.[10]

At the Field of Cloth of Gold as on many other occasions, jousts were part of a wide range of revels, including banquets, pageants, plays and masques. The courtiers who danced in the masques were often the same men who had earlier run in the tiltyard, and the King himself was frequently among them. At Greenwich in May 1527 he had to drop out of the tournament because he had hurt his foot playing tennis. However, he joined in the dancing, wearing black velvet slippers on account of his injury, and similar slippers were supplied to the other dancers so that the King would not feel out of place.[11] At times the feats of arms and the frolics became almost indistinguishable, especially with the advent of indoor tournaments: in 1522 a castle containing supposedly imprisoned damsels was stormed by Henry and his friends following a bombardment with dates and oranges.[12] Throughout Europe the future lay with similar less dangerous and more balletic combats. Elizabethan jousts were more allegorically sophisticated than Henry's; but they were further removed from the realities of armoured mounted warfare as it had been practised by the high medieval inventors of the tournament and, occasionally, by Henry's jousting courtiers amid the rising clouds of gunsmoke on the battlefields of France.

III.8 Pageants for Princess Mary's Ceremonial Entry into Paris, 1514

Henry's eighteen-year-old sister Mary made her ceremonial entry into Paris as the bride of Louis XII on 6 November 1514. In accordance with time-honoured tradition, familiar on both sides of the Channel, her processional route into the city, from Porte St Denis to the royal palace, was punctuated by elaborate tableaux symbolizing the new Anglo-French marriage alliance, with heavy emphasis on the allegorical union of the lily and the rose.

The scheme, devised by the court poet Pierre Gringore, is recorded in this unique manuscript, illustrated with seven miniatures in the style current among commercial book painters of Paris in the early sixteenth century. The manuscript may have been intended for presentation to Princess Mary herself. It is, in short, a souvenir programme of an event which Mary (as it turned out) wished only to forget. J.M.B.

Illuminated MS on vellum, 270 x 170 mm

Cotton MS Vespasian B II, British Library

Charles Read Baskervill, ed., *Pierre Gringore's Pageants for the Entry of Mary Tudor into Paris* (Chicago, 1934)

III.9 Portrait of Charles Brandon, Duke of Suffolk, and Mary Tudor

This painting still awaits detailed research. It would appear to be a marriage portrait in which the bride, Henry VIII's younger sister, wears black as widow of Louis XII of France. She also wears some of her magnificent jewels as queen dowager of France. Louis had died on 1 January 1515, having married Mary the previous October. Mary hated her dynastic marriage so much that she virtually commanded Brandon, who had been sent to bring her back to England, to marry her. The price of Henry's agreement included many of the jewels. Mary's prettiness is clear, as is Brandon's resemblance to Henry (though he was six years his senior). It was this similarity of build that enabled Brandon to serve so effectively as Henry's jousting partner and Hector to his Achilles. D.S.

Artist unknown

Oil on panel, 701 x 506

Earl of Yarborough

S. J. Gunn, *Charles Brandon, Duke of Suffolk* (Oxford, 1988)

IV The Field of Cloth of Gold, 1520

ON 20 MAY 1520 Henry VIII left Greenwich and, accompanied by a train of almost six thousand, made his way to Dover. On 30 May he embarked for Calais and the Field of Cloth of Gold.

The Field of Cloth of Gold, the meeting between Henry VIII and Francis I of France in June 1520, became a legend in its own day and has remained one ever since. Like most legends, it is misunderstood. We remember the magnificence, thanks to the resonance of 'cloth of gold'; we forget that 'field' (or *champ* in French) meant tiltyard. The tournament, which lasted (with some intermissions from 11 to 22 June, dominated the seventeen-day event, and the lists, set up in the no-man's-land between the English outpost of Guisnes and the French border town of Ardres, were the only common ground between the two kings; otherwise each lodged in his own territory. The 'Field of Cloth of Gold' painting shows this perfectly. In the foreground is Guisnes, and Henry's fairy-tale temporary palace; in the middle distance is the 'field', with the meeting of the two kings and the lists, and in the background Ardres, where Francis I stayed in his city of golden tents (IV.1).

The tilt was designed and sited (with some variations) according to a 'plat' devised by Henry (below, p. 145-50). It was 900 feet long and 320 feet broad; there were two triumphal arches at the English and French ends; galleries for spectators on either side, and accommodation for the kings to arm and rest. Dominating the field was the Tree of Honour. This was a lavish

artificial confection of a hawthorn (for England) and a raspberry (for France) intertwined, and was hung with the shields of the challengers and answerers. There were also, as usual, three shields by touching which the answerers enrolled for each of the different forms of combat: the jousts, the tourney and the foot combat (III.7). The two kings fought as brothers-in-arms (which spared them the embarrassment of fighting each other), and were assisted by a band of fourteen knights, half English, half French. According to the scores, the two kings did best in the jousts, each breaking six spears in a bout (the maximum score); while Suffolk (out of sorts or from tact) could only manage four. The jousts were followed by two days of tourneys. Here Henry VIII encountered M. de Fleuranges and broke his shoulder plate and disarmed him. The 'Fleuranges' armour (IV.3) was possibly the King's compensatory gift. Finally came the foot combat, in which a last-minute change of the rules, to require the combatants to wear a tonlet or skirt, led to the hasty cobbling together of the 'tonlet' armour for Henry (IV.2).

On 23 June the scene of mock war was transformed: the lists were turned into a chapel; the viewing galleries became the royal pews; Wolsey sang a solemn mass; Richard Pace, Henry VIII's secretary, gave a homily on peace, and the foundation-stone of a chapel, to be called Our Lady of Friendship, was laid. Strength had brought forth sweetness, and, as in the modern Olympics, it was hoped that, through friendly competition in sport, true friendship would grow and peace be nurtured. As with the modern Olympics, reality failed to match. Within a year relations between England and France were hostile and within two they were at war.

IV.1 The Field of Cloth of Gold

This painting, by various hands, is a composite of several events of the Field of Cloth of Gold. Bottom left is Henry VIII's entry into Guisnes. Before the King rides first Garter king-of-arms in his tabard between two serjeants-at-arms carrying maces, and then the marquess of Dorset bearing the sword; alongside Henry is Wolsey; while behind him come the duke of Suffolk (III.9) and the earl of Essex, the latter carrying his baton as marshal of the Kings train. Bottom right is Henry's fantastic temporary palace. This had brick foundations, walls of wood and painted canvas and real glass in the windows. Above centre is the meeting of Henry VIII and Francis I in a tent of cloth of gold (IV.4); above right, the jousts, with the two kings and queens watching, and immediately below the feeding of the gigantic host next to the field oven. Top left, the dragon firework released by the English on 23 June, just before the ceremonial mass, flies across the sky.

Despite the accuracy of some of the details in the painting, the picture dates from at least twenty years after the event: the dress of the yeomen of the Guard, in their red doublets embroidered with the crowned Tudor rose, is mid-Tudor, while the picture seems first to have been recorded in the Royal Collection in 1588-9. D.S.

Artists unknown, c.1545

Oil on canvas, 1689 x 3473

Royal Collection

J. G. Russell, *The Field of Cloth of Gold* (1969)

IV.3 Field Armour

IV.2 Foot Combat Armour of Henry VIII

This armour was almost certainly that worn by Henry at the Field of Cloth of Gold. The French king, Francis I, changed the rules for the foot combat in March 1520, only a few months before the event. The type of armour now required incorporated a tonlet (deep skirt) and a great basinet (helmet). It is likely that the armour was hastily assembled and decorated to be ready in time for the combat in June. The etched decoration includes the Tudor Rose, the Garter and the Garter collar and, on either side of the helmet and shoulder defences, St George and the Virgin and Child. In a foot combat two contestants fought in an enclosure with a variety of weapons which could include spears, swords, axes, daggers or staff-weapons. The contestants had a prescribed number of blows with each weapon (III.7). K.W.

According to a tradition already current in the seventeenth century, this armour belonged to Robert III de la Marck (1491-1537), seigneur de Fleuranges. Fleuranges took an active part in the Field of Cloth of Gold tournament. In one of the tourneys Henry VIII encountered Fleuranges whom he drove back and disarmed, breaking his pauldrons (shoulder defences). This armour shows characteristic features of the royal workshops at Greenwich, seen both in the distinctive rounded pauldrons, composed of lames articulated completely on internal leathers, and also in the stepped sight and concave profile of the visor. Fleuranges's memoirs are the source of some of the best stories about the Field of Cloth of Gold, including Francis bursting into Henry's privy chamber first thing in the morning proclaiming himself the King's prisoner, and, in more aggressive mood, giving Henry a severe fall in an impromptu wrestling bout. K.W.

Italian or Flemish craftsmen working in England, 1520

Steel etched, 1885 ht

II 7, Royal Armouries, HM Tower of London

Claude Blair, 'King Henry VIII's Tonlet Armour', *The Burlington House Fair Catalogue* (1983), pp. 16-20

Greenwich, c.1525

Steel, 1390 ht

G.46, H.57, Musée de l'Armée, Paris

Claude Blair, 'New Light on Four Almain Armours: 1', *Connoisseur* (August 1959), pp. 17-20.

J. P. Reverseau, *Musée de l'Armée: les Armes et la Vie* (Paris, 1982).

R. Goubaux and P-A Lemoisne, eds., *Mémoires du maréchal de Fleuranges*, Société de l'Histoire de France (Paris, 1913)

IV.4 Three Designs for Royal Tents

These three designs for tents were probably made for the Field of Cloth of Gold. One is in the Tudor livery colours of green and white; several tents similar to this appear in the painting of the 1520 meeting. In the most elaborate, coloured crimson and gold, the tent poles are crowned with the 'King's beasts' (lions, dragons, greyhounds, harts and heraldic antelopes);

royal badges appear along the ridge, and the royal mottoes, 'Dieu et mon droit' and 'Semper vivat in eterno', along the eves. The tents, in charge of the serjeant of the Tents, formed a major part of royal pageantry in peace and war. D.S.

Paper, 425 x 950, 460 x 640, 215 x 650

Cotton MS, Augustus III.11, 18, 19, British Library

R. Marks and A. Payne, *British Heraldry* (1978), no. 67

V The Banqueting House: the Reception of 1527

'THE YEAR 1527 saw more diplomatic activity between England and France than ... any other of Henry's reign apart from 1520.' The exchanges of 1527 are less famous than the Field of Cloth of Gold, but their effects were far longer lasting. At a political level they ushered in a decade of Anglo-French entente. This provided the vital diplomatic safety-net for Henry VIII's break with Rome, which was also, necessarily, a break with the long-standing Habsburg alliance. The same went for cultural exchanges. In 1520 the cloth of gold tents and pasteboard palaces had vanished as quickly as the unseasonal dust storms, which, much to the moralists' satisfaction, had enveloped their splendour. In 1527, however, the Court festivities were the seed-bed for much of the later cultural and artistic achievement of the reign: in miniature painting, the portrait, mapping and armour. And all this happened at Greenwich.

At the end of February 1527, a great French embassy came to England. Negotiations - for a treaty of 'eternal peace' to be cemented by a French marriage for the Princess Mary - were difficult but successful. On 5 May, Henry swore to the treaties, and to celebrate laid on one of the greatest but least well-known Renaissance court festivities.

It was held in a specially constructed banqueting house and theatre next to the tiltyard at Greenwich. We know every detail of these buildings (below, p. 65). The project was overseen by Sir Henry Guildford, the master of the Revels (V.4); the elaborate cosmographical ceiling in the theatre was designed by Nicolaus Kratzer, the King's horologer (V.13); the designs were executed by Hans Holbein the Younger (newly arrived in England and receiving his first royal commission - below, pp. 58-60), and the money was found by Sir Henry Wyatt, the treasurer of the Chamber (V.5). The jousts, held next door in the tiltyard, were a triumph for the master of the Horse, Sir Nicholas Carew (V.6).

As well as executing the decorations, which themselves played a major part in raising Henry VIII's 'map-consciousness' (below, pp. 145-50), Holbein painted the portraits of those who had worked with him in realizing the spectacular pageantry. This was the first portrait sequence in England; it also represented something of a change for Holbein himself, for whom portrait painting had not hitherto been very important. Carew of course was painted in Greenwich armour, a suit of which was also offered by Henry to the French ambassador, the vicomte de Turenne.

Shortly afterwards, Wolsey headed an equally lavish return embassy to France. He met Francis I at Amiens, and a fresh set of peace treaties was signed. The documents, as befitting an 'eternal peace', were of unparalleled magnificence, and in the initial letter of the French ratification appeared a new-fangled miniature portrait of Francis. Other French miniatures had been sent to England late the previous year (V.44) and Henry, not to be outdone, had recruited a family firm of illuminators and miniaturists: the shadowy Horenbout dynasty (below, pp. 88-90 and V.45-50).

Finally in November, the two kings exchanged their Orders of the Garter and St Michael, presenting each other with illuminated copies of the statutes of the two Orders (VI.1-12). Culture was important, but chivalry, even in an *annus mirabilis*, had the last word.

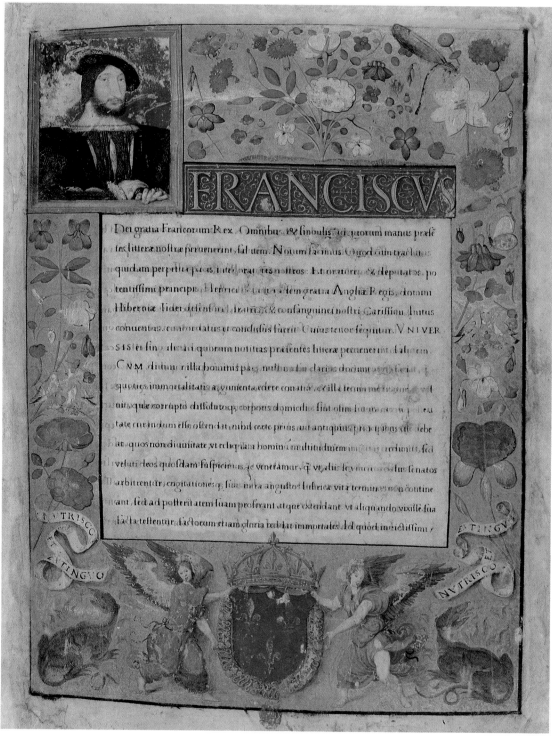

V.32 Confirmation of the Treaty of Amiens, 1527

Like the documents exchanged in August, the final ratification of the treaty of Amiens, sealed with a gold seal and brought to England in October, is richly illuminated - in this case in a polished style, associated with the French court rather than with the more general commercial book trade. The figures supporting Francis's arms link this book with the 1520s Hours Workshop, whose anonymous artists were influenced by Italians and the contemporary Antwerp Mannerists. The difference in quality is so marked that the personal taste of the French king himself was probably responsible. The portrait image of Francis follows a standard type current in 1526-7 and convincingly attributed in origin to Jean Clouet. It appears here as the last in the series of miniatures produced during the treaty negotiations. J.M.B.

Illuminated MS on vellum, 550 x 520

E 30/1109 [*LP* IV ii, 3356/6a], Public Record Office

Myra Orth, 'A French Illuminated Treaty of 1527', *Burlington Magazine* 122 (1980), pp. 125-6

The Political Background to the Diplomatic Revolution of 1527

Despite some dalliance with France, the whole thrust of English foreign policy had been pro-Habsburg - until Charles V's defeat and capture of Francis I of France at the battle of Pavia in 1525 made him too strong. Secret negotiations between England and France in 1525 were followed by the arrival of a major French embassy in spring 1527.

V.1 Charles V and Henry VIII

This double portrait, by an unknown artist, is being exhibited for the first time. To the left, bearing a sword and wearing the collar of the Golden Fleece, is the Emperor Charles V; to the right, with a sceptre and a carcanet or jewelled collar, from which hangs a medallion of St George, is Henry VIII. On the table before them is a document, presumably a treaty, and a globe with a nocturnal coastal scene; above is an elaborate canopy or cloth of estate. The two monarchs met three times: twice in 1520 and again in 1522 when Charles visited England. The picture is probably a composite image of this visit: the 'rich cloth of estate' at Greenwich is noted by Hall; while in their joint entry to London, the emperor and King were presented with two swords in Gracechurch Street, and at the conduit in the Stocks saw a remarkable pageant devised by John Rastell (below, p.146), which showed England as an island surrounded by 'water full of fish, and about it was the elements, the planets and stars'. This surely is the subject of the scene in the globe. The picture does not, however, appear in Henry VIII's Inventory (below, p. 167). D.S.

Artist unknown, 16th century

Oil on panel, 900 x 600; Private collection

E. Hall, [*The Chronicle*] (1550), fos. 95, 97v;

S. Anglo, *Spectacle, Paegentry and Early Tudor Policy* (Oxford, 1969) pp. 193-7

V.2 The Battle of Pavia

In the foreground, the French are gathered under the banner of the fleur-de-lis to the left and the Imperialists under the banner of the double-headed eagle to the right. In the background is the city of Pavia. Francis's defeat and capture at the battle transformed foreign affairs. Henry's first thought was to take advantage of Francis's impotence and seize France; his second (when Charles V showed no interest in Henry's aggrandizement) was to ally with France to counterbalance the overweening power of Charles. Hence the Anglo-French treaties of 1527. But the alliance proved unable to reverse the most important outcome of Pavia, which was imperial hegemony in Italy. And it was this in turn which, by preventing the pope from granting Henry his divorce from Catherine of Aragon, Charles's aunt, led to Henry's break with Rome. D.S.

Artist unknown, German school, c.1530

Oil on panel, 604 x 604

Royal Collection

The Personnel of the Greenwich Reception of 1527

The organizer of the reception for the French ambassadors was Sir Henry Guildford, master of the Revels; the paymaster was Sir Henry Wyatt, treasurer of the Chamber; while Sir Nicholas Carew, master of the Horse, was the leading jouster. All were painted by Holbein. The keeper of Greenwich Palace was William Carey, who died in 1528, leaving his portrait unfinished.

V.3 William Carey

William Carey (c.1500-1528), a distant royal cousin through the Beauforts, became keeper of Greenwich Palace in 1526. A gentleman of the Privy Chamber in 1519, he married Mary Boleyn in 1520 and when Anne replaced her sister as the King's mistress, seemed destined for real greatness. But in 1528 he died of the sweating sickness.

This painting is identified by an Elizabethan copy which includes the sitter's coat of arms. The copy was made after the original had been subjected to over-painting. Instead of a book, the copy shows him holding a pair of gloves and the lower part of the dress becomes Elizabethan. These changes, removed from the present picture when it was cleaned, were made because (as the cleaning also revealed) the original painting had been left unfinished. Finally, the cleaning uncovered an underpainting which resembles Holbein's drawing of 'M. Souch' (VII.10).

This underpainting, and the fact that the date of the sitter's death coincided with Holbein's departure from England at the end of his first visit, must lead to speculation that the painting was his, but despite the sensitive rendering of the face, an unknown French or Flemish artist (though not a Horenbout) cannot be ruled out. D.S.

Artist unknown, 16th cent.

Oil on panel, 790 x 660

Private collection

John Fletcher, 'A Portrait of William Carey and Lord Hunsdon's Long Gallery', *Burlington Magazine* 123 (1981), p. 304

Holbein as Court Painter

BY SUSAN FOISTER

When Hans Holbein the Younger left his adopted city of Basel in the summer of 1526 to try his fortunes in England, the summit of his ambitions must have been to attain the title of 'King's Painter' at the Court of Henry VIII. He probably made a similar attempt two years earlier when he visited France, but it was apparently unsuccessful. In August 1526 Erasmus wrote a letter of recommendation on Holbein's behalf to his friend Sir Thomas More, then busy in the service of Henry VIII as chancellor of the Duchy of Lancaster. In Basel, Erasmus explained, the arts were 'freezing' - the Reformation was encroaching - and Holbein was taking his services elsewhere. Sir Thomas More was not encouraging, but promised to help: 'Your painter', he wrote back in December 1526, 'is a wonderful artist, but I fear he will not find England such fruitful and fertile ground as he had hoped'.

More could hardly have been more in error. Within a couple of months of this letter a 'Master Hans' - undoubtedly Holbein - found himself employed at the Court of Henry VIII on the banqueting house and theatre being built at Greenwich. For this project he produced two spectacular paintings, both now lost along with the building for which they were designed (above, p. 66).

With the months spent on these, the portraits he painted (V.4, 5, 6, 13, VII.2) and the manuscript he illuminated (V.12), Holbein's first two-year visit to England appears to have been exceptionally busy as well as highly paid. Although he returned to Basel in 1528 - to avoid an absence longer than two years which would have meant forfeiting his Basel citizenship - the years 1526-8 marked the start of a long and successful association with the English Court.

The first surviving reference to Holbein as the 'King's Painter' occurs in a letter of 1536 and the first surviving payment of Holbein's salary as a royal painter (£30 a year paid quarterly) occurs in 1538. But earlier sequences of royal accounts are lost, and it is very likely that Holbein was a salaried artist much earlier than this, most probably very soon after his return to England in 1532. He may even have received a salary sometime between 1526 and 1528 - again the relevant accounts are missing - but even if he did not, the fact that 'Master Hans' was the most highly paid artist to work at Greenwich in 1527 clearly demonstrates his value to Henry VIII on his very first visit to England.

Holbein is known above all as a portraitist, especially as the creator of the imposing image of a bulky, overbearing Henry VIII. He certainly did paint portraits on his first visit to England - of Sir Thomas More (V.21), both individually and with his family; of William Warham, archbishop of Canterbury (VII.2); of Sir Henry Guildford, controller of the Royal Household (V.4, 20) who, like the first two, was a correspondent of Erasmus and the man with overall responsibility for the Greenwich revels; of Lady Guildford; and of Nicolaus Kratzer, the King's astronomer and a fellow German (V.13), who was also employed at Greenwich. But before his arrival in England he had painted relatively few portraits, and the work for which he was best known, apart from his woodcuts for Basel printers, was his decorative painting. He had painted the exteriors of houses with elaborate and vertiginous designs: one showed a horse which seemed about to jump over a balcony into the street below. And it was as a decorative painter that Holbein was employed at Greenwich.

Holbein's task was to paint two pictures in key positions in the two chambers of the Greenwich building. For the banqueting house, the centrepiece of the dining room of which was a magnificent gilded triumphal arch, Holbein was required to paint a picture of the *Battle of*

V.4 Sir Henry Guildford

Sir Henry Guildford (c.1489-1532), one of Henry VIII's intimates, became controller of the Household in 1522 and knight of the Garter in 1526. In this portrait he carries the white staff of controller and wears the Garter collar. He was also master of the Revels, and, as deviser of the 1527 Greenwich spectacle, would have worked closely with Holbein. The date 1527 is inscribed on the (repainted) label. Painter and subject were also linked through Erasmus (II.19-20), who was Guildford's correspondent. Guildford's interest in learning, rather unusual so early in the reign for a gentleman, is also suggested by his hat-badge. This is decorated with the instruments of the 'Typus Geometriae' which also appears in Dürer's engraving *Melancolia* . D.S.

Holbein, 1527
Oil on panel, 826 x 664
Royal Collection
Rowlands, no. 25

Thérouanne (*The Battle of the Spurs*), in which the English had defeated the French in 1513. This large painting, on canvas, was applied to the back of the triumphal arch. When the English and French had finished dining they left the room passing under the arch, and as they came through it the King indicated to his guests that they should look back and see Holbein's depiction of their defeat by the English fourteen years earlier. Not surprisingly, they did not find this nearly so amusing as Henry. The party then proceeded to the disguising house or theatre where, while seated ready for their entertainment to begin, they could look up at the canvas ceiling to see a detailed depiction of the heavens, including all the signs of the zodiac and the planets in their 'houses', again painted by Holbein.

Neither of these undoubtedly spectacular paintings survives. Fortunately we are informed about them by contemporaries, both by Edward Hall in his Chronicle and by the Venetian Spinelli. Much more information can be gleaned from the happy survival of nearly all of the payments to those who created the buildings at Greenwich and their splendid decorations. These accounts constitute the most detailed record of any project carried out by Holbein and even tell us precisely what pigments he used to create one of his lost paintings. Holbein evidently worked on the painting of the *Battle of Thérouanne* in a studio away from Greenwich: it was brought down by boat from London by one Lewis Demoron, a 'moulder of paper', on 4 April 1527. Holbein received a single payment for it of £4 10s, a very large sum, but as the commission was 'a bargain in great [gross]' the payment would have covered materials as well as his fee. The painting was a 'plat', or map-like panorama of the battle scene and siege (below, p. 146).

Much more can be deduced about the painted canvas ceiling. A variety of colours were used, which must have been necessary to show the planets in human form in their 'houses', as well as the stars and signs of the zodiac. There was much gilding: all 'the lines, the regiments, the stars and such', as the accounts described them, were gilded. Holbein worked on a similar depiction published in 1529 as a woodcut (V.12), which may even give some hint of what he painted in 1527. The accounts show that he worked in close collaboration with the King's astronomer Nicolaus Kratzer, whose portrait he painted in 1528 (V.13), and with whom he appears to have collaborated on a much smaller astronomical project for the King in 1528 (V.14). Kratzer must have laid down what was to appear in the design and advised Holbein on the proper characteristics of the figures and signs he was to paint.

Both of these great decorative paintings were on canvas. The technique of painting on canvas was well known to Holbein: these were not the only paintings of this type he produced in his career, and such paintings were far more common in northern Europe than their subsequent survival rate would suggest. One unusual feature of the ceiling though is suggested by Hall's description of the zodiac and the other 'girdles' encircling the earth appearing superimposed on it 'by a connyng makyng of another cloth'. Possibly this effect was contrived by suspending a semi-transparent painted cloth over the main ceiling. Work began on 6 February and finished on 4 March. On 11 March Henry VIII paid a visit and saw the 'cloths' hung up. He appears to have been satisfied.

Holbein did not, however, work on what must have been a very large painting alone with Kratzer, and this differentiates this part of his employment at Greenwich from the commission to paint the *Battle of Thérouanne*. It was clearly necessary not only to paint such a large ceiling-painting on the spot but also to have help: the accounts refer to 'Master Hans and his Company'. In this case Holbein's assistants were English painters, rather than the Italians in Henry VIII's employ who worked on the triumphal arch. These English painters were not regular salaried painters, but temporary help engaged at Court whenever such a large decorative project was needed, a pattern reflected in other northern European towns with a nearby court. None was paid much more than 1s a day whereas Holbein was paid at 4s a day, more highly than the Italians. There can be no doubt of his value to Henry VIII as a Court painter, even at this early date.

V.5 Sir Henry Wyatt

Sir Henry Wyatt (d. 1537) was treasurer of the Chamber, 1524-8, and as such paymaster for the 1527 Greenwich festivities. He paid Guildford (V.4) £660 for 'the making of two arches triumphant of antique works, [and] garnishing and trimming of a banquet house'. It is guessed that Holbein painted the original of this portrait, now in the Louvre, in the course of the following year. Wyatt's son, the poet Sir Thomas, was to be the archetype of the gentleman-scholar cum man of action. D.S.

After Holbein, 16th cent.
Oil on panel, 901 x 801
370, National Gallery of Ireland
PRO, E 36/227, fos. 2-3v
Rowlands, no. 29

Henry VIII, like other sixteenth-century European monarchs, needed painters to paint his royal palaces: from simply painting the window frames red to creating elaborate subject paintings and altarpieces. They were also needed to provide banners and heraldry for weddings, funerals and coronations; to paint cloths of honour and royal barges; to design and make stage properties for Court entertainments; to produce designs for the Court goldsmiths to work from; to paint portraits of the royal family as diplomatic presents or as a part of marriage negotiations. Such requirements were as true of Leonardo working for the Sforza court in late fifteenth-century Milan as they were of artists working for the early Tudor Court in London.

One artist might suffice for all of these tasks, with assistance where necessary, as Holbein had done at Greenwich, although painting a portrait required a very different order of skills from the regular run of Court work - say, painting hundreds of coats of arms at short notice. Henry VIII, as his predecessors had done, already employed a kind of painter-in-chief - known as the serjeant painter - who was in charge of all the regular painting work needed at Court. Until 1544 he was invariably an Englishman, and when he needed a large quantity of painting done in a short space of time he would bring in a band of other English painters. They were, like him, members of the London Painter-Stainers Guild, who strongly resented the presence of foreign artists as a threat to their livelihood.

However, Henry VIII, as his reign progressed, employed increasing numbers of foreign painters on a salaried basis to supplement the work of the serjeant painter and his assistants and to supply skills which, evidently, were in short supply among native English painters. The foreign painters seem to have been primarily concerned with the provision of wall-paintings in the royal palaces, and were mostly Italians. One of them, Antonio Toto, became the first foreign serjeant painter in 1544. Some of them, including Toto, also painted pictures. The Netherlandish painter Lucas Horenbout appears to have painted portrait miniatures but none could rival Holbein for the scope and quality of his work, and none could paint portraits with Holbein's dazzling verisimilitude and sophistication.

On his return to London from Basel in 1532 Holbein began to display his versatility as one of the King's painters: he designed a table ornament with Anne Boleyn's badge on it and he was involved in making a cradle for Princess Elizabeth (or another royal baby) with the royal goldsmith Cornelis Hayes, as well as other examples of royal plate (IX.14-17). He painted a large dynastic wall-painting in Whitehall Palace, and the portraits of princesses with whom Henry VIII contemplated marriage in 1538 and 1539.

His portrait group in Whitehall Palace was a spectacular example of his skills in depicting sitters at full-length which had already been seen in 1533 in the the double portrait of the French ambassadors, now in the National Gallery, which did not stay in London. A more permanent memorial to Holbein's compositional abilities - at least until the fire of 1698 which destroyed Whitehall Palace - was his depiction of Henry VIII and Jane Seymour with Henry's parents Henry VII and Elizabeth of York. With four figures standing round a tablet carved with a Latin poem in praise of the Tudors and an elaborate architectural background it must have dominated the room in Whitehall Palace for which it was painted (not necessarily the privy chamber as is often supposed from later descriptions). Certainly the image of Henry VIII Holbein created - which became the standard image of the King, repeated throughout the century - was imposing enough: Holbein's biographer van Mander said it would 'abash and annihilate' those who looked at it.

In order to paint the King's prospective wives - a task brought about by the death of Jane Seymour in 1537 - it was necessary for Holbein to travel abroad to have sittings with all the candidates. In Brussels in March 1538 Holbein had a sitting of three hours to take the portrait of Christina of Denmark. Presumably a drawing was the result and the full-length painting (now in the National Gallery), which Henry kept in his collection despite the failure of the marriage negotiations, was worked up later. We know Henry was delighted with the result, as he was with the portraits of Anne of Cleves taken in 1539, the full-size version (in the Louvre) and the miniature (in the Victoria & Albert Museum - Figure 8) which again Holbein probably worked up from drawings. Portraits of others considered by Henry and recorded by Holbein have not survived.

These are the only paintings we know Holbein executed for the King. The portrait of Prince Edward (in Washington) with Latin verses praising Henry is probably the one recorded as Holbein's gift to the King in the New Year of 1539. Other portraits of Henry and Jane Seymour by Holbein which are closely connected to the likenesses of the wall-painting may have been painted for the King, but we cannot be sure of this. Although so many of Henry VIII's courtiers sat to Holbein it is unlikely that his numerous surviving portraits of them were royal commissions. Both painted portraits and their preparatory drawings have survived, although the drawings far outnumber the paintings, probably because they were acquired by Henry VIII after Holbein's death: they are very likely to have been the 'patterns for physiognomies' owned by his son Edward VI.

These vivid and beautiful portrait drawings and paintings constitute the most remarkable visual record of a Renaissance court to have survived, hinting at the characters of Henry VIII's courtiers, as well as documenting their appearances. Although many of the corresponding paintings are lost, a number of the exquisite drawings in coloured chalks and ink have notes of colours, textures and details such as badges and jewellery which help us to visualize the lost painted portraits (for instance VII.5). Nearly all the drawings are of head and shoulders but this does not mean that the paintings produced from them were invariably limited to this format. Holbein needed only a detailed drawing of the facial features at a sitting to produce a convincing portrait: poses could be invented or modelled by others if necessary, and costumes and jewellery could always be lent to the artist by the sitter.

Holbein seems not merely to have used the drawings for reference, but to have transferred their outlines to the panels he painted on. Using a method similar to modern carbon paper he would have made a sandwich of the drawing, black chalk-covered paper and the panel to be painted, and traced over the outlines by means of a pointed instrument. Once the essential proportions of the face were on the panel, he would sometimes adapt or edit details of the portrait, perhaps according to the desires of the client. Thus the drawing of Sir Henry Guildford (VII.20) shows a fatter face than the final painted portrait (VII.4), which includes details such as the collar of the Order of the Garter, only cursorily indicated in the drawing, and a curtain in the background, which is not in the drawing at all.

The salary of £30 a year which Holbein received from the King was undoubtedly heavily supplemented by these portrait commissions, as well as by payments for designs for goldsmiths' work for private clients. This mixture of independence and royal service is crucial to our understanding of Holbein's position as a Court artist. Lucas Horenbout for instance, who earned slightly more than Holbein, was apparently much more of a personal servant than Holbein ever was. Horenbout was paid monthly with those retainers who attended closely on the King such as musicians and falconers; became an English denizen or national, and lived close to Whitehall Palace. Holbein was paid quarterly; lived at some distance from the Court in the City of London, in the parish of St Andrew Undershaft (conveniently near many goldsmiths), and never became an English citizen. Instead he appears to have maintained a complicated but successful balancing act, hedging his bets in both London and Basel.

On his visit to Basel in 1538, when he was said to be magnificently dressed, and was clearly prospering at Henry's Court, Holbein claimed he would leave England for good within two years. The Town Council - who had been demanding his return for some time - promised to support his family until he was back, but Holbein does not appear to have kept his side of the bargain, preferring the life of a Court painter in London to that of town painter in Basel. He died in London five years later, probably of the plague, leaving two illegitimate children.

V.6 Sir Nicholas Carew

Sir Nicholas Carew (c.1496-1539), 'well-mannered and having the French tongue' and of the King's 'own bringing up' (*LP* Add. I i, 196), was a favourite companion of the Privy Chamber and tiltyard. He succeeded Guildford (V.4) as master of the Horse in 1522 and in 1527 led the four challengers (who also included Sir Anthony Browne VI.9) at the celebratory jousts. Holbein's preparatory drawing survives at Basel, but whether the painting itself is by Holbein is disputed. In favour are three facts: the picture comes from the Lumley collection; dendrochronology dates the panel to c.1528, and finally the armour is a precise depiction of a Greenwich armour of c.1530, including the characteristic feature of the couters (elbow defences) with large removable wings. The painting would have been left unfinished when Holbein left England in the summer of 1528. D.S. K.W.

Holbein, perhaps with assistants, c.1528

Oil on panel, 1140 x 1230

Duke of Buccleuch and Queensberry

J. Fletcher and M. C. Trapper, 'Hans Holbein the Younger at Antwerp and in England, 1526-8', *Apollo* (Feb. 1983), pp. 87- 93

Rowlands, no. R.25

HENRY VIII: A EUROPEAN COURT IN ENGLAND

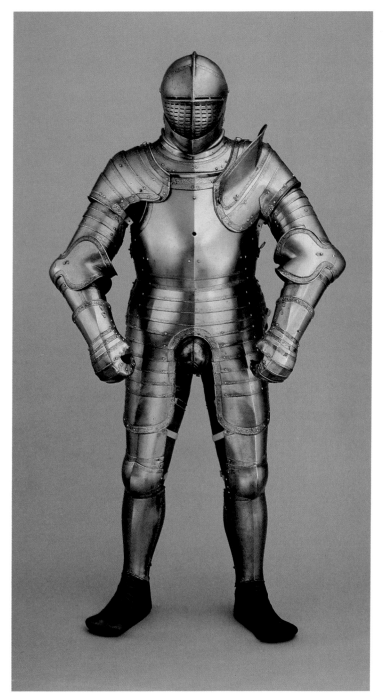

V.7 Tilt Reinforces for an Armour of Henry VIII

These pieces (above) are part of the large armour of Henry VIII (left), called a garniture. These reinforces allow the field armour to be adapted for the tilt. The tilt, one of the combat forms of the tournament, is jousting between individuals over a barrier. The combatants pass left side to left side, couching the lance across the horse's neck with their right hand. The manifer, pasguard and grandguard therefore protect the left hand, arm and upper body respectively, overlapping upwards to deflect the blow of an opponent's lance. The designs for the decorative etched borders are almost certainly by Holbein. K.W.

Greenwich, dated 1540
Steel, etched and gilt borders, 1880 ht
II 8, Royal Armouries, HM Tower of London

The Banqueting and Disguising Houses of 1527

BY SIMON THURLEY

On Sunday, 5 May 1527, after mass in the chapel at Greenwich, Henry VIII signed the treaties with France. Hard bargaining still continued behind the scenes, but Monday, 6 May was devoted to public rejoicing. All day there were jousts in the Greenwich tiltyard; then in the evening there was a banquet, followed by a masque and dancing till dawn. This came early, an Italian observer thought, since the sun had 'greatly hastened his course, having perhaps had a hint from Mercury of so rare a sight'.[1]

The architectural setting in which this lavish evening's entertainment took place was one of the most important created in the first part of Henry's reign. Edward Hall's description allows the architectural shell to be reconstructed: 'The King against that night had caused a banquet house to be made on the one side of the tiltyard at Greenwich of an hundred foot of length and thirty foot breadth ... the windows were all clerestories ... at the one side was a halpace for heralds and minstrels ... at the nether end were two broad arches ... from thence they passed by a long gallery richly hanged to a chamber fair and large, the doors whereof were made of masonry.'[2]

The long gallery, which Hall speaks of, was clearly the tiltyard gallery built in the early part of Henry's reign for viewing jousts in the tiltyard next door. At either end of the gallery lay the two houses of which Hall writes (Figure 2). Wyngaerde's views of Greenwich show this arrangement in some detail, (Figure 4). The northern building, which measured 33.5 x 9 metres (110 x 30 ft), is shown with its high clerestory windows, exactly as in the description. This building was the banqueting house and it abutted the tiltyard gallery which led, at its far end, to the disguising house shown with a windowless west wall with two chimney stacks. A view of the east side of the complex shows that there were windows on that side.

The interiors of these new buildings are minutely recorded in the revels accounts.[3] The descriptions are important because they enable us to visualize, with great precision, the decorations set up for an important international diplomatic event. They were clearly the best the King could afford and some of those involved, Hans Holbein the Younger, Giovanni da Maiano and Nicolaus Kratzer, were figures of international standing. The banqueting house was approached by a gallery from the Queen's apartments in the palace. In itself, it was a fairly unremarkable building, somewhat like the surviving great watching chamber at Hampton Court. Its walls were hung with rich tapestries in the time-honoured way. The top of the tapestries were divided from, and hung beneath, the clerestory windows by a cornice or 'jowpy' decorated with grotesque work. The timber-work of the roof, quickly erected, was concealed by red buckram decorated with roses and pomegranates. The exposed timber members were disguised with gilded lead roses and leaves. The room was lit with gilded iron sconces and candelabra fashioned after the antique.[4]

At the far end of the room, acting as a screen and screens' passage, was a tripartite arched exit with a musicians' gallery above. Although the function of this structure was entirely traditional - it can be closely compared to the screen in the great hall at Hampton Court - its decoration was more elaborate. The King's arms, antique (probably terracotta) busts and illusionistic and decorative painting of 'gargoyles and serpents' and other 'sundry antiques and devices' adorned the structure. Its form has often been compared to the triumphal arches *à l'antique* such as that designed by Holbein for Anne Boleyn's coronation.[5] Yet closer parallels may be the Holbein and King Street gates of Whitehall Palace.[6] The latter structures featured heraldic and antique motifs, busts and highly decorated surfaces on a tripartite archway.

On the reverse of the screen there was a painting executed by Hans Holbein the Younger depicting the Siege of Thérouanne, an inappropriate choice, one might think, for a structure designed to honour the French delegation. What relation this painting of the siege had to the surviving paintings, *The Battle of the Spurs* and *The Meeting of Henry VIII with the Emperor Maximilian* (both compositions based on the same event) is unclear.[7] Beyond the archway the tiltyard gallery led to the disguising house 'ordained to be made for pastime and to do solace to strangers, the preparements of an house called the long house to be furnished of work of pleasure for revels of disguising and masking'.[8]

The room was laid out like an amphitheatre with seats lining three sides of the room in three tiers. The floor area was covered with silk embroidered with gold lilies and had, in the centre, a great arch again decorated with classical busts but also with papier-mâché figures. The ceiling of this room was most magnificent, and was painted to represent the world surrounded by the planets and the twelve signs of the zodiac. The composition was a collaboration between the King's astronomer, Nicolaus Kratzer, and Hans Holbein the Younger who also painted canvases for the back wall of the house. To the modern mind the employment of a painter such as Holbein for an ephemeral decoration seems absurd, but for Henry and for the artist himself it was all in a day's work. Holbein's work was probably replaced within a short space of time as the house was stripped of its decoration and left as a shell waiting for the next state occasion.

Henry used the houses overlooking the tiltyard many times more - the first for a reception for another French embassy which came in the autumn of 1527 to ratify the treaty of Amiens and invest Henry VIII with the Order of St Michael (below, p. 94). The celebrations took place on 10 November: first came the investiture; then a joust, which had to be cut short because of the early dusk, and finally a banquet and a revel. The 'new Banqueting Chamber ... was hanged with a costly verdure [tapestry] all new', with flowers of satin silver on a gold ground; while the disguising house was similarly transformed with a symbolic white marble fountain and two silk trees a hawthorn for England and a mulberry for France. In other words, within a few months the *mise-en-scène* of May 1527 had vanished. The gilded candelabra and sconces, for instance, were taken down and put in a special store;[9] the tapestries, a set of hangings representing the History of David, were taken back to the great wardrobe (V.8). As for Holbein's paintings, we hear nothing more: presumably they were discarded as old scenery. For the houses, more even than most rooms in a Tudor palace, were stages: they remained empty until required and then were dressed with rich fabrics and movable furniture.

After Henry's death Elizabeth kept the banqueting houses in repair and, indeed, built another one in 1559. During 1582-3 more radical works were undertaken to the structure of the building: its walls were rendered and lined out in imitation of ashlar; at the same time the building was propped up with additional timber posts and the existing posts were underpinned.[10] These works underline the temporary nature of the 1527 buildings. Yet, though built almost overnight for a particular occasion they survived, repaired and patched-up, for at least eighty years as settings for Tudor state functions. The ephemeral decorations of 1527 were long forgotten as over and over again the Tudor revels department created new interiors as a backdrop to new celebrations.

The Banqueting House

In the banqueting house, the two features noted by the Italian observer, Spinelli (apart from the usual towering cupboard of plate - below, p. 131), were the 'antique' triumphal arch at the end of the chamber and the walls, which 'were hung with the most costly tapestry in England, representing the history of David'. A recent recalculation of the size of the ten-piece set of the 'rich history of David' in Henry VIII's Inventory by Mr Tom Campbell demonstrates that (contrary to what had been thought) they were of the same size as the 'History of David' tapestries now at the Musée de la Renaissance at Ecouen. Either, therefore, these are Henry's tapestries, or the King owned another set woven from the same cartoons.

Francis Salet, *David et Bethsabée* (Paris, Editions de la Réunion des Musées Nationaux, 1980)

V.8 Photographs: Two Tapestries from the History of David and Bathsheba

The Ark of the Covenant is transported to Jerusalem (2 Samuel VI, 3-23). The first tapestry of the series commences with a representation of the narrator, in this case the author of the Book of Samuel. Like the other figures of the tapestry he is shown in contemporary costume. The main narrative begins in the upper left corner of the principal scene, and shows the Ark, in the form of an elaborate gothic chest, being transported to Jerusalem. It is preceded by David who carries a harp. Uzzah, who incurred the wrath of God by touching the Ark, has just been struck dead. In the foreground the arrival of the Ark at the sacred capital is shown. David, now bareheaded and barefoot, is surrounded by officers who carry the symbols of his office. Above, his first wife Michal looks on disapprovingly. David orders his generals to recommence the campaign against the Ammonites (2 Samuel XI, I) - illustrated. In the second tapestry of the series David is shown at the porch of his palace surrounded by his generals and advisers. Before him stands his chief officer, Joab, with drawn sword. According to the inscription on the first tapestry this scene represents the council at which David ordered his troops to recommence the campaign against the Ammonites, and in the background troops are already departing to lay siege to Rabbah. T.C.

Brussels tapestry series of ten pieces, early 16th cent.
1613-1622, Château d'Ecouen

V.9 Musicians on a Balcony

There are no grounds for the traditional assumption that the musicians' gallery at Whitehall is depicted. Instead, the slit windows and the turret to the left clearly suggest the temporary setting of some Court festivity, like the reception for the French ambassadors at Greenwich in 1527, when we know there was a musicians' gallery over the triumphal arch in the banqueting house. The musicians shown are members of the King's band of shawms and sackbuts, augmented with a straight trumpet with a banner. D.S.

Hans Holbein, attrib.
Ink and wash on paper, 129 x 181
1852-5-19-2, British Museum

The Theatre

On the back of the triumphal arch was a painting of Henry VIII's victory over the French at the siege of Thérouanne in 1513; then the tiltyard gallery, hung with tapestries, linked the banqueting house to a theatre. The feature of the theatre which impressed all observers was the ceiling: a world map over which the stars and the zodiac seemed to soar, 'by a cunning making of another cloth'. This ceiling was devised by the King's astronomer, Nicolaus Kratzer, and was painted, like the siege of Thérouanne, by Hans Holbein. Holbein's precise source for his 'plot of Thérouanne' cannot be traced but its nature is easily guessed at.

V.10 Photograph: Triumphal Arch of Maximilian I

In 1512, Maximilian commissioned Albrecht Dürer to supervise the creation of a set of woodcuts in the form of a decorated arch commemorating his triumphs. Completed in 1515, it was published in 1518. One of the panels shows Henry VIII meeting Maximilian at the siege of Thérouanne in 1513, and is identical in composition to the painting of the same subject at Hampton Court. Holbein may well have known the 'Triumphal Arch': Kratzer was Dürer's correspondent and in 1524 had written to ask him the price of a complete set of his prints. Even the archway format, albeit common in the Renaissance, looks forward to the triumphal arch in the Greenwich festivities. P.B., S.F.

Albrecht Dürer, attrib.; cut by Hieronymus Andrea, 1515

V.11 Photograph: The Battle of the Spurs

The map-like depiction of the siege of Thérouanne in bird's-eye perspective in the background suggests that it is closely related to Holbein's painting of the siege on the triumphal arch at Greenwich. Holbein's painting itself is described as a a 'plot', or pictorial plan, and was probably copied from a 'plot' which had been created shortly after the siege by a Flemish or Italian engineer in Emperor Maximilian's forces. Such 'plots' become increasingly common in northern Europe after 1500 (below, pp. 145-50). P.B.

Unknown artist, c.1530 (?)

Royal Collection

Christopher Lloyd and Simon Thurley, *Henry VIII: Images of a Tudor King* (1990), pp. 48-9, 55, 120, no. 20, 124-6

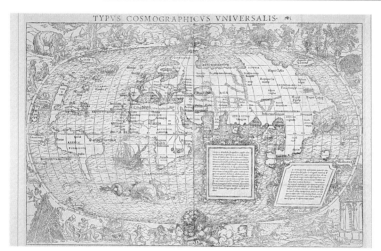

V.12 World Map: 'Typus cosmographicus universalis'

Although traditionally ascribed to Sebastian Munster, with Holbein as draughtsman, rather than to Kratzer, this map reflects the geographical knowledge of the 1520s and bears a striking resemblance to contemporary descriptions of the ceiling painted by Holbein for the festivities at Greenwich in 1527. The chronicler, Edward Hall, described this as showing 'the whole earth environed with the sea, like a very map or cart' - or, in the words of the Venetian ambassador, a 'mappamondo' in which could be read all the names of the principal provinces. It made a startling contrast to decorated ceilings at earlier Court festivities with their generalized geographical or astronomical depictions. This map is also novel in placing the ethnographic scenes around the borders instead of, in medieval style, inside the continents to which they relate. P.B.

Sebastian Munster and Hans Holbein the Younger (?)

Woodcut on paper, 355 x 545

From Johann Huttich and Simon Grynaeus, *Novus Orbis Regionum* (Basel, 1532)

1895-1-22-113, British Museum

Rodney Shirley, *The Mapping of the World: Early Printed World Maps 1472-1700* (1984), pp. 74-5, no. 67

Nicolaus Kratzer: the King's Astronomer and Renaissance Instrument-Maker

BY WILLEM HACKMANN

According to Holbein's portrait of him, Kratzer was born in 1487[1] in Munich, Bavaria, the son of a sawsmith. Although he learnt some of the metalworking skills of his father's trade, his mind turned to scholarship. He matriculated at Cologne in 1506 to read mathematics and astronomy and took his BA in 1509. He next went to the small university town of Wittenberg, where he may well have heard Martin Luther lecturing on scholastic theology. However, Kratzer left before the confrontation between Luther and the Catholic Church came to a head, and for the next few years he disappears from view. Certainly, he was for some time in the Carthusian monastery of Maurbach near Vienna, where he copied a number of astronomical treatises.
He may also have been practising as an instrument-maker.

In January 1517 Peter Giles wrote to his erstwhile teacher Erasmus that the skilled mathematician Kratzer was on his way to England with astrolabes, armillary spheres, and a Greek book.[2] The purpose of this move is shrouded in mystery known only to an anxious Erasmus and his correspondents. Erasmus may have worried about the hostility shown to foreigners in the riots of May Day 1517, which prevented his own return to this country. Kratzer must have had powerful English acquaintances to be accepted so readily by the Court of Henry VIII. By 1519 he was in the King's household, as astronomer and 'deviser of the King's horologes'. Almost nothing is known of his duties at Court. As the King's astronomer he may have been involved in casting judicial horoscopes, a common (if not altogether uncontroversial) practice at that time. He was

V.13 Nicolaus Kratzer

Kratzer is shown making a polyhedral dial, surrounded by tools and other instruments: on the wall behind him hang dividers and ruler; while on the shelf are two types of dial (V.15-18, IX.17, XI.42-3). The paper on the table is inscribed with the date 1528. The original of the picture, now in the Louvre, was probably in the earl of Arundel's collection; this copy has a provenance which takes it back, through Holland House and Sir Walter Cope, to Andreas de Loo in the early seventeenth century. The under-drawing is a careful record in chalk of details present in the finished painting, like shadows in the face and hands. It is quite different from Holbein's own fluent brush drawing and suggests a painter working close to Holbein and direct from the original finished portrait. Holbein and Kratzer struck up a friendship when they co-operated on the Greenwich ceiling in 1527: they collaborated in a royal New Year gift in 1528 (V.14); that year Holbein painted Kratzer, and in 1533, after Holbein's return to England, Kratzer seems to have lent the painter some of the instruments which appear in Kratzer's portrait to create the *mise-en-scène* for *The Ambassadors* (below, p. 73). S.F.

After Holbein, 16th cent.

Oil on panel, 819 x 648

5245, National Portrait Gallery

also employed by the King in other ways. He was sent on a diplomatic mission to the Low Countries in 1520 because of his knowledge of 'high Almain' and the German scene, and in 1529 he surveyed the Cornish tin mines, a chief source of income to the crown. He probably received regular payments from the royal purse between 1519 and 1531 of £5 per quarter, supplemented by a licence to trade in wine and woad.[3]

Supplementing his role at Court were a variety of other employments. In 1521 he was engaged to teach astronomy to the children of Sir Thomas More. More exulted in their good fortune to find such a teacher: 'In the space of a month, and with only a little effort on your part, you will learn so many and such sublime wonders of the Eternal Artificer, which so many men of pre-eminent and almost superhuman intelligence have discovered only with toil and study, not to say with shivering cold and nightly vigils down the ages.'[4]

Kratzer's next move was to Oxford for which Cardinal Wolsey was certainly in part responsible. His status in the university is open to some doubt, not least because of the old collegiate custom of claiming great men as Fellows.[5] On Kratzer's own evidence he lectured on elementary astronomy, the construction of the astrolabe, and the geography of Ptolemy 'at the King's command'.[6] Like his colleague, the Spanish humanist Juan Luis Vives, he was probably one of Wolsey's lecturers who resided at Corpus Christi pending the completion of Cardinal College (now Christ Church).[7]

Kratzer's stay in Oxford was short, probably from 1521 (or 1522) until late October 1524, barely time enough to construct two famous large polyhedral sundials. Although there is some conflicting evidence as to the date, they were probably made in 1523. The one for the University Church of St Mary survived until 1744, the other in the orchard of Corpus Christi College had disappeared by 1710. The only known representation of the former is in Loggan's print in *Oxonia Illustrata* of 1675.[8] This dial consisted of a rectangular prism with its long edges vertical and above this a four-sided rectangular prism surmounted by an orb with a cross, and stood perhaps about five feet above the church's perimeter wall. It achieved some notoriety as Kratzer affixed

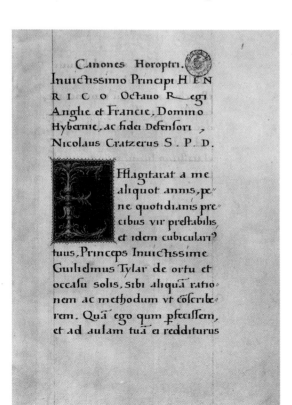

V.14 Nicolaus Kratzer, 'Canones Horoptri'

The text is a set of instructions for the use of an instrument called an 'horoptrum'. Invented by Kratzer, the 'horoptrum' was to be used for finding the times of sunrise and sunset and other key indicators. In the preface, Kratzer explains to Henry VIII how William Tyler 'of your Privy Chamber' had begged him daily for some years to explain these questions in writing. He had now done so, but thought the matter worthy of presentation to the King. Written out by the Flemish scribe, Peter Meghen, and with illuminated capitals by Holbein, it became Kratzer's New Year's gift to the King in 1529. Tyler was also the leading enthusiast for hawking at Court (XI.35). D.S.

Written by Peter Meghen, decorated by Hans Holbein,
1 January 1529
MS on vellum, 280 x 330
Bodley 504, Bodleian Library, Oxford
More: NPG, no. 188

V.15   Wolsey's Portable Polyhedral Sundial

The instrument consists of nine dials on a block of gilt brass. The dials are set to show the equinoctial hours in approximately latitude 51°N - that is, for London and the south of England. The compass is marked with a line of declination with a deviation of about 9° east. This accords reasonably well for the period. On the base of the north and south slopes of the stand are engraved cardinal's hats; on the west face are the arms of Wolsey and on the east, the arms of the archbishopric of York with, unusually for the period, a mitre rather than a crown. Aspects of this instrument, such as the declination of the compass and the inhomogeneity of the brass alloy, indicate authenticity, but the relatively crude workmanship, lack of provenance, and the error in the arms of the cathedral church of York, cast a certain doubt. If genuine, the dial was probably made between 1522, when Kratzer came to Oxford as Wolsey's lecturer, and the cardinal's death in 1530.   W.H.

Probably by Nicolaus Kratzer, 1522-30

Brass gilt, 100 ht, base 48 x 48

246, Museum of the History of Science, Oxford

L. Evans, 'On a Portable Sundial of Gilt Brass Made for Cardinal Wolsey', *Archaeologia* 62 (1901), pp. 1-2, pl. XLV

V.16   German Pillar Dial

The pillar or cylinder dial is a portable altitude dial made for a particular latitude. The cap is rotated until the gnomon lies above the required month indicated at the foot of the cylinder. The gnomon is then made to face the sun, so that the shadow falls straight down the side of the pillar. The time is indicated by the shadow of the tip of the gnomon on the scale. There is a fine pillar dial on the shelf on the left-hand of Holbein's Kratzer portrait (V.13).   W.H.

Prob. 17th cent.

Boxwood, brass, 110 ht, base 30 dia.

G 7, Museum of the History of Science, Oxford

V.17   Dividers

Of massive construction, with finely cut mouldings and engraved decorations. The limbs are adjusted by means of the wing-nut fixed in one of the arms and mounted so as to be free to rotate. This nut moves along a finely cut threaded arc (90°) of steel attached to the other arm. The detachable drawing-pen can be replaced by another point. Similar dividers hang on the wall to the right of Holbein's Kratzer portrait (V.13).   W.H.

French or Italian, 17th cent.

Brass, polished steel, 254 lgth

57-84/254, Museum of the History of Science, Oxford

M. Hambly, *Drawing Instruments 1580-1980* (Sotheby's Publications, 1988), pp. 69-88

V.18   Facsimile: Terrestrial Globe

This globe is virtually identical with that shown in Holbein's *Ambassadors*, except that it lacks the homes of the ambassadors that appear in the painting. It shows the division of the world agreed between Portugal and Castile under the treaty of Tordesillas of 1494. The division - which neither England nor France recognized - created a difficult strategic problem for the formulation of English naval and mercantile policy. The globe was long thought to have been the work of the Nuremberg instrument-maker Georg Hartmann, but analysis of its core and comparison with the Yale University globe, and other gores (the shaped paper covering) in the New York Public Library revealed during 1972 that both its core and gores were reproductions produced about 1890 in Munich.   R.B.

Facsimile after Georg Hartmann

G33, Hydrographic Collection, National Maritime Museum

A. D. Baynes Cope, 'Investigation of Some Globes', *Imago Mundi* 33 (1981), pp. 9-20

to it a notice advertising the University's condemnation of the doctrines of Luther. Some fine manuscript drawings have survived of the Corpus Christi dial made by the sundial enthusiast Robert Hegge, of which the earlier version dates from 1624-5.[9]

The appellation 'deviser of the king's horologes' may simply refer to Kratzer's work on sundials and not to mechanical clocks. Indeed, there is no evidence that he possessed any skills in this direction while his interest in the construction of sundials is well known, especially of polyhedral dials. The one that has survived is the so-called portable gilt brass Wolsey dial (V.15) which, as so often happens, has no provenance. The only link with Kratzer's patron are Wolsey's arms and the cardinal's hats engraved on the instrument. Two other dials have been attributed to Kratzer: the celebrated dial at the Palace of Whitehall,[10] and the badly damaged dial recently discovered at Iron Acton Court, which has the better claim (VIII.1). It bears the date '1520' and the initials 'N.K.', and if these are indeed the initials of Nicolaus Kratzer then this is the only dial signed by him and the earliest dated English polyhedral dial recorded.[11]

That Kratzer not only designed but also made instruments is strongly suggested by the Holbein portrait (V.13),[12] which depicts him holding an incomplete decahedron dial with its gnomons lying on the table. The same complete instrument (now with a small magnetic compass) is shown in *The Ambassadors* (1533). In the portrait Kratzer is also holding a pair of dividers (V.17), and he is surrounded by devices of the sundial trade: a pivoted rule, a ruling knife, a burin, scissors, and another dialing instrument. On the wall hang large dividers, another ruler, and what appears to be a combined parallel rule and square. On the shelf behind is a pillar dial (V.16) and an unusual form of adjustable vertical dial with a semicircular scale.

Many of the same instruments reappear in Holbein's great double portrait of *The Ambassadors*.[13] But the effect is very different as here they form part of a rich allegory. At one level the combination of musical and scientific instruments symbolizes the Renaissance university learning, age and origins of the two subjects, Jean de Dinteville and Georges de Selve. But above all the painting is a meditation on the embassy which had brought Dinteville to England in 1533. It has been suggested that the pillar dial gives the day as Good Friday, 11 April 1533, the deadline set by Henry VIII for Clement VII to agree to his divorce. This was a black day for those who, like the sitters, hoped for the unity of Christendom. Hence the prominence of symbols of death and disharmony: the crucifix, the broken lute string, the distorted skull. But hope of reconciliation continued, as the inclusion of two works by Luther suggests. Kratzer no doubt advised on the technical aspects of all this, but there is nothing to suggest that the programme was anything other than the sitter's own.

Kratzer lived at the beginning of the great colonial expansion with its impact on astronomy, 'practical' mathematics, navigation, surveying, and on a burgeoning instrument-making trade.[14] In 1530 Gemma Frisius suggested the use of the small portable clock developed at Nuremberg (XI.19) for determining longitude at sea, but clock technology would not be practical for this purpose until the eighteenth century.[15] Kratzer brought German science and technical arts to the Court of Henry VIII. As an astronomer he probably made his own instruments, although he would have made use of skilled labour as required. All the evidence suggests that he was a competent craftsman and teacher. He died in about 1550.

The Return Embassy to France

In July 1527 Wolsey left for France as the King's lieutenant (or plenipotentiary) to negotiate another set of treaties. In August he met Francis I at Amiens and treated with him as an equal. The cardinal's suite was large and magnificent, and a significant proportion of them were drawn by Holbein. The temptation (which should probably be resisted) is to assume that exposure to French culture heightened visual awareness.

V.19   Edward Stanley, 3rd Earl of Derby

V.20   Sir Henry Guildford

The Stanleys were a satellite family of the Tudors. Thomas, Lord Stanley had married Lady Margaret Beaufort, mother of Henry Tudor, as her last husband. His forces, engaged at the last moment, clinched his step-son's victory at Bosworth in 1485 and he was rewarded with the earldom of Derby. His great-grandson, Edward Stanley (1508-72) succeeded to the earldom in 1521 as a minor. He was Wolsey's ward (being allowed ten personal servants in the cardinal's household) and in this capacity accompanied him to France in 1527. At the coronation of Anne Boleyn he was cupbearer and was created knight of the Bath. No painted portrait from this drawing appears to survive. D.S.

This is the preparatory drawing for Guildford's magnificent painted portrait (V.4). On his previous mission to France in 1521, Wolsey had also taken Guildford and Sir Thomas More (V.21) together with others of the inner royal entourage. This led to a request from Henry VIII for Guildford's return as he was bare of attendants. In 1527 most of Wolsey's suite was made up of members of his own household (V.19, 23) - but he took Guildford and More once more. The chain of the Garter (to which Guildford had been elected the previous year) is sketched in, but the face is fatter and less powerfully lined than in the final painting. D.S.

Hans Holbein

Chalks and ink on pink-primed paper, 282 x 197

12243, Royal Collection

Foister/Parker, no. 52

R. S. Sylvester and D. P. Harding, eds., *Two Early Tudor Lives* (London and New Haven, 1962), p. 21

Hans Holbein

Chalks on white paper, 384 x 294

12266, Royal Collection

Foister/Parker, no. 10

LP III ii, 1597; IV ii, 3216

Tho:Moor L.Chancelour

V.21 Sir Thomas More

Like Guildford, More had links to Holbein through
Erasmus, who in 1526 had written him a letter of
recommendation for Holbein, then planning to come
to England in search of work. Nor did More need the
embassy to France to introduce him to continental
culture. Indeed, ever since his first mission abroad to
Flanders in 1515, when the conversations that were
reworked into Book I of *Utopia* took place, More had
felt more at home with the civic culture of the
European cities than the chivalric ethos (however
disguised) of the English Court.

    This is a preparatory drawing for Holbein's lost
group portrait of the More family; the drawing for
Holbein's individual portrait of More is also in the
Royal Collection. D.S.

Hans Holbein

Chalks on white paper, 376 x 256

12225, Royal Collection

Foister/Parker, nos. 2-3

V.22 Thomas, Lord Vaux of Harrowden

Lord Vaux (c.1510-1556) accompanied Wolsey to
France in 1527; went with Henry VIII and Anne
Boleyn to their meeting at Calais with Francis I in
1532, and was dubbed a knight of the Bath at Anne's
coronation in 1533. But, disapproving of the religious
changes consequent on Henry's second marriage,
he withdrew from public life and consoled himself
by writing poetry, some of which was published
posthumously. He sat twice to Holbein. D.S.

Hans Holbein

Chalks, etc. on pink-primed paper, 278 x 293

12245, Royal Collection

Foister/Parker, nos. 24, 30

Reskemeer a Cornish   Gent:

V.23 John or William Reskimer

John and William were the sons of John Reskimer of
Merthen, Cornwall. John, the elder, after being
Wolsey's servant and accompanying him to France in
1527, ran the family estates; William, the younger,
became a minor courtier. But John retained his central
contacts, and William never lost touch with his local
roots. In these circumstances, the inscription
'Reskemeer, a Cornish gent.', could apply to either. D.S.

Hans Holbein

Chalks on pink-primed paper, 290 x 208

12237, Royal Collection

Foister/Parker, no. 31

History of Parliament III, pp. 188-9

The Treaties

By mid-August agreement was reached and Wolsey hoped that the treaties of Amiens would be 'ratified, sworn and confirmed' on the 15th. But the ceremonies had to be put off till the 18th, 'the engrossing and penning thereof ... is so great, requiring such a tract of time'. The delays were caused not only by the quantity of the work but by its quality. For the decision had been taken that this 'eternal peace' should be embodied in appropriately splendid documents.

V.24 Ratification of the Treaty of London, 1518

The treaty of London was designed to be a 'perpetual peace', primarily between England and France, but also incorporating all the other European powers in a mutually enforceable security system. Despite its ambitions, the document itself was modest and workaday. It is signed by Francis I; countersigned by Florimond Robertet, the secretary of State, and sealed with the great seal of France on a green and red cord. D.S.

MS on vellum, 630 x 870

E 30/829, [*LP* II ii, 4649] Public Record Office

V.25 Confirmation of the Treaty of the More, 1525

Practical considerations also dominated the treaty of the More. This marked the first rapprochement between England and France after the battle of Pavia. Negotiations were more or less secret, and England's prime concern was making the treaty (in particular its financial clauses) stick in the enforced absence of Francis I, who was Charles V's prisoner. So the treaty is signed by Louise of Savoy as regent, and registered by four of the *parlements* or 'sovereign courts'. D.S.

MS on vellum, 400 x 510

E 30/922, [*LP* IV i, 1663] Public Record Office

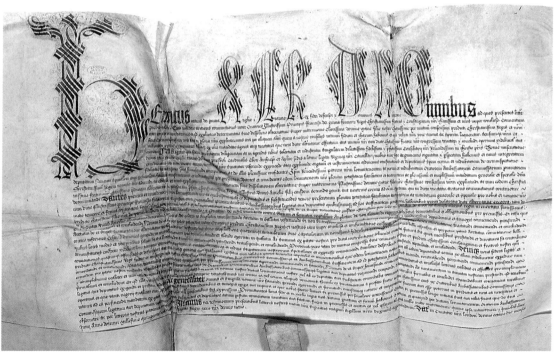

V.26 Cardinal Wolsey's Letters of Credence

This document represents the Letters of Credence issued to Wolsey as Henry's representative when he set out for France in the summer of 1527. It is dated 18 June 1527. Although the ornamental element consists only of simple strapwork, enhanced by delicate pen decoration of flowers and foliage, it is

clearly in the same tradition as the much more elaborate work seen on the patents produced by the Chancery in favour of Wolsey's own educational foundations during the late 1520s (V.37). J.M.B.

MS on vellum, 400 x 670; seal 120 dia.

AE III 75, Archives Nationales, CARAN, Paris

LP IV ii, 3186

A Diplomatic Revolution? Anglo-French Relations and the Treaties of 1527

BY CHARLES GIRY-DELOISON

On 30 April 1527 at Westminster, after long and arduous negotiations, Francis I's ambassadors signed a treaty of perpetual peace between the kingdoms of France and England, in the presence of Cardinal Wolsey and the English negotiators.[1] At first sight, the treaty of Westminster was a turning point in England's foreign policy towards the continental powers. It marks the end of the hostilities with France, opened in May 1522,[2] and seals the reversal of alliances for which Thomas Wolsey had so assiduously striven since 1525. It affirmed the humanist ideals of peace and concord in the heart of Christendom, and above all it proclaimed the definite end of the age-old rivalry between the kingdoms of France and England. The ideals of Erasmus had triumphed. But this is a short to medium term view. In a longer perspective, the treaty of Westminster signalled no lasting change in relations between the two countries. The real change of policy adopted by the English towards the European powers, and particularly towards France, had begun on 22 April 1509.[3] The Venetian ambassador in London, Andrea Badoer, reported that on the very day Henry VIII succeeded his father, he swore to wage war on the king of France. The young King's proclamation delighted the Venetians, for France's enemy would 'be the Signory's friend';[4] it also put an end to the prudent policy of disengagement from continental quarrels that had been the key-note of Henry VII's policy. Henry VIII's declaration reveals his determination to pick up the mantle of the all-conquering Henry V and make a reality of his title of 'King of France'.[5] He was as good as his word. Twice, in 1513 and 1522, he sent troops to wage war in northern France, and in 1513 he personally led his army to the gates of Tournai.[6] His joy on hearing the news of the French defeat at Pavia on 14 February 1525, and of the capture of the French king,[7] witness to his abiding dream of the reconquest of 'English-France'.[8] This 'Great Enterprise' was resolutely turned towards the past.

Henry VIII's adoption of a forward policy had two consequences: England began to play an active part on the European scene, but, owing to lack of means in both men and money, she could only act in association with another dominant power: France, or Spain and the Empire, which were soon to fuse into one in the hands of Charles V. After 1519, the fragile balance of power between France and the Empire made an English alliance a key element in diplomatic agreements and it was this role of arbiter that England strove to play. At this game, Henry acquired an international prestige exceeded only by Charles and Francis, and Wolsey became the incontestable intermediary of monarchs. To these two aspirations - to play a part on the continent and to revive the claim to France - was added a third: the search for a general peace. Here is not the place to try to determine the roles played by Cardinal Wolsey and Henry VIII in England's foreign policy,[9] but on at least two occasions, in 1518 and 1527, England tried to impose a peaceful settlement on the rest of Europe. On both occasions, Wolsey personally conducted negotiations. It is extremely difficult to say if a peace settlement, which (so long as it lasted) removed any hope of Henry regaining the French crown, corresponded to Wolsey's or the King's true desires, or simply showed their adaptation to the necessities of the time. In either case, Henry VIII and Wolsey became, at important moments and with apparent conviction, advocates of a peaceful settlement to current conflicts. The result of these contradictory aims was that, after 1509, Anglo-French relations (like English foreign policy in general) followed an erratic and sometimes devious path. War and cold war alternated with peace, and the transition was made, with maximum dramatic impact, in 1518 and 1527. In both years, a comprehensive reversal of previous treaty obligations to the Habsburgs was linked with - and partially masked by - treaties of universal peace. In this sense 1527 was no more than a re-run

V.27 Confirmation of the Treaty of Amiens, 18 August 1527: See page 9

The formal treaty documents prepared in France in August 1527 for presentation to Wolsey and the English delegation were written out in book form and professionally illuminated. Their ornaments incorporate figures and subject matter both symbolic of their individual contents and appropriate to the occasion in general. The amount of time involved in their preparation is actually commented upon in Wolsey's letters which note that the ceremonies of ratification had to be postponed for three days,

'the engrossing and penning thereof ... is so great'. This general confirmation of the treaty of Amiens concentrates on the theme of eternal peace. A classical figure of Peace stands between the arms of France and England, which are surrounded by lilies and roses respectively. In the lower margin the benefits of peace are exemplified by shepherds and shepherdesses dancing as they tend their flocks, while trees heavy with fruit symbolize plenty. J.M.B.

Illuminated MS on vellum, 520 x 600
E 30/1110, [LP IV ii, 3356/6b] Public Record Office

of 1518, though the fact was disguised by the public relations. The celebrations were magnificent; the language was near blasphemous in its extravagance (an 'eternal' peace to endure 'in secula seculorum'); the treaties were lavishly illuminated and sealed with gold seals (V.24-34); while Wolsey himself showed off the seals in Star Chamber, to prove that the peace was as 'noble' as the metal!

Secret negotiations between the two crowns were opened in the spring of 1524, first in Calais then in London where, on 22 July or a few days before, Jean-Joachim de Passano, lord of Vaux, arrived, sent by Louise of Savoy, mother of Francis I, under the pretext of private affairs.[10] The negotiations seem to have been fruitful, since in the winter of 1524-5, Jean Brinon, first president of the parlement of Rouen crossed the Channel to join Passano in London. He arrived on 22 January 1525.[11] If Henry had not desired these negotiations, at least he had accepted them. Yet on the very day (9 March) the news of Francis I's defeat and capture at Pavia reached London, the King cancelled the meeting he had for the first time granted the emissaries.[12] He ordered public rejoicings throughout the country and a mass at St Paul's and seriously contemplated a military operation in France. The French ambassadors left London on 21 March 1525.[13] It is difficult to know what to make of all this. Henry VIII's warlike intentions against France did not last; they contrasted with Wolsey's more pacific endeavours, and they were summarily ended when Charles V showed no interest in helping Henry recapture the French crown. It is also true that Passano returned to London on 22 June[14] and Brinon on 26 July.[15] But, with all these reservations, it remains the case that in 1525 the King had not completely given up the 'Great Enterprise'.

And of course, whatever their intentions, neither Henry nor Wolsey enjoyed a free hand. In particular, two domestic problems impinged largely on the conduct of foreign policy. The first was financial. When in March 1525 the news of Pavia was received at Court, it was decided to ask the population (without the preliminary consent of Parliament) to contribute again towards the war effort to reconquer France. Already in 1523 similar contributions had been imposed to finance war in France and the second instalment, due on 9 February 1525, had not been entirely collected by March 1525. This time, the sum asked for under the wishful title of the Amicable Grant,[16] was much heavier: about a sixth of the income of the laity and a third of the income of the clergy. It was asking too much and the commissioners appointed on 21 March to collect the Grant encountered strong resistance,[17] particularly in Kent and London. The message was clear: the population was not ready to support another war with France. On 26 April, Henry VIII announced that he was renouncing the Amicable Grant,[18] pretending moreover that he had not been informed of its existence. Whatever Henry's equivocations, however, one thing was certain: without the money to have been raised by the Amicable Grant, he could not launch a military expedition to France.

Later, a second but more important problem was the affair of Henry's divorce. In spring 1527,

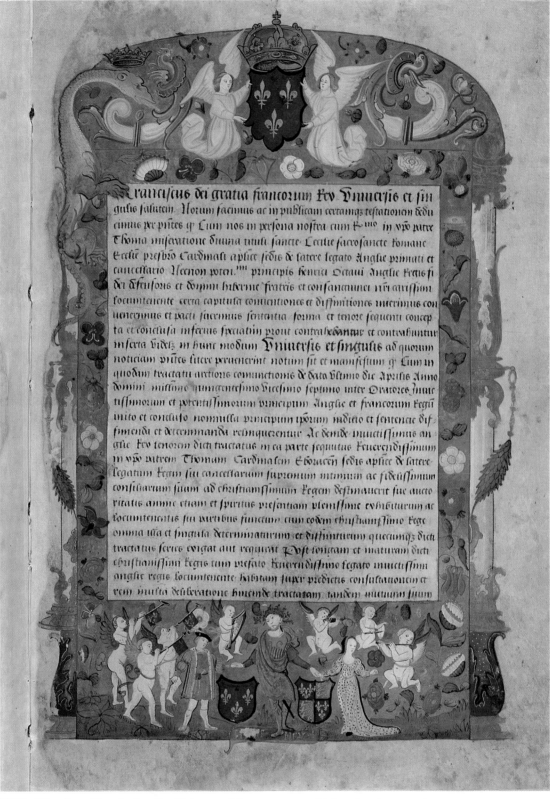

V.28 Marriage Treaty for the Princess Mary and the Duke of Orléans, 18 August 1527

The treaty of Amiens was to be given concrete expression through a marriage between the children of the two kings. At the foot of this document the classical god of marriage, Hymenaeus, unites figures representing the young royal couple, Henry's eleven- year-old daughter Mary and Francis's second son, eight-year-old Henry, who was ultimately to succeed his father as Henry II. Francis's salamander device forms the introductory initial and the royal arms of France appear in the upper border. J.M.B.

Illuminated MS on vellum, 520 x 550

E 30/1112, [*LP* IV ii, 3356/7] Public Record Office

V.29 The Mercantile Treaty, 18 August 1527

The commercial treaty of 1527 was intended, optimistically, to substitute trade with France for trade with the Netherlands. A seascape in the lower margin represents trade between England and France via the English Channel, the traffic passing through waters somewhat improbably infested with sea monsters. The arms of France at the top of the document are flanked by symbolic lilies. The blue snakelike forms in the right-hand margin may possibly be intended as an oblique reference to French involvement in northern Italy. J.M.B.

Illuminated MS on vellum, 560 x 600

E 30/1113, [*LP* IV ii, 3356/2] Public Record Office

V.30 Treaty to Withhold Consent to a General Council while the Pope Remains a Prisoner, 18 August 1527 (Detail)

At the period of Wolsey's sojourn in France, the pope remained the emperor's prisoner following the Sack of Rome. The miniature in the upper margin of this document represents the Church in captivity. At the foot of the page, Henry and Francis are shown in a fictitious encounter. Although the illumination is not of the first quality, both men are readily recognizable and must have been drawn after available portrait types. Two of Henry's attendants wear doublets in his livery colours of green and white, embroidered with the crowned rose, and carry a halbard and a longbow. They are intended to represent yeomen of the Guard, whose old livery this was. Francis's salamander badge decorates the righthand margin over a ground of fleurs-de-lis, on either side of the French royal arms. J.M.B.

Illuminated MS on vellum, 560 x 510
E 30/1114, [*LP* IV ii, 3356/3] Public Record Office

it had become patent that Henry VIII had decided to divorce Catherine.[19] The legal arguments on which the King based his divorce action required the help of the papacy and, in particular, a papal dispensation was required for a remarriage. It was clear, both to Wolsey and to Henry, that Charles V would do his utmost to prevent the divorce and that he would profit from his supremacy in Italy (conferred by Pavia in 1525 and confirmed by the Sack of Rome in 1527) to bring pressure to bear on Pope Clement VII. A rapprochement with France was thus imperative in order to ensure that Clement VII aligned himself with Francis. The Holy League of Cognac, concluded on 22 May 1526[20] between France, the papacy, Venice, Florence and Milan, and to which Henry agreed to be 'protector', was the ideal setting for such a manoeuvre. Considering the uncertain chronology, it is difficult to say if the affair of Henry's divorce played an important part in the signing of the treaty of Westminster. On the other hand, it is undeniable that it was at the centre of Wolsey's preoccupations when he went to France a few months later in July 1527 and concluded a treaty with Francis I at Amiens on 18 August.

Finally, the Anglo-French rapprochement was also due to the fact that, as we have seen, in either war or peace England could only act in Europe in concert with one of the two great powers. Charles V had shown himself unwilling to extend this necessary co-operation before as well as after Pavia; moreover imperial hegemony after Pavia represented a double risk for England: first, to be excluded from any direct settlement of the conflict between France and the Empire (after all England's mediation was not indispensable for the signing of a treaty of peace between the two belligerents); and second, to be at the mercy of a far too powerful Empire and its satellites. An agreement with France would thus be both a safeguard and an opportunity: it would enable England to oppose imperial domination and to take part in the settlement of the conflict.

Consequently, as soon as Henry VIII and Wolsey were convinced of the need to side with France, the rapprochement was swift. On 30 August 1525, the French ambassadors Passano and Brinon signed five treaties collectively known as the treaty of the More. The first was both a peace and a defensive alliance between the two countries, by which Henry agreed to instigate the prompt release of Francis from his captivity at the hands of Charles V;[21] the second bound Francis to pay Henry two million écus in annual instalments of 100,000;[22] the third provided for the settlement of maritime disputes;[23] the fourth agreed to include Scotland, under certain conditions (namely that Albany was not to return to Scotland during James V's minority), in the treaty of peace;[24] while by the fifth the French undertook to pay compensation to Mary, duchess of Suffolk and widow of Louis XII, for any losses suffered because of the war.[25] On 22 May 1526, Henry VIII accepted the title of 'protector' of the League of Cognac and on 8 August 1526, Jean-Joachim de Passano signed the treaty of Hampton Court, by which France and England agreed not to deal individually with Charles V. Finally, the treaty of Westminster was signed on 30 April 1527.

As usual, the diplomatic terms were complemented by a projected dynastic alliance. If war broke out between Charles and the new allies, Mary would marry Francis I's second son, Henry, duke of Orleans, while Francis I would marry Eleanor, sister of Charles V. It was also agreed that a meeting between Henry VIII and Francis I should take place, but on a lesser scale than the Field of Cloth of Gold. Finally, an Anglo-French embassy was to be sent to Spain: to inform the Emperor of the terms of the treaty, to negotiate for the release of Francis's sons and for the payment of the Emperor's debt to Henry, and to persuade him to agree to a general peace.[26] Undoubtedly, the French gained from the treaty of Westminster in as much as it gave Francis further diplomatic and, if necessary, military support for obtaining the release of his sons and later driving Charles out of Italy. It also put an end, albeit temporarily, to the feud with England and enabled Francis to concentrate on restoring France to its previous grandeur. For the English, and for Wolsey in particular, Westminster did not achieve the international diplomatic success desired and which he had anticipated. Charles did not agree to the terms put to him by the joint Anglo-French

V.31 Ratification of the Treaty of Amiens by Wolsey as King's Lieutenant, 18 August 1527

A personification of Peace presides over the treaty, standing between the royal arms of France and England. The introductory initial incorporates Francis's salamander device within a thicket of Henry's roses. The decorative borders, areas of which take the form of golden fleur-de-lis, are of a type which was first fashionable in France in the late fifteenth century and may be regarded as somewhat old-fashioned in the context of the 1520s. Wolsey's commission as the King's lieutenant entitled him to royal honours: French towns greeted him with pageants in his honour; Francis I treated him as an equal and the title 'Cardinal Peacemaker' was inscribed on the door of his lodgings. J.M.B.

Illuminated MS on vellum, 540 x 330
E 30/1111, [*LP* IV ii, 3356/8] Public Record Office
R. Strong, *Gloriana: the Portrait of Queen Elizabeth I* (1987), p. 74

V.32 Confirmation of the Treaty of Amiens, 1527: See page 55

embassy and the Sack of Rome (6 May 1527) and the ensuing treaty between Clement VII and the viceroy of Naples (5 June 1527) gave the emperor total control of the papacy. Wolsey's hope for a general peace under his auspices was shattered.

As Francis was spreading his spider's web of counter-alliances against Charles across Europe, England was quickly brought into even closer collaboration with France after the Sack of Rome. Henry, far more than Francis, needed to free the pope, for his divorce was at stake. He therefore also agreed to contribute financially to the French army which had just crossed the Alps under the command of Marshal Odet de Foix, lord of Lautrec.[27] On 11 July 1527, Wolsey crossed the Channel[28] and met Francis at Amiens on 9 August.[29] On the l8th, the treaty of Amiens was signed.[30] Wolsey agreed, on Henry's behalf, that Mary should marry Henry, duke of Orleans (V.28), and that if there were to be war, English merchants could enjoy similar privileges in France as they had done in the Netherlands (V.29), and that neither France nor England would take part in a General Council of the Church as long as Pope Clement VII remained Charles's prisoner (V.30). In September 1527, Anne de Montmorency, great master of France, was commissioned to confer the Order of St Michael on Henry VIII (V.1-4).[31] This was to prove a costly agreement. Between 1527 and 1529, Henry's contribution to Francis's wars in Italy amounted to £112,437 11s, though only £49,148 was paid out of the King's coffers. The rest of the contribution was met in jewellery and by foregoing part of the pension Francis had agreed to pay Henry.[32] But the major blow for England came from Wolsey's decision to join France in a combined invasion of The Netherlands. For Wolsey, this was to be the finishing touch to the reversal of alliances, while the expected Anglo-French victory over Margaret of Savoy, the regent of the Netherlands, was to force Charles V to negotiate under Wolsey's auspices. But, though war was declared, the invasion never took place and the English threat was ridiculed by Margaret and Charles. The non-invasion was a serious diplomatic blunder and England was dragged even further into hostilities with the Empire. More damaging still was the fact that the intended war with Margaret cut the vital economic links with Antwerp and the other great cloth markets of the Netherlands, and seriously impeded English cloth exports. For the English merchants, Calais and the French market, despite what had been agreed at Amiens, were never more than a poor substitute for the Netherlands.

In the long term, the consequences of the treaties of Westminster and Amiens were twofold. The French alliance proved a disaster to Wolsey. It did not prevent Clement VII from signing peace with Charles V on 29 June 1529[33] and then from taking, on 16 July 1529,[34] the decision to revoke Henry's divorce suit to the Curia. Furthermore, at Cambrai on 5 August 1529, Louise of Savoy and Margaret of Savoy[35] agreed to a peace, known as the Ladies' Peace, from which England was almost completely excluded.[36] Wolsey's plans to be the peacemaker in Europe had failed. The peace talks in Cambrai, the pope's decision in the divorce suit, and the growing opposition in England to the French alliance precipitated Wolsey's fall. They also led to the breach with Rome.But equally, the Anglo-French rapprochement made the breach possible: if it had destroyed Wolsey, it helped preserve Henry. The result was that the rapprochement long survived Wolsey's fall and peace lasted until early 1543. In June 1542 Henry VIII had made a secret alliance with the Emperor to invade France[57] and on 22 June 1543 war was declared.[37] The reasons for the declaration of war remained the same: France's failure to keep up payments in English pensions, maritime disputes between the two countries and the struggle in Scotland between pro-English and pro-French factions. By 16 July 1544, a hundred years after the English defeats of Formigny and Castillon had ended the Hundred Years War, Henry VIII had crossed the Channel to recover the crown of France.[38] The 'eternal' peace had lasted for less than twenty years; on the other hand, twenty years in politics is almost an eternity.

V.33 The Golden 'Bulla' used to Seal the Treaty of Amiens

The golden 'bulla' used to seal the final ratification of the treaty of Amiens shows on the face Francis I seated in majesty under a rich cloth of estate, the curtains of which are drawn back by angels (the supporters of the French royal arms). Lions form the footstool and the Latin of the inscription reads 'Most things are preserved by a treaty made in good faith'. On the obverse are the arms of France, encircled with the collar of the Order of St Michael and surmounted by a closed or arched crown topped with a fleur-de-lis. This device had been used by Francis for his shield on the Tree of Honour at the Field of Cloth of Gold, and had excited much comment. D.S.

Gold on ? core, 107 dia.
Public Record Office
More: NPG, no. 195
J. G. Russell, *The Field of Cloth of Gold* (1969), p. 121

V.34 Confirmation of the Treaty of Amiens, 1527

This elaborately embellished copy of the confirmation of the treaty of Amiens, dated 18 September 1527, was signed by Henry VIII in person for transmission to Francis I by the French embassy that waited upon him in England shortly thereafter. Although now severely damaged, it is clear that the document was originally decorated by the most accomplished hand at the disposal of the chancery. Stylistically the work is extremely close to the illumination in an Epistolary and a Gospel Lectionary made in 1528-9 for Cardinal Wolsey. These two books have been tentatively ascribed to the Flemish book-painter, Gerard Horenbout, one-time court painter to Margaret of Austria, regent of the Netherlands. Horenbout (sometimes called Hornebolte in English contexts) is known to have entered Henry's service in the mid-1520s, along with his son Lucas and daughter Susanna. However, the decoration may equally well be due to Lucas, who was in Henry's service from at least the autumn of 1525 until his death in 1544. J.M.B.

Illuminated MS on vellum, 330 x 260
AE III 25, Archives Nationales, CARAN, Paris

V.35 Golden 'Bulla' used to Seal the Treaty

The English 'bulla' is clearly designed as the pendant to the French one. On the obverse is the King seated in majesty. The image is Renaissance in character, in marked contrast to the great seal, which remained wholly gothic until 1542. Both the figure of the King and the architectural throne, with its shell niche, are derived from the historiated initials of the letters patent for Wolsey's colleges, which are attributed to the Horenbouts (V.45-50). The exaggerated size of

Henry's arched crown answers Francis I's pretensions to imperial status, as does the reverse of the 'bulla'. This shows the royal arms encircled with the Garter collar as on the French seal, and surmounted by an emphatically arched crown. The Latin motto translates: 'They are united by Order, and stand firmly together by treaty'. D.S.

Gold on ? core, 90 dia.
Archives Nationales, CARAN, Paris
A. B. and A. Wyon, *The Great Seals of England* (1887), p. 71

V.36 The Casket for the Ratification of the Treaty of Amiens

Important treaties often came complete with a special casket or box. It is not known whether this one was made expressly; if so, it differs from the 'bulla' in being purely gothic in style. D.S.

150 ht, 302 w, 410 lgth
Archives Nationales, CARAN, Paris

V.37 Letters Patent for Cardinal College, Oxford

Wolsey's twin foundations at Oxford and his birth-place at Ipswich were intended as monuments to his patronage of humanist scholarship. Everything about them was to be of the latest and the best, including the decoration of their foundation deeds. The pen-and-ink drawing in the initial 'H' of (1) shows Henry VIII in majesty on an architectural throne with a shell niche; in (2) the King, similarly represented, is flanked by figures representing Wolsey and Norfolk. In 1528-9 there is a payment to 'Gerarde [Horenbout]' for work in preparing letters patent for Cardinal College, Oxford. This would include (1), and (2) is evidently by the same hand. The pattern of the royal image established in these documents was used for the golden 'bulla' of 1527 (V.35), and continued to be employed in the 1530s (V.38). (2) has a good impression of the gothic first great seal of Henry VIII. D.S.

1. 5 May 1526: Decorated MS on vellum, 850 x 1090
E 24/6/1, [*LP* IV i, 2152] Public Record Office
2. 25 May 1529: Decorated MS on vellum, 950 x 820
E 24/20/1, [*LP* IV iii, 5593] Public Record Office
Strong, *Renaissance Miniature*, pp. 30-32 and fig. 12

V.38   The Treaty of Windsor, 1532

V.39   Ratification of the Treaty of Camp [Ardres], 1546

This Anglo-French agreement, in which Anne Boleyn's father, Thomas, is named as Henry's principal representative, was concluded at Windsor on 1 September 1532. It was a preliminary to the meeting between the two kings which took place a few weeks later at Boulogne.

The document, in the form of letters patent under the great seal, is decorated in a style very similar to that first found in the late 1520s on the patents for Wolsey's colleges (V.37). It has been suggested that Gerard Horenbout was responsible for the Wolsey patents. However the relatively late date of this example makes Lucas Horenbout a more likely candidate. Some politically motivated changes have also been made, like replacing the figure of Wolsey in a cardinal's hat on the King's right with a mitred archbishop. J.M.B.

The French ambassador, Odet de Selve, received this formal copy of the ratification of the Anglo-French treaty of Camp (7 June 1546) for transmission to Francis I on 17 July 1546. The document, written in a fine italic script, is elaborately illuminated in a restrained version of the mannerist style already well established on the continent. In England this style is particularly associated with the influence of Guillim Scrots, formerly (1537) court painter to Mary of Austria, regent of the Netherlands. Scrots first appears in Henry VIII's accounts in January 1546, receiving an annuity backdated to the previous September. A circular miniature portrait of Henry, very old and grey, is an integral part of the decoration of the initial letter. The figure of Peace presides over the arms of England and France at the top of the page, while Prudence and Wisdom are seated on the lower margin. J.M.B.

Decorated MS on vellum, (i) 530 x 900; (ii) 570 x 900; seal 120 dia.

AE III 31, Archives Nationales, CARAN, Paris

Illuminated MS on vellum

AE III 33, Archives Nationales, CARAN, Paris

LP XXI i, 1014, 1240

Portrait Miniatures and Book Illumination

If treaties became works of art, works of art also carried a heavy diplomatic content. This was most marked in the case of portrait miniatures, whether free-standing or as part of book decoration. Once again, French influence is strongest, while the key artists are the Flemish Horenbout family. They came to England in the mid-1520s from Flanders, the main centre for the production of luxury illustrated books.

V.40 Les Commentaires de la Guerre Gallique, vol. I, 1519

This is the first in a series of three volumes ordered by Louise of Savoy to flatter the imperial pretensions of her son, Francis I, by placing him on an equal

footing with Julius Caesar. The miniatures were painted early in 1519, and Charles V was elected emperor in June. The author, François du Moulin, was frequently employed by Louise. The artist who collaborated with him, Godefroy le Batave, was a Fleming whose style betrays an Antwerp background. The mansucript, however, studiously emulates the most elegant Italian humanist work of the day. Circular portraits of the two main protagonists appear at the beginning of the volume. That of Francis, painted in the semi-grisaille (imitation stone relief) which is characteristic of the volume as a whole, is somewhere between a medal and a naturalistic portrait. J.M.B.

Illuminated MS on vellum, 250 x 125
Harley MS 6205, British Library
Myra Orth, 'François du Moulin and Albert Pigghe,
Les Commentaires de la guerre gallique', in Thomas Kren, ed.
*Renaissance Painting in Manuscripts: Treasures from the British
Library* (New York, 1983), pp. 181-6

V.41 Les Commentaires de la Guerre Gallique, vol. II, 1519

The second volume of du Moulin's *Commentaires*, also produced in 1519, includes circular naturalistic portraits of the heroes of the French victory at Maringo (1515) by which Francis I had reasserted his claim to the duchy of Milan. These portraits, derived from drawings now preserved at Chantilly, are attributable not to Godefroy le Batave, as in the first volume (V.40), but to the portrait specialist Jean Clouet. They display many of the characteristics of later independent portrait miniatures, including gold framing lines and intense blue backgrounds. However, their appearance on the pages of a book, accompanied by passages of text, is entirely consistent with the practices of earlier manuscript-painters in Italy and they cannot therefore be regarded as an indication of the existence of the independent portrait miniature in France at this date. J.M.B.

Illuminated MS on vellum, 250 x 125
MS fr. 13429, Bibliothèque Nationale, Paris

Illuminated Manuscripts and the Development of the Portrait Miniature

BY JANET BACKHOUSE

Throughout the reign of Henry VIII it remained customary for prestigious books and documents to be decorated by hand, just as they had been in earlier centuries. Even presentation copies of printed books often had further hand-painted decoration added to them. No evidence has been found, however, to suggest that craftsmen were employed at the English Court solely to act as illuminators. Only a single reference in surviving royal accounts has been noted as mentioning a 'lymner of books', an Englishman named Richard James who is recorded in 1525.[1] Some of the work commissioned at various times for the King but not specifically documented is far from expert. English native illuminators in the early decades of the reign often tried to emulate the work of their Flemish contemporaries, but with variable success. The presentation copy of the work which earned Henry his title of 'Fidei defensor', the *Assertio septem sacramentorum adversus Lutherum*, sent to the pope in 1521 and still preserved in the Vatican Library, is a good example.[2] The craftsmen whose work as illuminators can be identified and is of high quality were on the whole foreigners and are usually known to have received their emoluments for a very varied range of services.

The most significant event in the history of early Tudor book painting was the arrival in England from Flanders in the mid-1520s of three members of the Horenbout family, Gerard and his children, Lucas and Susanna.[3] In English sources they are often called Hornebolte. The widespread influence of this event was to be felt not just in book decoration but also in the increasingly important field of portraiture. Gerard Horenbout, born apparently during the 1460s, is a major figure in the history of Flemish illumination at its zenith. Well documented during the last two decades of the fifteenth century, he was employed from 1515 by Margaret of Austria, regent of the Netherlands, by whom he was paid some five years later for providing a series of additions to the Hours of Bona Sforza (V. 42). Both his children were also illuminators and had presumably been trained in his own workshop. Susanna's work was admired by Dürer in 1521, when she was only eighteen, but details of her subsequent career are lacking. Lucas was to become Henry VIII's Court painter and remained in his service until his death in 1544.

The first identifiable reference to the Horenbouts in English sources is the record of payment to Lucas in the royal accounts in the autumn of 1525. The series of accounts is imperfect and there is no means of knowing how long he had been in the country at the time. Gerard received monthly payments between October 1528 and April 1531, but gaps in the records both before and after these dates obscure his actual movements. He had apparently returned to Flanders by the beginning of 1538, and possibly considerably earlier.

Some very accomplished and distinctive manuscript decoration was carried out in the late 1520s, including work on the patents for Cardinal Wolsey's two colleges and illumination in liturgical manuscripts ordered for his use. Coincidence of date suggests that this work may be associated with the Horenbouts.[4] Two additional items not previously discussed in this context but clearly related to the Wolsey material are the English Ratification of the treaty of Amiens, produced in the autumn of 1527 (V. 34), and the 1532 Anglo-French agreement of Windsor, (V. 38). The work has usually been assigned to Gerard, largely on account of his prior reputation, but it does not seem overwhelmingly similar to work attributed to his Flemish period and could equally well have been carried out by Lucas or by his sister. Its Flemish character is, however, unassailable.

Of far greater long-term significance is the now generally accepted link between Lucas Horenbout and the earliest portrait miniatures to be produced in England. The connection was

V.42 Leaf from the Sforza Hours, c.1490 and 1520

The Sforza Hours was originally designed about 1490 for Bona of Savoy, and illuminated by the Milanese artist Giovan Pietro Birago. It passed to Bona's niece by marriage, Margaret of Austria, regent of the Netherlands. In 1519-20, Margaret ordered replacements for sixteen missing miniatures, together with two 'vignettes'. Payments for these to Gerard Horenbout of Ghent, her own Court painter, appear in her accounts. On this particular page, which marks the beginning of the Penitential Psalms, Italian and Flemish work are combined. The upper and lateral borders are by Birago. The panel in the lower border, enclosing an oval portrait image of Margaret's nephew, the newly-elected Emperor Charles V, dated 1520, is a 'vignette' painted for the regent. The image itself, which echoes Italian marginal elements elsewhere in the manuscript, appears to be based on a medal. J.M.B.

Illuminated MS on vellum, 130 x 95

Additional MS 34294, fo. 213, British Library

Mark Evans and Thomas Kren, 'Hours of Bona Sforza', in Thomas Kren, ed., *Renaissance Painting in Manuscripts: Treasures from the British Library* (New York, 1983), pp. 113-22

first proposed about forty years ago.[5] The initial example is thought to be the small circular image of Henry, set within a border of red and gold Flemish ornament incorporating the letters H and K linked by a knotted cord, which is now in the Fitzwilliam Museum.[6] An inscription describes the King as 'an[o] xxxv', but whether this means 'in the thirty-fifth year of his age', i.e. between 28 June 1525 and 27 June 1526, or 'at the age of thirty-five', between 28 June 1526 and 27 June 1527, is obscure. Several detached versions of the circular image exist (e.g. V. 45) and there are apparently contemporary images of Catherine of Aragon (V. 46) and of Princess Mary (V. 47). Other members of the immediate royal circle were also portrayed.[7]

The new form of portraiture received great impetus in the diplomatic exchanges preceding the treaty of Amiens. In the autumn of 1526 Henry received from a French embassy portraits of Francis I and his two young sons, by then held hostage in Spain as a surety for their father. From written descriptions it appears that these were miniatures enclosed in symbolically decorated lockets.[8] The miniature of the Dauphin attributed to Clouet (V. 44) is probably a version of one of them. However, the settings appear to have excited greater attention than their contents. Henry reciprocated early in the following year with portraits of himself and of Mary, whose proposed betrothal to the younger prince was to be a feature of the treaty (see V. 28). These too were symbolically mounted.[9] The image of Mary was no doubt a version of the surviving Horenbout miniature (V. 47) and the reference to 'The Emperor' on the ornament at her breast could be interpreted as a reminder of the political potential of her blood relationship to Francis's antagonist, Charles V.

Mary had however been officially betrothed to Charles V from August 1521 until her repudiation in June 1525. The proposed match had been greatly favoured by her Spanish mother, who was Charles's aunt. It is not impossible that her portrait pre-dates the summer of 1525 and that the first portrait of Henry should be assigned to the earliest possible date consistent with its inscription. The Fitzwilliam miniature of the King, like the half-length portrait of Catherine of Aragon in the Buccleuch collection, is essentially a small square page of vellum and not a detached circular image. Instances of miniature portraits bound into small books as personal mementos are not unusual in the sixteenth century.[10] Surviving gold girdle book-covers, including the panels assigned to the 1520s (VII. 17) are in general extremely close in size to the two rectangular royal miniatures. In August 1525 Mary was sent to establish her own court as Princess of Wales at Ludlow, which suggests a suitable occasion for an exchange of miniature portraits between the King, his wife and his daughter. During the following year or more, opportunities for Lucas Horenbout to take her likeness were infrequent.

In the past, historians of portrait-miniature painting have often given too little consideration to its dependence upon manuscript illumination, in which both circular picture spaces and realistic portraiture had long been commonplace. There is evidence to suggest that portrait specialists were in fact employed to contribute to fifteenth-century manuscript work.[11]

The techniques and materials seen in early miniatures have now been acknowledged to be the same as those in manuscripts.[12] At what point and in which country someone finally took the step of detaching such an image from the vellum page and allowing it to stand in its own right we do not and may never know.

V.43 The Croke Girdle Book, c.1540

The smallest surviving early Tudor girdle book contains an English translation of the Penitential Psalms by Master John Croke, who was one of the six clerks in Chancery during the greater part of the reign of Henry VIII. The translation was made at the request of Croke's wife, Prudentia Cave, and this elegant little copy, written out by Coke himself and bound in gold filigree with traces of black enamel, was no doubt intended for her use. The psalms are prefaced by a tiny portrait of Henry VIII, following the pattern established by Holbein at the end of the 1530s. Although it is not very expertly painted and has sometimes been regarded as a later addition,

the image is of exactly the right date for the manuscript in which it appears. There is increasing evidence to suggest that it was unusual for miniature portraits to be bound in to girdle books, which were worn as jewels by their owners. J.M.B.

Illuminated MS on vellum, 40 x 35

Stowe MS 956, British Library

Hugh Tait, 'Historiated Tudor jewellery', *Antiquaries Journal* 42 (1962), 232-7, p. 235.

Janet Backhouse, 'Illuminated Manuscripts and the Early Development of the Portrait Miniature', in Daniel Williams, ed., *Early Tudor England: Proceedings of the 1987 Harlaxton Symposium* (Woodbridge,1989), 1-17, pp. 15-16

V.44   The Dauphin François

In March 1526, François (1518-36), eldest son of
Francis I, and his brother Henry were handed over to
Charles V as hostages for the payment of the ransom
for their father, Francis I, captured at the battle of
Pavia (V.2). In late 1526 Marguerite, Francis's sister,
sent Henry VIII an elaborate locket with portraits of
her two captive nephews to excite English sympathy.
This miniature is probably a copy of the portrait of
François. Henry reciprocated the following year with
portraits of himself and Mary (V.47).   D.S.

Jean Clouet, attrib.

Watercolour on vellum, 62 dia.

Royal Collection

Strong, *Renaissance Miniature*, pp.27-9, fig. 11

V.45   Henry VIII with a Beard

This image of the King is dated by its inscription 'anno
xxxv' to 1525-7. This allows for two possibilities: either
that the sitting took place in 1527, when Henry sent his
miniature as a return gift to France (IV.44); or, nearly
two years earlier in 1525, when, with Mary about to go
to Ludlow as princess of Wales, the King and his
daughter may have exchanged miniatures (IV.47).   D.S.

Lucas Horenbout attrib., 1525-7

Watercolour on vellum, 47 dia.

Royal Collection

Strong, *Renaissance Miniature*, pp.27-9, fig. 11

V.47   Princess Mary

There are two possible dates for this miniature: either
1527, when Mary's miniature was sent to Francis I,
to whose younger son Henry she was now betrothed;
or 1525, when Mary and Henry may have exchanged
miniatures. If this was the version sent to France,
the huge 'Emperour' brooch she wears would either
be a reminder to France of the potential of her blood
ties to his enemy Charles V or a sign of Mary's own
intransigent commitment to the imperial cause. There
remains another possibility that this miniature was
prepared for Charles V himself, to whom Mary was
betrothed from August 1521 to June 1525. This would
make it perhaps the earliest English miniature.   D.S.

Lucas Horenbout attrib., 1525-7

Watercolour on vellum, 40 dia.

Brian Pilkington Esq.

Strong, *Renaissance Miniature*, p. 189 no. 9

V.46   Catherine of Aragon

The Latin inscription, 'Queen Catherine his wife',
presupposes it to be a pendant to one of the King.
Therefore it too probably dates to 1525-7. The contrast
between this and (N.49) helps explain the divorce.   D.S.

Lucas Horenbout attrib., 1525-7

Watercolour on vellum, 38 dia.

4682, National Portrait Gallery

Strong, *Renaissance Miniature*, p. 189 no. 8

V.48   Charles V

This miniature is a version of a portrait of the emperor
still in the Royal Collection. It probably belongs to
c.1525, as thereafter relations between Henry VIII and
Charles V remained frigid at best until the 1540s.   D.S.

Lucas Horenbout attrib.

Watercolour on vellum, 42 dia.

P.22-1942, Victoria and Albert Museum

Strong, *Renaissance Miniature*, p. 189 no. 10

V.49 Anne Boleyn

Sir Roy Strong's suggestion that the sitter is Anne
Boleyn is greatly strengthened by the recent dating of
Anne's birth to 1501. The Ontario version of this
miniature gives the sitter's age as twenty-five.
This would date the miniature to 1525-7 - that is, to the
moment when members of the royal family were first
portrayed in this way and when Anne herself first
joined the royal circle as Henry VIII's acknowledged
mistress. The jewel at her breast is therefore the falcon
(Anne's badge), not the phoenix (Jane Seymour's). D.S.

Lucas Horenbout attrib., 1525-7
Watercolour on vellum, 42 dia.
Duke of Buccleuch and Queensberry
Strong, *Renaissance Miniature*, p. 189 nos 15-16

V.50 Henry Fitzroy, Duke of Richmond

Henry Fitzroy was the issue of Henry VIII's liaison
with Elizabeth Blount. In 1525 the King, desperately
anxious about the lack a of male heir, created him
duke of Richmond and made him titular head of the
Council of the North. Richmond spent a happy year
at the French court in 1532-3, in company with his
friend and brother-in-law, the earl of Surrey. But he
caught tuberculosis and died in 1536. This miniature,
in his shirt and nightcap, must show him on his
sickbed. D.S.

Lucas Horenbout attrib., c.1534-5
Watercolour on vellum, 44 dia.
Royal Collection
Strong, *Renaissance Miniature*, p. 189-90 no. 17

Medals: Continental and English

Often the medal and the miniature are closely related. But in England, though the miniature
quickly became domesticated the medal did not. Very few English medals were produced and
the ones that were (V.54) were quite unlike continental examples.

V.51 Medal of Francis I, c.1515

The inscription F I REX FRANCO PRI DOM
HELVETIOR (Francis I, king of the French,
first conqueror of the Swiss) must refer to Francis's
victory at the battle of Marignano. G.F. Hill suggests
that this medal is by the same artist as a medal of
Ercole Gonzaga, of the same period, and concludes
that it is likely to be Italian. M.J.

Cast lead, 122 dia.
Department of coins and medals, British Museum
G.F. Hill, *A Corpus of Italian Medals of the Renaissance* (1930), nos.
258, 259.
M.P. Jones, *A Catalogue of French Medals in the British Museum* I, no. 18

V.52   Medal of Francis I, c.1525

This is a later copy of a medal possibly made c.1525, after a drawing by Jean Clouet. M.J.

Cast lead, 53 dia.

Department of coins and medals, British Museum

M.P. Jones, *A Catalogue of French Medals in the British Museum* I, no. 33

V.53   Medal of Henry VIII

This unique lead medal, which has been attributed to the German medallist Hans Schwarz, was probably made in the mid-1520s. It shows the King in profile, wearing a hat with drapery looped under the brim, a cloak and a riband, from which a medal or jewel would have hung, around his neck. M.J.

Cast lead, 60 dia.

Department of coins and medals, British Museum

E. Hawkins, A. W. Franks and H. A. Grubber, *Medallic Illustrations of Great Britain and Ireland* (1885), p. 30, no.14.

G. F. Hill and J. G. Pollard, *Medals of the Renaissance* (1978), p. 106

V.54   Henry VIII, 1545

This gold medal representing Henry VIII as 'defender of the faith and, under Christ, the supreme head on earth of the Church of England and Ireland', and a similar piece made in 1547 to commemorate the coronation of Edward VI, seem to have been made in England. They have been attributed to Henry Bayse, who was chief engraver at the Tower Mint from 1544-7. It is quite unlike contemporary European medals, in its primitive portrait, its coin-like appearance, and in the way the scholarship of its designer is advertised by the translation of the legend into Greek and Hebrew. M.J.

Struck gold, 54.5 dia.

Department of coins and medals, British Museum

E. Hawkins, A.W. Franks and H.A. Grubber, *Medallic Illustration of the History of Great Britain and Ireland* (1885 and 1969) p. 47, no. 44

G.F. Hill 'A Medal of Henry VIII as Supreme Head of the Church', *Numismatic Chronicle* (1916), pp. 194-5

V.55   Medal of Clement VII, 1534

This medal by Cellini commemorates the construction of Antonio da Sangallo's well at Orvieto, built on the orders of Clement VII. The circumstances of the commission are described by Cellini in his autobiography. The obverse was initially created for a medal celebrating peace in Italy, begun in 1533. The medal was finished only three days before Clement's death. Cellini made great claims for his screw-press, yet (as is not uncommon) there is a double image on the reverse. P.A.

Silver, 41 dia.; Department of coins and medals, British Museum

Benvenuto Cellini, *Autobiography* (Harmondsworth, 1985), p. 133.

J. Graham Pollard, *Medaglie Italiane del Rinascimento nel Museo Nazionale del Bargello*, II (Florence, 1985), no. 517

VI The Orders of the Garter and St Michael

ON SUNDAY, 10 NOVEMBER 1527 at Greenwich, Henry VIII was installed as a knight of the French Order of St Michael by Anne de Montmorency, Great Master of France; the same day Arthur Plantagenet, viscount Lisle, invested Francis I with the Garter at Paris. The banqueting and disguising houses at Greenwich, constructed for the celebrations of the peace treaty with France the previous May, were used again, with another lavish *mise-en-scène* run up inside. So other-worldly were its splendours, Cavendish (I.5) thought, that the next day it seemed 'but as a fantastical dream'. The Orders of Chivalry themselves now seem another 'fantastical dream'. But in their day they were a central part of an essentially aristocratic politics, and of international relations which followed the same rules.

The initiative in the exchange of Orders had come from Francis I in a conversation with Wolsey at Amiens. 'Now the the King my Brother and I be thus knit and married in our hearts together', Wolsey reported him as saying, 'it were well done ... that we should be knit "par collets et jambes" [by collars and legs] - meaning thereby that you should interchangeably take and receive each other's Order.' Henry VIII agreed and the symbolism of the exchange of Orders figured prominently in the special gold seals of the English and French ratifications of the treaty of Amiens that were exchanged at the same time (V.33, 35).

The exchange of the two Orders was unprecedented. The Garter was the oldest Order of chivalry. It had been established by Edward III on St George's Day, 23 April 1348 at Windsor, and consisted of the sovereign and twenty-five knights-companions, including the Black Prince. All had taken part in the recent campaigns in France as the king's brothers-in-arms. The reason for both the adoption of the Garter device and the motto 'Honi soit qui mal y pense' ('Evil be to him who evil thinks') are obscure. The knights met in annual Chapter on St George's Day to discuss the business of the Order; elect new knights to replace companions who had died, and hold a commemorative feast. Subsequent kings went out of their way to identify themselves with the Order. Edward IV began the rebuilding of St George's Chapel, Windsor and is buried there (along with Henry VI, whom he dethroned). The rebuilding was finished under Henry VII and paid for largely out of the estates of his councillor, Sir Reginald Bray, KG, whose punning badge of the hemp-press or 'bray' appears in the bosses of the vault. Henry VIII also took a strong personal interest in the Order: he gave definitive form to the collar which had been added to the insignia by Henry VII; reformed the statutes and commissioned the illuminated register known as the Black Book (VI.5). But there was no corresponding interest in Windsor itself: instead Chapters were held in whichever palace the King happened to be (more often than not Greenwich) and Henry often arranged for a deputy to preside over the feast.

The Order of St Michael was founded by Louis XI of France in 1469 and consisted of the king and thirty-six knights. The original seat of Mont St Michel was soon abandoned for Paris. The Chapter was supposed to meet at Michaelmas, 29 September, but was hardly ever convened. Instead, appoinment lay solely in the king's hands.

The insignia of the Order consisted of a mantle and a collar of cockle-shells (VI.7- 8). The Order had been founded in imitation of the Burgundian Order of the Golden Fleece. But its political purpose was to isolate Burgundy. Francis I, like Henry VIII, augmented the splendour of his Order. But the English envoy, Sir Anthony Browne (VI.9), was not impressed with the result: 'they would fain follow the fashion of your Order', he wrote to Henry VIII after witnessing the ceremonies of the St Michael, 'but they fail in everything ... I think in all the world there is no such Order as yours.'

Browne's was a prejudiced view. But the future of the two Orders rather bore him out. In the later sixteenth century the number of knights of the St Michael inflated enormously. The prestige of the Order collapsed, and in 1578 Henry III founded the new, superior Order of the Holy Spirit. England founded a second Order too. But it was the Order of the Bath, which was not established until 1725 and then as a second-best, to take those excluded from the Garter.

VI.5 The Black Book of the Garter

The Black Book, named after its (renewed) black velvet binding, is the first surviving register of the Garter. It was begun in 1534 but incorporates material from an earlier register (now lost) started under Henry V. Written in Latin, it contains the statutes, an account of the foundation of the Order, and the record of ceremonies and elections. It is finely written and richly (if sometimes rather roughly) illuminated in the Flemish style. There are representations, in illuminated initials, of the founder, Edward III and Queen Philippa, and the Lancastrian, Yorkist and Tudor kings. The greatest of them, Henry V, is shown as a clear likeness of Henry VIII. Henry VIII's own reign begins with a double-page representation of the ceremonies of the Order for 1534: above left, Henry VIII surrounded by twenty-five knights in the robes of the Order; bottom left and right, the knights, in armorial surcoats, process to chapel, where, above right, the three junior knights arrive.

The Black Book shows the impact of the Reformation: the hand becomes rougher in 1540-1 and the decorations have been mutilated and sponged to eliminate 'superstitious' elements. D.S.

Illuminated MS on vellum, 420 x 300

G 1, Windsor Aerary

Lent by the Most Noble Order of the Garter and with the Gracious Permission of Her Majesty the Queen

J. Anstis, *The Register of the Most Noble Order of the Garter*, 2 vols. (1724)

E. Ashmole, *The Institution, Laws and Ceremonies of the Most Noble Order of the Garter* (1672), pp.198-201

E. Auerbach, 'The Black Book of the Garter', *Report of the Society of the Friends of St George's* 5 (1972-3), pp. 149-53

VI.1 Election of Henry VIII to the Order of St Michael

On 15 September 1527 at Compiègne Henry VIII was elected to the French Order of St Michael. The same day, Francis I's favourite and chief adviser, Anne de Montmorency, was commissioned to go to England to inform Henry of his election and install him. Both the commission and the notice of election are sealed with the seal of the Order, and subscribed by Robertet, the *greffier* or registrary of the Order, 'By order of the king, chief and sovereign of the Order, in the presence of the brother knights and companions of the same being the electors'. D. S.

1. Commission, 15 September 1527: MS on vellum, 560 x 510
2. Notice of election, 15 September 1527: MS on vellum, 630 x 650
E 30/1447, 1448, Public Record Office
LP IV ii, 3428/1, 2

VI.2 Election of Francis I to the Order of the Garter

On 14 October 1527 Montmorency landed at Dover and made his way to the English Court at Greenwich. There, on 21 October, Henry VIII and fourteen knights of the Garter met in chapter. Francis I was nominated unanimously and his election confirmed by the King. On 22 October Arthur Plantagenet, viscount Lisle, the King's bastard uncle, was made head of a commission to install the French king; on 25 October Henry VIII wrote formally to Francis I to ask him to accept the Order; Henry also personally corrected the draft terms (softening the usual rules) for Francis's acceptance. The documents were heavily influenced by their French equivalents: the exact wording of the

subscription 'By order of the King ...' was copied and the name of the Order adjusted to the 'Order of My Lord St George, called the Garter' to make it correspond to the French. D.S.

1. Commission, 22 October 1527: MS on vellum, 360 x 710
Additional MS 5712, fo. 30, British Library
2. Letter from Henry VIII to Francis I, 25 October 1527:
MS on paper, 265 x 200
Additional MS 5712, fos. 27-8, British Library
3. Draft certificate, corrected by Henry VIII, 10 November 1527:
MS on paper, 330 x 300
Additional MS 5712, fo. 29, British Library
LP IV ii, 3494, 3508, 3516, 3565/2
J. Anstis, *The Register of the Most Noble Order of the Garter*,
2 vols. (1724) II, pp. 380-83

VI.3 Statutes of the Order of St Michael

This is the copy of the statutes of the Order of
St Michael presented to Henry VIII on the occasion of
his installation as a knight of the Order in November
1527. It is embellished with a full-page miniature
representing the foundation of the Order by Louis XI
in 1469. Copies of these statutes traditionally included
such a miniature but this example, although it
represents the commercial rather than the de luxe
level of French illumination in the late 1520s, is of a

standard appropriate to a royal diplomatic gift.
Records of payment reveal that copies of the statutes
were being written and illuminated in batches
during the 1520s, and other surviving contemporary
copies are in the main of very indifferent quality. J.M.B.

Illuminated MS on vellum, 300 x 420
E 36/276, [*LP* IV ii, 3428/4] Public Record Office
Paul Durrieu, 'Les manuscrits des Statuts de l'Ordre de Saint-
Michel', *Bulletin de la Société française de reproductions de
manuscrits à peintures* 1 (Paris, 1911), 17-47, pp. 29-32

VI.4 Statutes of the Order of the Garter

This is the copy of the statutes of the Order of the
Garter, which was presented to Francis I when he was
installed as a knight of the Garter in November 1527.
The frontispiece was specially designed for the
occasion. The solid golden background is patterned
with stylized roses and fleurs-de-lis. The arms of the
Order, of Henry as its sovereign and of Francis I as a
member, and all encircled with Garters, are placed
between the symbolic roses and lilies of the two

kingdoms which are themselves united by a gold cord
held by the fashionably attired figure of Concord.
The latter must also represent Princess Mary,
whose marriage to Francis I's younger son was to
cement the treaty. J.M.B.

Illuminated MS on vellum, 275 x 390
Additional MS 5712 [*LP* IV ii, 3566], British Museum

VI.5 The Black Book of the Garter: See page 95

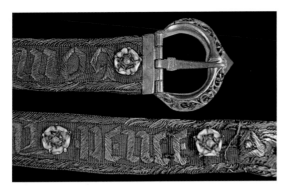

VI.6   Garter of Maximilian I, King of the Romans, c.1489

The silk Garter has a gold and enamelled buckle and Tudor roses. The roses are set between the words of the motto, 'Honi soit qui mal y pense', which are embroidered in gold thread. On the back is a plate engraved with the arms of Maximilian as king of the Romans. Maximilian was elected king of the Romans in 1486 and knight of the Garter three years later. This is the earliest surviving Garter. Garters, like the other insignia of the Order, are very rare as the statutes required that they be returned to the sovereign on the death of the knight. The Garter is the chief and oldest insignia of the Order; the Collar was only instituted under Henry VII. D.S.

Silk, enamelled gold and gold thread, 540 lgth

The National Trust: Anglesey Abbey

C. R. Beard, 'The Emperor Maximilian's Garter', *The Connoisseur* 131 (1953), pp. 108-9

VI.7   Pendant of the Order of St Michael, 1607

As with the Garter, and for the same reason, early insignia of the St Michael are very rare. This pendant was presented to Marin de Vanssay in 1607. It shows, within a miniature collar of the Order, the Archangel Michael, the chief knight of Heaven, slaying the Dragon-Devil. The pendant hung from the collar of the Order. The earlier versions of the pendant were more sculptuarl in form, without the encircling miniature collar. D.S.

Gold enamelled, 450ht, 400w

Musée National de la Légion d'Honneur, Paris

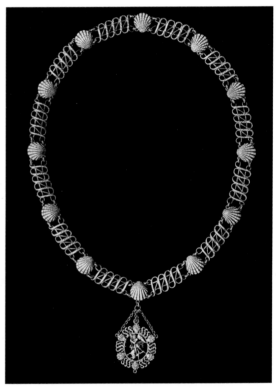

VI.8   Collar of the Order of St Michael, 1662

The original collar of the St Michael consisted of cockle-shells (the emblem of Mont St Michel, the first seat of the Order) alternating with knots. Under Francis I the cockle-shells were paired and the knots (too near probably to the Garter collar) were replaced in 1516 by a double friar's girdle. The paired shells disappeared but the girdle remained, as in this late sixteenth-century example, presented in 1662 to Corneille-Lampsins. D.S.

Gold with white enamel, 250 lgth

Rijksmuseum, Amsterdam

De l'Ordre de Saint-Michel à la Légion d'Honneur, catalogue of an exhibition at the Hôtel de Ville, Amboise (1970), no. 10

VI.9 Sir Anthony Browne, c.1500-48

This portrait, as the inscription suggests, was probably posthumous. But it is based on a likeness taken many years before, when the sitter was young. This likeness is French in style, and may well have been painted when Browne was in France. He was ambassador there in 1527, and was one of those commissioned to deliver the Garter to Francis I. He was present at the ceremonies of the St Michael at Michaelmas (29 September) 1527, and compared them very unfavourably with the Garter: some knights wore collars, some only escutcheons of St Michael and none robes. 'I think in all the world is no such Order as yours,' he wrote to Henry. Browne himself became a knight of the Garter in 1540 and is here shown with the Lesser George on a blue ribbon round his neck. The Lesser George was instituted by Henry VIII in 1521 as the everyday mark of knights of the Garter. D.S.

Artist unknown, c.1550
Oil on panel, 924 x 749
5186, National Portrait Gallery

VI.10 Garter Stall-Plate of Sir Anthony Browne, 1540

Sir Anthony Browne was, as the inscription on this plate tells us, installed as a knight of the Garter in 1540. The plate would normally have been placed among those of other knights on the back of the stalls in St George's Chapel, Windsor. However, it appears to have been rejected, perhaps because of errors in the tinctures, the quarterings and the inscriptions, all of which are slightly different on the far finer version that is still in the Chapel at Windsor. It is unclear why the incorrect plate was not destroyed. H.T.

Gilt copper, engraved and enamelled, 167 x 123
OA 85, British Museum
E.H. Fellowes, *The Knights of the Garter 1348-1939 with a Complete List of the Stall-Plates in St George's Chapel* (1939), p. 23
R. Marks and A Payne, eds., *British Heraldry from its Origins to c.1800*, British Museum and British Library exhib. cat. (1978), no. 258

VI.11 A Knight of the Garter's Stirrup

The unusual width of this stirrup is designed to accommodate the wide and square-toed sabatons of the fashionable suits of armour that were made from about 1515 onwards, as on Henry VIII's three suits of armour now preserved in the Tower of London and at Windsor Castle (IV.2). The two lost roundels formerly applied within the Garter and Motto (in relief) at each side may have borne the enamelled coat-of-arms of the sovereign or of one of his twenty-five knights of the Garter. The naturalistic, branch-like form of the arches, found in combination with decorative motifs in relief of a purely Renaissance character (at the sides and in the centre of the stirrup), was probably at its most fashionable in English Court circles around 1520. H.T.

Gilt metal, 176 ht, 164 w.
S1. 1451, British Museum

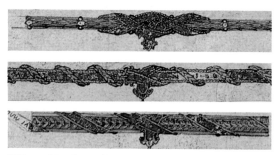

VI.12 Designs for Jewellery, including Garters

The three Garter designs are elegant variations on the usual pattern (VI.6) and lace or twine the characteristic blue of the Garter with gold laurel. They could have been intended either as decorative borders or as designs for actual Garters. D.S.

Hans Holbein
Pen and brown ink, with yellow wash on blue body-colour on paper, 77 lgth
5308-82, 82*, 82**, British Museum

VII The Great Hall: a Royal Christening, 1533

ELIZABETH, daughter of Henry VIII and his second Queen, Anne Boleyn, was christened and confirmed in a single ceremony at Greenwich on 10 September 1533. Anne, secretly married to Henry on 25 January and crowned in a blaze of publicity on 1 June, had 'taken to her chamber' at Greenwich on 26 August. This was the custom by which a pregnant queen took leave of the masculine world until the moment of her delivery. The carpenters at Greenwich had been busy preparing her apartment since the start of the month: putting a false ceiling in her bedchamber and hanging it with arras; building a cupboard of state for her plate, and 'making a great bed of state in the Queen's chamber of presence'. On this frame was mounted 'one of the richest and most triumphant beds' in the royal wardrobe. Buoyed up by the assurances of his astrologers and physicians, Henry's hopes of a son were high: jousts were organized and the French ambassador was approached to see if he had authority to carry the prince to the font. All this was hastily abandoned when Anne was delivered of a girl on 7 September.

It was resolved to put on a good show nevertheless. Immediately the carpenters were set to work to frame the way from the door of the great hall to the Friars' Church and hang it with tapestry (VII.1), while inside the church, also hung with tapestry, they built a three-stepped platform on which to stand the silver font. At 1 p.m. on Wednesday, 10 September the mayor, aldermen and leading citizens of London were rowed to Greenwich in two barges and joined the procession. Mary Howard, duchess of Richmond (VII.5) bore the chrism; the child 'in a mantle of purple velvet, with a long train furred with ermine' was carried by the dowager duchess of Norfolk, supported by the duke of Norfolk (VII.4), 'with his marshal's rod', on the right, and the duke of Suffolk (III.9) on the left, while the dowager marchioness of Dorset (VII.6) was one of the godmothers and the dowager duchess of Norfolk the other.

Despite the relatively low-key appropriate to the birth of a princess, the christening was a triumph for Anne Boleyn and her uncle the duke of Norfolk. Norfolk, who had used his niece's coronation to regain the family office of earl marshal from Suffolk, now officiated again, while members of his family dominated the ceremony. For Anne, the very site of the ceremony was a sweet revenge as the observant friars of Greenwich had been among the most vocal and outspoken opponents of the divorce. The Friary was dissolved the following year. Yet the triumph was a hollow one. Until Anne produced a son she would never be secure - and the son never came. Instead, three years later at the Mayday jousts at Greenwich, Anne and her leading supporters in the Privy Chamber, including her brother Lord Rochford and the musician Mark Smeaton (VII.7), were arrested, charged with multiple adultery and executed.

Yet Anne's reign, despite its shortness and its shameful end, was not barren. Instead, historians are now coming to endorse the contemporary judgment of both friends and enemies and see Anne as one of the first patrons of religious reform in England: she used her own example, her patronage of men and books, and her power over the King (VII.10). Particularly striking is the role of France. Understanding with France provided the diplomatic precondition for the divorce (VII.25); while Anne's own education, whether in the Netherlands or in France itself, was French; so were many of the books she bought and the men she patronized (VII.9-12); even Henry VIII's love letters to her were almost all in that language too. Here we see how Court culture, even the culture of courtly love, and religious reform could be allies, not enemies. The combination receives its highest expression in the poetry of the Boleyn circle, in particular the work of Sir Thomas Wyatt (VII.13). But it was not only a Court phenomenon as the progress of 1535 shows (VIII).

VII.10 Mrs Anne Zouche [?], by Hans Holbein

Inscribed 'M Souch', the identification of the sitter turns on the meaning of the 'M'. If 'Mary', then the sitter is the daughter of John, Lord Zouche of Haringworth. Unhappy at home after her father's remarriage, she sought a place at Court; became a member of Jane Seymour's household and eventually received an annuity of £10 in consideration of her service. But if 'Mrs' is meant, then the subject is probably Anne Gainsford, lady-in-waiting to Anne Boleyn and fiancée and later wife of George Zouche of Codnor. The couple shared Anne Boleyn's religious views and Anne Gainsford was the unwitting instrument of Anne Boleyn's introducing Henry VIII to Tyndale's *Obedience of a Christian Man*. D.S.

Chalk and ink on pink-primed paper, 294 x 210
Royal Collection
Parker/Foister, no. 72

101

The Politics and the Setting

Two events heralded the Boleyn marriage: the death of Archbishop Warham (VII.2) in August 1532, and the meeting between Francis I and Henry and Anne in October 1532. Emboldened, the couple first slept together in November and were secretly married on 25 January 1533. On 10 September Elizabeth was carried along a tapestry-hung route to be christened in the Friars' Church.

VII.1   The Story of Esther: Esther Hearing of Haman's Plot

VII.2   Archbishop William Warham of Canterbury, c.1450-1532

This tapestry depicts Esther's reaction to news of the plot which Haman, the favourite minister of King Ahasuerus, has instigated against the Jews.

Like David and Bathsheba, Esther was an exceedingly popular subject in fifteenth- and sixteenth-century tapestries. In the reign of Henry VIII it received a particular application to the overthrow of wicked ministers (Wolsey or Cromwell) by good Queens (Anne Boleyn or Catherine Howard). Henry's Inventory lists at least four sets of the subject and while there is no evidence to identify this piece as being from the royal collection it is nonetheless an interesting example of the sort of medium-quality tapestry with which Henry's palaces were hung on a daily basis. T.C.

For a long time, this painting was thought to be Holbein's original and the version in the Louvre the copy; then, as a result of an inspired guess by Roy Strong followed by dendrochronological analysis, the status of the two was reversed.

Warham, a rather legalistic royal servant for most of his life, was finally galvanized into resisting Henry's claims to royal supremacy over the English Church. But his death in 1532 opened the way for the appointment of Thomas Cranmer as his successor. Cranmer, a Boleyn protégé, was conscientiously committed both to the Boleyn marriage and to religious reform. D.S.

Brussels tapestry, c.1500-1525
Wool and silk, 3420 x 4000
5669-1859, Victoria and Albert Museum
G. W. Digby, Victoria and Albert Museum: *The Tapestry Collection: Medieval and Renaissance* (1980), pp. 42-3

After Holbein, c.1580-90
Oil on panel, 709 x 606
Lambeth Palace
E. Foucart-Walter, *Les peintures de Hans Holbein le Jeune au Louvre* (Editions de la Réunion des Musées Nationaux: Paris, 1985), pp. 32-3

Participants in the Ceremony

Elizabeth's christening was dominated by members of Anne Boleyn's family and her Howard cousins. Thomas Cranmer, the Boleyn client who was Warham's successor as archbishop of Canterbury, officiated, and the duke of Norfolk, Anne's uncle, presided as earl marshal, while Norfolk's stepmother and daughter played other leading roles.

VII.3   Anne Boleyn, 1501-36

This is a good version of the standard portrait type of Anne Boleyn. Its accuracy has been argued for by Eric Ives, Anne's latest biographer, using a ring which combines a miniature version of this image with a profile portrait of Queen Elizabeth, Anne's daughter. But (V.49), with the reconsideration of its dating and badges, probably has the claim to primacy, for it is certainly contemporary. D.S.

Artist unknown
Oil on panel, 572 x 432
The Dean and Chapter of Ripon
E. W. Ives, *Anne Boleyn* (Oxford, 1986), pp. 54-6, plates 1, 6-7

VII.4   Thomas Howard, Duke of Norfolk, 1473-1554

This is one of several good versions of Holbein's original in the Royal Collection. The duke holds the staff of the lord treasurer in his left hand and the baton of earl marshal in his right. He exercised the office for the first time at Anne's coronation. At the christening, Norfolk and Suffolk walked on either side of the dowager duchess of Norfolk, who carried the baby. D.S.

Oil on panel, 901 x 705
Duke of Norfolk
Rowlands, no. 68

VII.5   Mary Howard, Duchess of Richmond, 1519-57, by Hans Holbein

Mary married Henry Fitzroy, duke of Richmond (V.50) in 1533. The marriage was never consummated. At Elizabeth's christening she carried the chrism for the confirmation which followed immediately after the child's baptism. D.S.

Chalks and ink on pink-primed paper, 267 x 201
Royal Collection
Foister/Parker, no. 16

VII.6   Margaret, Marchioness of Dorset (d. 1541), by Hans Holbein

Margaret Wotton married Thomas Grey, 2nd marquess of Dorset, in 1509. He died in 1530. At Elizabeth's christening his widow - referred to as the 'old marchioness' and shown here grasping a walking staff - was one of the baby's godmothers. Several copies of a painting after this drawing survive. D.S.

Chalks and ink on pink-primed paper, 333 x 238
Royal Collection
Foister/Parker, no. 28

Music at the Court of Henry VIII

BY PETER HOLMAN

Music was important to the Tudor age. It was a prominent feature of the mental world of an educated man by virtue of its role as an expression of the harmony of the cosmos, and by its traditional place in the university syllabus. On a practical level, music was thought to be, as Castiglione put it, 'not only an ornament, but necessary for a courtier.'[1] But the aristocracy cultivated it in limited and specific ways: their children normally learned solo instruments, on which they would have played solo music or accompanied their own singing. Most of the Tudors played the lute, or, in the case of Henry VIII's sister Mary and his children Mary and Elizabeth, the lute and the keyboard. Playing and singing in ensembles was left largely to professionals, because amateurs lacked the more advanced skills it required, and because it was still thought, in the words of Sir Thomas Elyot, 'that a gentleman, playing or singing in a common audience, appaireth his estimation'.[2]

Thus Henry VIII was exceptionally musical by the standards of his time. As well as playing the lute, the keyboard and, probably, the harp (he appears with one in an illumination in his psalter, (XI. 31), he could sing 'from book at sight', and could play ensemble instruments such as the recorder.[3] He was even a composer of sorts, though his achievements in that direction have been exaggerated: he did not write 'Greensleeves', as is popularly thought (it is based on an Italian chord progression that became known in England only after his death), and some of the pieces attributed to him in 'Henry VIII's Manuscript' (XI. 23) are arrangements rather than original compositions. Even 'Pastime with good company' may not be all his own work, for the melody also appears in a chanson published in Paris in 1529.[4] 'Henry VIII's Manuscript' was not

VII.7 Music Book Written for Anne Boleyn, perhaps by Mark Smeaton

This rather old-fashioned collection of thirty-nine Latin motets and five French chansons of the Franco-Flemish school (dominated by the works of Josquin and Mouton) was compiled for Anne Boleyn. On page 4 an illuminated initial shows a falcon (Anne's badge) furiously pecking a pomegranate (the badge of Catherine of Aragon, Anne's displaced predecessor); the music book opens with a motet perhaps composed for her coronation festivities in May-June 1533; and on page 157 musical notation is used to symbolize her execution three years later. It has been suggested that the compiler of the manuscript was Mark Smeaton, a favourite musician of the King's Privy Chamber. He was infatuated with Anne, who scornfully rejected him as 'an inferior person'. At the time of Anne's fall he was forced, probably under torture, to confess to committing adultery with her, so destroying them both. The attribution of the music book to Smeaton has recently been challenged. D.S.

MS on paper, 285 x 190

MS 1070, Royal College of Music

E. Lowinsky, 'A Music Book for Anne Boleyn' in J.G. Rowe and W.H. Stockdale, eds., *Florilegium Historiale* (Toronto & Buffalo, 1971)

VII.8 'Queen Elizabeth's Virginals'

This pair of virginals is strikingly similar to one made by Benedetto Floriano in 1571 in Venice, but the original keyboard layout was distinctively English. All the forward-facing parts of the case (which alone are visible inside the more robust, and later, outer case) are decorated with red and blue varnishes over a gold ground leaving a reserved pattern of gold moresques. The English royal arms as borne by the Tudor monarchs appear in the panel to the left of the keyboard while the panel on the extreme right shows Anne Boleyn's badge of a falcon on a stump. There is no sign of any alterations to the decoration. The instrument has been traditionally associated with Queen Elizabeth I throughout its recorded history. But the use of Anne Boleyn's device, which is rare in Elizabethan iconography, remains a puzzle. F.P.

1524 x 178 x 406

H. Schott, *Victoria and Albert Museum Catalogue of Musical Instruments, Volume I, Keyboard Instruments* (2nd edn, 1985)

actually compiled by or for the King: it seems to have belonged to the controller of the Household, Sir Henry Guildford (see V.4 and V.20). But it certainly reflects the diverse musical life of the Court in the first years of the reign. The King and his cronies presumably sang the many simple English rounds and part-songs it contains, including two versions of 'Pastime with good company'. There is also a selection of popular continental chansons and instrumental pieces that belong more to the sphere of professional music-making; some of them were clearly models for pieces by English court composers. The King showed less interest in music making as he got older, which may be the reason why we have no 'Henry VIII Book' for the 1530s or 40s, though there are several sources of lute and keyboard music, including a recently- discovered manuscript that has associations with the playwright and Côurt virginal player John Heywood (c.1497-1580).[5]

The King left his most enduring mark on music through his patronage of professional musicians. All Court musicians were members of the Chamber under the lord chamberlain, but they were divided into a number of separate ensembles. The Chapel Royal, the oldest (it dates from the thirteenth century), provided the King with daily choral services, though its members also took part in Court pageants and disguisings.[6] The Chapel Royal was the leading choir in England at the time - in 1515 a Venetian diplomat thought their voices 'really rather divine than human' - and it became still more pre-eminent later in the reign, when many of its rivals were disrupted by the dissolution of the monasteries.[7] We can presume that its repertory was founded on works by its members, including Robert Fayrfax, William Cornish, Avery Burton and Thomas Tallis, though choirbooks of continental motets were copied for Henry and Catherine of Aragon by the Flemish scribe Pierre Alamire, and for Anne Boleyn by, possibly, Mark Smeaton, the musician who ensured Anne's downfall by confessing to their adultery (VII. 7).[8]

Smeaton was a musician of the Privy Chamber. This meant that he belonged to the elite of secular musicians. They were divided into two: the minority, who had access to the privy chamber, and the majority, who worked outside in the presence chamber. This distinction, of course, only dates from the establishment of the Privy Chamber itself in the 1490s, and its embodiment in the Eltham Ordinances of 1526; before then the minstrels were a single body. But such an arrangement was foreshadowed by the medieval distinction between those who played *bas* instruments in small rooms, and those who played *haut* instruments outdoors or in large halls.[9] Musicians were usually granted access to the privy chamber on an unofficial basis; most do not appear in its lists, and we know of their status only from casual references in other documents. They tended to be lutenists, like the Netherlands composer Philip Van Wilder, or keyboard players, like Mark Smeaton, and must have spent most of their time teaching members of the royal family or entertaining them with solo music. Towards the end of the reign, however, Van Wilder ran a group of 'singing men and children' in the privy chamber; they were distinct from the Chapel Royal, and probably sang vocal chamber music, including his own French chansons.[10]

The Presence Chamber musicians can be divided in turn into those who were more functionaries than musicians, such as the trumpeters and the fife and drum players, and those who were musicians first and foremost. The numbers of the second category greatly increased during Henry VIII's reign, in part because the last exponents of the solo minstrelsy of the middle ages were giving way to organized groups of four, five or six, who played polyphonic music on sets of instruments of different sizes. The earliest example of the latter at Court was an *alta capella*, the dance-band of Flemish towns that consisted of two or three shawms improvising over a plainsong-like melody played by a slide trumpet or sackbut.[11] Holbein's *Musicians on a balcony* (V.9) may represent such a group, perhaps playing for dancing at a revel, though the musical accuracy of the drawing is called into question by the inclusion of a straight trumpet with a banner - a herald's instrument that is unlikely to have been used in a polyphonic ensemble.

Most of Henry VIII's instrumentalists came from abroad. This was not because native musicians were thought to be inferior - the Chapel Royal lists are full of English names - but because the skills needed to make and play sets of instruments had been developed on the continent; were still fairly novel, and could most easily be provided by groups of travelling musicians. Cases in point are the five recorder-playing members of the Bassano family and the consort of six string-players who arrived in London in the spring of 1540; they were recruited in Venice on the orders of Thomas Cromwell as part of the preparations for Henry's marriage to Anne of Cleves (below, pp. 140-43).[12] Recent research has revealed that they were Jews in flight from the Inquisition. England gave them refuge, provided they were prepared to conform to the established religion; they proved to be reliable servants who, in Roger Prior's words, 'owed loyalty neither to the pope or to Luther'.[13] The Bassanos later became famous for their instruments, some of which still survive, and descendants of the members of both the 1540 groups served the Crown until the Civil War.[14]

The reign of Henry VIII set the pattern for music at Court for the next hundred years and beyond. Indeed, the distinction between Privy Chamber and Presence Chamber musicians only finally disappeared when James II reformed the royal household in 1685. One Henrician foundation lasted much longer: the six-man string consort of 1540 was the ancestor of Charles II's Twenty-four Violins, and the twenty-four places of the royal band remained, on paper at least, until it finally disappeared during the Great War.[15]

Anne Boleyn as Patron

BY MARIA DOWLING

Anne Boleyn has been regarded as something of a lightweight in the history of Renaissance and Reformation: a frivolous butterfly who, if she thought of religion at all, perceived of it only as a weapon in politics. The opposite is true and ample evidence exists that she was a woman of some culture, an active promoter of the Reformation, and a practitioner of evangelical devotion.

Anne spent part of her youth at the French Court, and possibly some time too in the household of Margaret of Austria in the Netherlands. She returned to England fluent in French (though not in Latin) and with a taste for beautiful books and ornaments. The manuscript volumes she owned were exquisitely illuminated and elegantly bound (VII.11-12). Her artistic taste is also shown by the metalwork she commissioned. There is a silver standing cup, now in Cirencester parish church, topped by her device of the falcon; English in make, it is Italian in inspiration (IX.11). And it was Holbein himself who designed the table fountain which she presented to Henry VIII at New Year 1534. His sketch incorporates the Boleyn falcon into a Renaissance design of satyrs, nymphs and antique heads (IX.16).[1]

A striking picture of Anne as she was in these years is given in a biography by her chaplain, William Latymer. The biography is hagiographic, but much of the detail can be checked. Anne was, Latymer wrote, 'very expert in the French tongue, exercising herself continually in reading the French Bible and other French books of like effect, and conceived great pleasure in the same. Wherefore her highness charged her chaplains to be furnished of all kind of French books that reverently treated of the holy scriptures'.[2] Another witness, Rose Hickman, daughter of the mercer William Locke, recalled, 'I have heard my father say that when he was a young

Nicholas Borbonius Poeta.

VII.9 Nicolas Bourbon (1503-c.1550), by Hans Holbein

Bourbon, a French poet and Protestant, sought refuge in England in 1535. He was maintained at Anne Boleyn's expense in Dr Butts's house (XI.4). He returned to France after Anne's fall. In his collection of occasional verses entitled *Nugae* (Trifles) he included poems addressed to Anne, Butts, and other members of the evangelical circle at Court, like Cranmer, Cromwell (IX.3) and Sir Edward Baynton (below, p.118). The frontispiece to the collection was a woodcut, based on this drawing and dated 1535. Holbein, who shows Bourbon in fashionable profile and writing, was also mentioned in the dedicatory letter to *Nugae* as 'the royal painter, the Apelles of our time'. D.S.

Chalks and ink on pink-primed paper, 307 x 260
Royal Collection
Foister/Parker, no. 37
Maria Dowling, *Humanism in the Age of Henry VIII* (1986), p. 146

VII.10 Mrs Anne Zouche [?], by Hans Holbein: See page 101

merchant and used to go beyond sea Queen Anne Boleyn ... caused him to get her the gospels and epistles written in parchment in French, together with the psalms'.[3]

Books corresponding to these descriptions survive. Anne owned a copy of the French translation of the Bible by the humanist Jacques Lefevre of Etaples, printed at Antwerp in 1534 (VII. 12). while an unknown kinsman presented her with a manuscript volume of 'The Epistles and Gospels for the Fifty-Two Sundays in the Year, with an Exhortation to Each in English', the scriptural text being Lefevre's French translation. Similarly, Anne had an illuminated manuscript of Ecclesiastes, with the text in French and a commentary in English. She also had an exquisite French psalter.[4]

These books were used as much for public demonstrations of piety as for personal devotion, as Loys de Brun made clear in dedicating a treatise on letter-writing to Anne at New Year 1530: 'When I consider your great affection and perfect desire for the French tongue, I am not surprised that you are not to be found (when the occasion is fitting) without some French book in your hand which is useful and necessary for teaching and discovering the true and straight path of all virtue: such as approved translations from holy scripture, filled with all good doctrines; or equally, other good books by erudite men, giving salutary remedies for this mortal life and consolation to the immortal soul. And chiefly I have seen you this last Lent, when I was in this magnificent, excellent and triumphant Court, reading the salutary epistles of St Paul, in which are contained the whole manner and rule of a good life.'[5]

Latymer says that Anne encouraged discussion of scripture during meals, and recalls a prolonged debate leading to correspondence between the King and Sir James Boleyn on one side and Anne's chaplains Hugh Latimer and Nicholas Shaxton on the other.

Tradition holds that Anne gave her ladies prayer books to hang from their girdles. Two manuscripts compete for the honour of being one of these gifts, but in neither case does the claim seem likely (V.43, VII.14). In contrast, Latymer relates that Mary Shelton, Anne's cousin and waiting-woman, was rebuked by her for having 'certain idle poesies' written in her prayer book. Latymer's anecdote has two points. Mary Shelton was thought to have had an affair or at least a flirtation with Henry VIII after his marriage to Anne, and this incident would contrast her light immorality with Anne's serious piety; and more generally, Latymer sought to correct the image of Anne as a frivolous and wanton being and present her instead as a responsible princess and devout reformer.

Latymer's austere portrait of Anne must be tempered by knowledge of her interest in music, shown by her book of 'motets and chansons' (VII.7), and by the poetry read and produced by her associates. A book of poems by Jean Lefevre contains the signatures of George Boleyn and Mark Smeaton. (VII.13) The 'Devonshire MS', an anthology of poetry owned by Anne's cousin Mary, duchess of Richmond (VII.5), contains entries written up by Mary Shelton and Margaret Douglas,

VII.11 Clément Marot, Le Pasteur Evangélique

This is a version of Marot's *Sermon du bon pasteur et du mauvais*. The original, a compilation of Scriptural texts on the theme of the Good Shepherd, elegantly versified into French, has been retitled and adapted for presentation to Anne Boleyn. The frontispiece shows Anne's arms as Queen, imperially crowned, wreathed and with her badge of the white falcon beneath and there are complimentary verses celebrating the uniting of the royal families of England and France, and in particular, the two great ladies, Marguerite of Navarre and Anne Boleyn, who were committed to reform. The poem ends by assuring Anne that Christ would give her a son, the image of his father, and that the King and Queen would live to see him grow into manhood. D.S.

Illuminated MS on vellum, 197 x 140

Royal MS 16 E XIII, fos. 1v-2, British Library

Lowinsky, 'A Music Book for Anne Boleyn', pp. 189-90

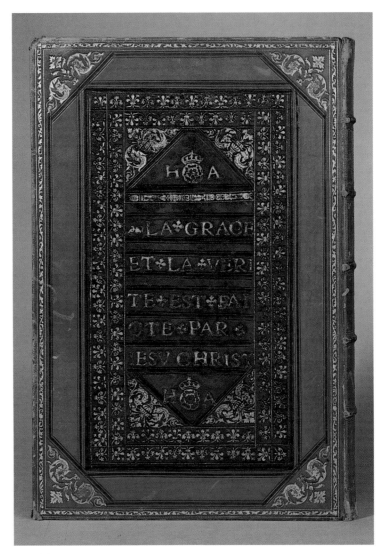

VII.12 La Saincte Bible en Francoys, translated by Jacques Lefevre d'Etaples, vol. II

The Bible in the vernacular was central to the 'evangalism' espoused by Anne. This copy of the 1534 Antwerp edition has been bound for Henry VIII and Anne Boleyn. Crowned Tudor roses and 'HA' ciphers appear on the binding of both volumes, together with evangelical texts in French emphasizing the contrast between the Old Law and the New. On the front of this volume is written: 'The Law has been given by Moses', and on the back, 'Grace and the Truth [have been given] by Jesus Christ'. The same motto appears in Latin on another book from Henry VIII's library (XI.28). D.S.

Printed book, 379 x 265
C 18 c 9, British Library

the King's niece.[6] At the same time, two of the courtier-poets in Anne's circle displayed deep religious sentiment. Sir Thomas Wyatt's devotional poetry is marked by scriptural piety, while Anne's brother George spoke from the scaffold of his own shortcomings as a Gospeller: 'Men do common and say that I have been a setter-forth of the word of God and one that hath favoured the gospel of Christ; and because I would not that God's word should be slandered by me, I say unto you all that if I had followed God's word in deed as I did read it and set it forth to my power, I had not come to this.'[7]

Two French poets are associated with Anne: Clément Marot and Nicolas Bourbon. She owned an extremely fine manuscript of the *Sermon du bon pasteur et du mauvais* by the evangelical Clément Marot (VII.11). Anne's version is retitled *Le Pasteur évangélique*, and differs from the

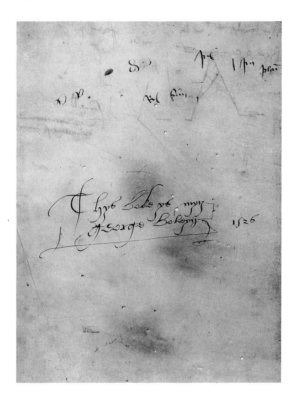

VII.13 Jean Lefevre, 'Les Lamentations de Matheolus' and 'Le Livre de Leesce'

The signatures in this book, which contains two fifteenth-century French poems in manuscript, one a satire against women and marriage and the other a reply, show how the volume was passed round the Boleyn circle. First it was owned by Anne's brother, Viscount Rochford, who wrote at the beginning 'Thys boke ys myne, George Boleyn 1526'; he then gave it to Mark Smeaton who added 'A moi M. Marc S.' at the end of the text; finally the poet Sir Thomas Wyatt acquired it and scribbled proverbs in Latin, French, Spanish and Italian on the back flyleaves. These include one in French - 'He that is an ass, and thinks himself an hind,/On leaping the ditch will realize the truth' - which may well represent Wyatt's verdict on Smeaton's career. D.S.

MS on vellum, 286 x 210
Royal MS 20 B XXI, fos. 2v-3, British Library
Lowinsky, 'A Music Book for Anne Boleyn', pp. 197-200

printed text in that it contains complimentary references to the French and English royal families. Henry VIII appears as a second Ezekiel sent by heaven to reform abuses, while Anne receives good wishes for herself and, by implication, for the cause of reform in England: 'O lady Anne, O queen incomparable, may this good shepherd with whom you find favour give you a son, the image of his father the king, and may he live and flourish so that you may both see him come to manhood.'[8]

Latymer states that the royal physician William Butts (XI.4) received letters from Nicolas Bourbon of Vandoevre (VII.9) who had been imprisoned in France for speaking against the pope. Butts appealed to Anne, and 'did not only obtain by her grace's means the king's letters for his delivery, but also after he was come into England his maintenance at the queen's only charges in the house of the said Mr Butts'. Anne also made him tutor to three youths, Henry Norris, Thomas Howard or Harvey, and her nephew Henry, son of William Carey (V.3). Bourbon himself wrote verses of gratitude to Anne, Henry and Butts.[9]

Foreign evangelicals looked to Anne for protection. Thomas Alwaye, prosecuted for buying English New Testaments and other forbidden books, spoke in his petition to Anne of her goodness 'as well to strangers and aliens as to many of this land'. Latymer mentions a French gentlewoman named 'Marye', who 'fled out of France into England for religion'. Anne sent for her on her arrival and 'entertained her so lovingly and so honourably, as she confessed that her trouble had purchased her liberty'. Anne may also have invited Sturmius to England.[10]

Crucial to the operation of Anne's patronage were lesser sponsors and intermediaries who brought suitors to her notice: courtiers like Dr Butts and her vice-chamberlain Sir Edward Baynton (below, p. 118), and her own chaplains. These last included Hugh Latimer, Nicholas Shaxton, John Skip and Matthew Parker, later respectively bishops of Worcester, Salisbury and Hereford and archbishop of Canterbury. A letter of John Cheke to Parker of September 1535 shows the chaplains dispensing Anne's bounty. Cheke wrote on behalf of William Bill, a poor scholar of Cambridge. Praising Anne's generosity, he said that it was well known that suitors merely had to be recommended by Parker, Skip or another chaplain. Cheke's petition was successful.[11]

While Anne placed her clients in influential positions in the Church she also drew Henry's attention to books which might alter his religious and ecclesiastical policy. The martyrologist Foxe records that she was sent a copy of Simon Fish's *Supplication for the Beggars*, and that at her brother's suggestion she showed it to Henry. However, Foxe also prints another account involving two merchants and a royal footman which does not mention Anne. Perhaps Foxe confused Fish's book with another Anne promoted; perhaps Henry heard about the *Supplication* from both sources.[12] It is more certain that Anne introduced Henry to Tyndale's *Obedience of a Christian Man*, since the story is found in two separate accounts. Anne obtained a copy of the *Obedience* and allegedly marked some passages in it with her fingernail to show the King. Her waiting-woman Anne Gainsford (VII.10) read it and passed it to George Zouche, her future husband. It was snatched from his hands by Wolsey's henchman Richard Sampson, dean of the King's chapel, who presumably hoped to use it to incriminate Anne Boleyn. Moving swiftly, and vowing that it would be the dearest book that dean or cardinal ever took away, Anne begged the King for its return and then 'besought his grace most tenderly' to read it. He did so, and declared that it was 'for me and all kings to read'.[13]

Some evangelical translators approached Anne as a possible intermediary with Henry. William Marshall in 1535 published a translation of the poor relief regulations of Ypres which he dedicated to 'the flower of all queens': 'My very mind, intent and meaning is (by putting of this honourable and charitable provision in mind) to occasion your Grace (which at all times is ready to further all goodness) to be a mediatrice and mean unto our most dread sovereign lord ... for the establishing and practising of the same (if it shall seem so worthy) or of some other, as good or better.'[14]

George Joye, in exile at Bergen-op-Zoom in 1533, 'printed two leaves of Genesis in a great form, and sent one copy to the King, and another to the new Queen, with a letter to N. to deliver them; and to purchase licence that he might so go through all the Bible'.[15] Joye was unlucky in that Henry was not yet ready for an authorized English Bible, which would not appear until 1539. Similarly unfortunate was Tristram Revell. Hoping for Anne's patronage of his studies, he dedicated to her his printed translation of François Lambert's *The Sum of Christianity Gathered out almost of all Places of Scripture*. Revell chose the dangerous early days of 1536 to present his work, but this apart, the book was so radical that even Hugh Latimer found parts of it unacceptable, and Anne could not sponsor it.[16]

Anne Boleyn's great enemy, the imperial ambassador Chapuys, spoke of 'the heretical doctrines and practices of the concubine - the principal cause of the spread of Lutheranism in this country'.[17] Evangelicals were horrified at her fall, and sought to disassociate the 'guilty' woman from the cause she had promoted. In the reign of Elizabeth (indeed, even before this) Anne was acclaimed as a reformer; the first to kindle the light of Reformation at the Court of England.[18] The physical traces of her activity - her books and the documents which show her patronage - demonstrate that the assessment of her friends and her enemies was accurate.

Goldsmiths and their Work at the Court of Henry VIII

BY HUGH TAIT

Silver and gold, gem-set and elaborately chased and embossed, had never been more in demand at the English Court than when the Tudors came to power. Henry VII was as conspicuous a patron of the goldsmith as his son, Henry VIII. But both monarchs depended on foreign goldsmiths and artists residing in London for work of the highest quality.

Unfortunately, almost nothing has survived from the earlier of these two reigns: perhaps the only extant piece that ranks as a high quality Court object is the famous silver-gilt cup and cover of Lady Margaret Beaufort at Christ's College, Cambridge.[1] It has lost its jewels from the castellated foot but otherwise is well-preserved and its simple beaker-like tapering form, with sinuous ogee outlines, crenellated rims and heraldic decoration, is wholly characteristic of the late-gothic style. This cup reveals no awareness of the Italian Renaissance nor of its vast new vocabulary of ornament.

On the other hand, Henry VIII's spectacular gift to Queen Jane Seymour was a tall jewelled gold cup and cover of typical Renaissance design. Both Holbein's preliminary design and his final presentation drawing have survived (IX.14). But, however fine the detail, the basic design of the cup and cover, with its slender stem on a domed foot and its tall bowl divided into horizontal zones or bands of ornament, is not at all innovatory. Holbein, in his comings and goings from Basel to London, could have acquired from any number of goldsmiths' workshops on the continent - if not in England - designs of a comparable nature. In particular, the zone of projecting classical busts or 'antique heads' within roundels on the side of the bowl was one of the most popular Italian Renaissance forms of decoration. It came to be frequently employed by architects and metalworkers north of the Alps, especially in France, and can be seen, for example, in the carved mannerist cameo-heads on the French Clock Salt (IX.9) that is known to have

VII.14 Designs for a Girdle Prayer Book and a Jewellery Casket, by Hans Holbein

The two designs for girdle prayer books were probably alternatives for the same commission. They were to be executed in black enamel on gold (like the spine of VII.16), and both contain the letters 'TWI'. These have been conjectured to be the initials of Sir Thomas Wyatt the Younger and his wife Jane Haute who were married in 1537. A Wyatt girdle prayer book, extant until the nineteenth century, had covers similar to the first design, but without the initials. Tradition had it that either this book or (V.43) had been given to a lady of the Wyatt family by Anne Boleyn on the scaffold. The dating of the contents makes the story unlikely in either case. The designs for the ends of a jewellery casket (below) are so similar that they could have been part of the same commission. D.S.

Ink with washes on paper, 79 x 59, 81 x 60, 115 x 79, 113 x 79
5308-8, 10, 1, 5, British Museum
J. Rowlands, *The Age of Dürer and Holbein*, Exhibition catalogue: British Museum (1988), no. 207
E. W. Ives, *Anne Boleyn* (Oxford, 1986), p. 315 n. 50

VII.15 'Hans von Antwerpen', after Holbein

The traditional identification as Hans of Antwerp, a prosperous goldsmith and member of the Steelyard in London, rests on the much damaged inscription of Holbein's portrait of the same sitter in the Royal Collection. This is dated 1532, the year of Holbein's return to England, when he painted several other Steelyard merchants. But the seal-stamp in front of the sitter is marked with a 'W', which tells heavily against the traditional identification. Holbein designed a cup incorporating Hans's name; he was also a witness of Holbein's will in 1543. D.S.

Oil on panel, 130 dia.
P.158-1910, Victoria and Albert Museum
Rowlands, no. 36 (b)

belonged to Henry VIII. In contrast to this competent conventionality, in 1540 Cellini designed and executed for Francis I a gold salt-cellar of the utmost originality, unique both in its iconography and technical craftsmanship. Cellini's masterpiece survives and is fully documented;[2] unfortunately, nothing is known of the goldsmith - not even his name - who was given the task of interpreting Holbein's final design, while the Cup itself was melted down in 1629/30.

Previous writers have conjectured that Holbein may have succeeded in obtaining this prestigious commission for his goldsmith friend, Hans von Antwerpen (John of Antwerp) who witnessed his will in 1543 (VII.15); the evidence, however, is inconclusive. Hans von Antwerpen had come to England in the first decade of the sixteenth century. He and his like were not seeking refuge from religious persecution but were hoping to make a more prosperous livelihood.[3] Indeed, the numbers of foreigners coming to live in London was steadily growing, with far more being Flemish- or German-speaking than French. The resulting anti-alien sentiment periodically got out of hand and after the worst outbreak, the 'Evil May Day' riots of 1517, some fifteen Londoners were sentenced to be hanged, drawn and quartered. Hans von Antwerpen married an Englishwoman and had a large family; indeed, the last reference to him occurs in July 1550, when another son was born to him and was baptized at St Nicholas Acon in Lombard Street, the church where London goldsmiths traditionally congregated.

He had clearly been accepted but it was not always so. In 1528 four of his apprentices, all with Flemish-sounding names were admitted to the freedom of the Goldsmiths' Company, even though he himself had not been made a freeman. Shortly afterwards, he (and three Dutchmen) were found guilty by the Company of refashioning old plate and returning it to the owners without submitting it for assay and marking at Goldsmiths' Hall. By 1536, the year when Jane Seymour's Royal Gold Cup was being designed, Hans von Antwerpen was sent to prison for employing in his workshop, without the necessary approval of the Goldsmiths' Company, a foreign craftsman named Andrew Pomert. However, within ten months the Company withdrew its objections and on 27 September 1537 admitted him to the freedom. This *volte-face* was the direct result of a letter of recommendation to the Company dated 9 April 1537 from the minister Thomas Cromwell. In the previous months Hans von Antwerpen's name had appeared in the Privy Purse Expenses of Henry VIII's daughter, the Princess Mary, while in 1539 he was paid for carrying despatches to Germany for the King. Had this Court patronage come in time for him to have been chosen for the great honour of making the Jane Seymour Cup?

VII.16   Girdle Prayer Book, c.1540

This girdle prayer book, made of gold, embossed and enamelled, has on the front cover the scene of the Brazen Serpent (Numbers xxi, 8) and, on the back cover, the Judgment of Solomon (3 Kings iii, 27), each surrounded by the appropriate inscription copied from either the 1539 or the 1540 printed English Bible. The goldsmith's work is probably by Hans von Antwerpen, while the original contents were removed and replaced by two printed works, one dated 1574. H.T.

English, c.1540; Gold, embossed and enamelled, 64 ht
94. 7-29. 1, British Museum
H. Tait, 'The girdle-prayerbook or "tablett"': *Jewellery Studies* 2 (1985), pp. 29-57, figs. 11-13

The Goldsmith's Company would have hardly dared imprison him in 1536 if he already had the King for a client and by October 1537 Jane was dead.

Although he may not have made the Jane Seymour Cup, his close connections with Antwerp, its goldsmiths and their young apprentices makes it seem highly probable that his London workshop produced the famous Tudor girdle prayer-book (VII.16), which was made very soon after 1540 for a lady of the English Court.[4] One of its gold covers has the enamelled relief of the Brazen Serpent copied directly from a panel of identical size on Abbot Arnoldus de Dyest's monumental silver-gilt book-cover at the Abbey of Tongerlo. This was made in Antwerp by Hieronymus Mamacker, goldsmith of Antwerp, and finished in 1543. It is the earliest Flemish piece of goldsmith's work in the fully-fledged Renaissance style to have survived. It remains conjectural, therefore, whether Hans von Antwerpen obtained access to the original relief of the Brazen Serpent in Mamacker's workshop in Antwerp while he was travelling on the King's behalf to Germany in 1539, or whether it was brought to him by one of his foreign assistants who had previously been employed in Mamacker's workshop in Antwerp. These two reliefs of the Brazen Serpent, one in gold and one in silver, are exactly contemporary and, although their minor differences indicate that they were made individually, they were undoubtedly based on the same original source.

Such attempts at up-to-the-minute modishness apart, the London goldsmiths were probably more concerned to produce strong, well-proportioned silver-plate, similar to the Rochester tazzas (IX.13). These sturdy pieces, when given simple surface decoration, such as the scallop or shell pattern, and then gilded, would look imposing enough from a distance. Although they lacked finesse and required little knowledge of Renaissance ornament, these pieces of plate were often well-designed as, for example, is the graceful Boleyn covered cup, which was made in London in 1535-6 (IX.11). But place any of these English pieces of plate alongside the Founder's covered tazza at Emmanuel College, Cambridge, which was made in Antwerp in 1541-2, and the superiority of the latter is overwhelmingly obvious. Its originality of design, its sculptural features and high technical finish are incomparably finer than anything produced by English goldsmiths. Little wonder that discerning patrons in England still preferred to buy the work of foreign goldsmiths, even towards the end of Henry VIII's reign.

VII.17 Pair of Panels from the Speke Girdle Prayer Book

Made of gold, embossed and enamelled, these two panels depict the Judgment of Solomon and the scene of Susanna, falsely accused by the Elders, and the judgment of Daniel (Daniel xiii, 49). Recently, a portrait of Philippa Speke dated 1592 was discovered in which the sitter is portrayed wearing a girdle prayer book with an identical scene (and inscription) on the cover as occurs on the Susanna and the Elders panel. It seems likely, therefore, that the two panels come from the now lost Speke girdle prayer book, which was probably made for Anne, wife of Sir Thomas Speke (1508-51), one of Henry VIII's gentlemen of the Privy Chamber. The lingering late-gothic quality of these panels would suggest a date about a decade earlier than (VII.16). H.T.

English, c.1530s

Gold, embossed and enamelled, 66 x 44

AF 2852-3, British Museum

Jewellery and Jewellery Designs

Tudor jewellery was, like jewellery in general, both ornamental and precious. But it was often symbolic as well: jewels for masking costume (VII.18) often made elaborate visual puns; classical motifs were invoked, more or less seriously (VII.18-21), but most frequent were mottoes and ciphers of initials (VII.23-4).

VII.18 Miniature Whistle Pendant

This pendant is in the form of a pistol, chased with scrolling foliage, and containing cosmetic tools within the barrel. By family tradition, this trinket was Henry VIII's first gift to Anne Boleyn. It is apparently a rare survivor of the gold devices which were sewn in such profusion onto the King's masque costumes. In September 1510, for instance, Robert Amadas was paid £266 for 'wreaths, hearts and roses of fine gold'; many of these were 'lost off the King's back', stolen or 'given away at his pleasure'. P.G.

English, c.1520

Gold, 47 lgth, 27 h, 10 dia.

Private Collection

P. Glanville 'Robert Amadas, Court Goldsmith to Henry VIII', *Proceedings of the Silver Society* 3 (1986), pp. 106-13

VII.19 Jester Cameo

It has been suggested that the cameo represents Henry VIII's jester, a rare example of a non-royal, if courtly, portrait. Contemporary interest in cameos reflected the revived concern of the Renaissance with the techniques of ancient jewellery. An inventory of the collection of Thomas Cromwell in 1527 included rings with classical intaglios. P.G.

French or English, c.1500-1550

Onyx, 20 x 16

Private Collection

C. Oman, *British Rings* (1974), pp. 131-2

VII.20 Cap Badge

This cap badge is in the form of a decorated roundel enclosing an embossed bust of a Roman emperor on a matted ground. Renaissance hat jewels originated in northern Italy around 1450, soon becoming widespread throughout Europe. This example has been attributed to an English workshop on the evidence of similar hat badges surviving with English inscriptions. Comparison can also be made with the contemporary Renaissance decoration being applied to Hampton Court by Italian craftsmen. P.G.

English or Italian, c.1530-40
Gold, 47 dia.
630-1884, Victoria and Albert Museum
A. Somers-Cocks, *Courtly Jewellery* (Victoria and Albert Museum, 1980), pp.16-17

VII.21 Seal Ring with Intaglio of Henry VIII

The King is shown full-face, wearing a flat-cap, moustache and full beard, with a fur-trimmed robe, flanked by the initials H and R. An impression of this intaglio appears as the seal of Dorothy Abington of Hindip, Worcestershire, dated 31 October 1576, concerning a lease of crown land. The intaglio, which depicts the King late in his life, may well have been cut after his death. Henry is known to have employed intaglio cutters and at Christmas 1529 sent Cardinal Wolsey an intaglio portrait of himself as a gesture of his continuing goodwill, at the time of the cardinal's disgrace. A sardonyx intaglio of Henry is recorded in a drawing by George Vertue. P.G.

English, c.1545 or later
Gold and chalcedony, 26 dia.
M5-1960, Victoria and Albert Musuem
A. Somers-Cocks, ed., *Princely Magnificence: Court Jewels of the Renaissance, exhibition catalogue:* Victoria and Albert Museum (1980), no. 17

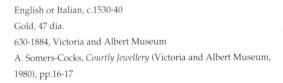

VII.22 Pomander or Musk Ball

Found 'on the Surrey bank of the Thames' in 1854, the frame of the pomander has survived intact, together with five of the twelve pearls but none of the original enamel decoration. Its construction is simple. The central tubular shaft contains a thread in the upper section (now visible through the split in the seam) and the small ring-topped gold screw fastens the remaining five separate elements together once they have been assembled. This enabled the pomander to be taken apart and refilled easily. H.T.

English, early 16th cent.
Gold, 52 ht, 43 dia.
54.124, British Museum
H. Tait, ed., *Seven Thousand Years of Jewellery* (1986), p. 154, col. pl. 353

116

VII.24 Designs for Jewellery and Goldsmith's Work, by Hans Holbein

These designs for chains, book clasps and jewels include three associated with Henry's children: there are two alternative designs for a jewel with the words 'MI LADI PRINSIS', and one for a chain made of ostrich plumes, or Prince of Wales feathers. William Scrots's portrait of Prince Edward in late 1546 shows him wearing a jewel with this ornament. D.S.

Ink and washes on paper

5308.77, 84, 71, 27, 142, 137, 135, 144, 145, 152, British Museum

Strong, NPG I, p. 92, II pl. 171

VII.25 Boxwood Model for a Medallion of Charles de Solier, Sieur de Moret, by Christoph Weiditz

This model, inscribed in Latin with the subject's name and age, enabled Holbein's great portrait of the same sitter to be firmly identified. This painting was executed between April and July 1534, when Moret was French ambassador to England. He had first come here in 1518 for the celebrations of the treaty of Universal Peace, and had remained for several months as one of the French hostages for the payment of an indemnity for the restoration of Tournai. Like others of this group, he continued to maintain close connections with England. These personal ties were particularly important during the ascendency of the Francophile Anne Boleyn. D.S.

VII.23 Designs for Ciphers and Jewellery Formed with Ciphers, by Hans Holbein

Ciphers, or word-games using initial letters, were a favourite Tudor pastime, especially for lovers. Henry's love letters to Anne Boleyn are full of them; they were also used on buildings, objects and jewellery. Holbein designed many, using both Roman letters and more florid forms. Several of these are associated with Anne Boleyn. Most straightforward is 'HA'. These form a pendant set with a single square-cut stone, and appear, joined with a lover's knot, on a small shield which is also shown in section. More complex is 'HISA'. The King's love letters would suggest that this means 'Henri immuable serviteur Anne'. 'ABCE' appears in three variations. At first sight it defies interpretation, but if the 'HR' of Henry's signature be understood, it probably means 'Henri cherche Anne Boleyn'. D.S.

Ink and washes on paper

5308.119, 110, 120, 108, 113, 9, 38, 14, 4, 7, 6, 3, 11, 114, 36, 46, 79, 115, British Museum

J. Rowlands, *The Age of Dürer and Holbein*, Exhibition catalogue: British Museum (1988), no. 209

Henry Savage, ed., *The Love Letters of Henry VIII* (1949), pp. 97-111

Boxwood, 59 dia.

Victoria and Albert Museum

E. Hall, [Chronicle] (1550), fo. 65v: *LP* II ii, 4409

Rowlands, no. 53

VIII Acton Court and the Progress of 1535

IN EARLY JUNE 1535 Henry VIII and his Court left Greenwich; made their way by easy stages to Windsor, and started the summer progress to the west country and Hampshire at the beginning of July. The progress was to be the usual mixture of business and pleasure 'hunting and visiting ... with a view to gain popularity with his subjects' as the imperial ambassador put it. But, unusually for the reign of Henry VIII, business came first. The reason was the Reformation. In 1534 Parliament had passed the torrent of controversial legislation which completed the break with Rome and protected the King's new title of Supreme Head of the Church of England with the terrible penalties of treason. All this, as historians have long realized, presented a major problem of local enforcement. What they have not realized (though the imperial ambassador did) was the part played by the progress of 1535.

The first leg of the progress lay through Gloucestershire and Wiltshire. This was the second most important region after the south east; it was also (like the south east) an area where reform had local roots. Everything was done to strengthen them. Local gentlemen who favoured reform, like Sir John Walshe at Little Sodbury or Sir Edward Baynton at Bromham, were singled out for the honour of a royal visit, as were towns with strong reforming parties, above all Bristol. In the event, plague prevented the intended royal visit to Bristol. But when instead a delegation of townsmen waited on the King and Queen at nearby Thornbury Castle, Anne, all graciousness, promised Bristol another visit in future. Throughout the progress, in fact, Anne was the more active of the royal couple: at Winchcombe she ordered an investigation into the famous relic of Christ's blood at Hailes Abbey; while at Bromham she gave money to 'an earnest and zealous embracer of God's word' who had fallen on hard times. What really showed that the Court meant business, however, was the fact that the King's minister, Thomas Cromwell, caught up with the progress at Winchcombe on 23 July and accompanied it for the next two months. In January Cromwell had been made the King's vicegerent in spirituals, with power to visit all the monasteries in England. So far nothing had been done; now, however, Cromwell decided to launch the visitation of the monasteries in the west country, with himself on the spot to direct operations and, apparently, to visit some monasteries in person.

The result was, literally, a triumphal progress for reform. It culminated on 19 September with the consecration of three reforming bishops in Winchester Cathedral, while the Court lay nearby at Bishop's Waltham. But at this point the wind shifted. The original intention had been that the Court should turn back towards London. Cromwell stuck to it but Henry and Anne decided to linger in Hampshire for another month. Immediately, the progress reverted to type and the religious complexion of the King's hosts altered. Sir William Paulet (who entertained Henry at Basing) was a covert conservative; Lord Sandys, the lord chamberlain (who received the Court at The Vyne) was an open one. The effects were immediate. Cromwell thought he had got the prior of Worcester on a treason charge; two days after the King had left her roof, however, Lady Sandys wrote to Cromwell to plead for the prior's pardon as 'a true monk to God and the King'. She was successful.

The two principal surviving monuments of this progress correspond to its contrasting halves. One is The Vyne itself, with its panelling still richly carved with the badges of Catherine of Aragon. The other is Iron Acton in Gloucestershire, where Nicholas Poyntz built a splendid new lodging for Henry VIII and Anne Boleyn and decorated and furnished it in the latest Renaissance taste. D.S., S.W.

Figure 5: Sir Nicholas Poyntz of Acton Court, by Hans Holbein. (Royal Collection)

The Royal Visit to Acton Court in 1535

BY ROBERT BELL

'Saturday, 21 August, Bristol to Acton, Mr. Poyntz's place, and there Sunday, 7 miles. Monday, 23 August, Acton to Mr. Walshe's [at Little Sodbury].'[1] This is the only written reference to the visit to Acton Court by Henry VIII, accompanied by Queen Anne Boleyn and their retinue, during the course of the royal progress through the west of England in the summer of 1535. But recent archaeological and architectural research by English Heritage has demonstrated that a much more substantial memorial to the event survives in the form of the east range of the house, which was built by Nicholas Poyntz in anticipation of the royal visit. It still stands to its full height and contains original wall paintings of extremely high quality.

Acton Court, on the outskirts of the village of Iron Acton in south Gloucestershire, now Avon, was a moated manor house constructed in the thirteenth century as the capital messuage of the Acton family. It had been inherited by Sir John Poyntz in 1364 through an agreement with his aunt, the widow of the last of the Actons,[2] and was to remain in the ownership of the Poyntzs until 1683. Until the late fifteenth century, no member of the Poyntz family held any position of more than local significance. However, Robert Poyntz was a protégé of Anthony Woodville, Earl Rivers, whose sister was Edward IV's queen, and whose illegitimate daughter Poyntz married in 1479.[3] Poyntz became a courtier; survived the reign of Richard III, and (like many Woodville connections) was a supporter of Henry Tudor. He was knighted at Bosworth Field,[4] and when Henry VII legitimized his succession by marrying Elizabeth of York, the daughter of Edward IV, and the mother of Henry VIII, the family links with the Crown through the Woodville connection were continued under the new regime.

It is thus hardly surprising that Henry VIII's visit to Acton Court was not the first by a Tudor monarch. Indeed, his father dined with Sir Robert at his house on 23 May 1486, while on his way to Bristol during the course of a royal progress,[5] and the following year Poyntz was rewarded with the sum of £50, probably as reimbursement for his expenses. He remained in favour after Henry VIII succeeded to the throne, achieving successively the positions of vice-

Figure 6: The east range of Acton Court, built for the royal visit of 1535, from the east. The chimney-stacks, of which there were originally three, one for each of the principal first-floor rooms, are original. All the windows on this façade are later, however. The plain exterior gives no indication of the original richness of the interior decoration.

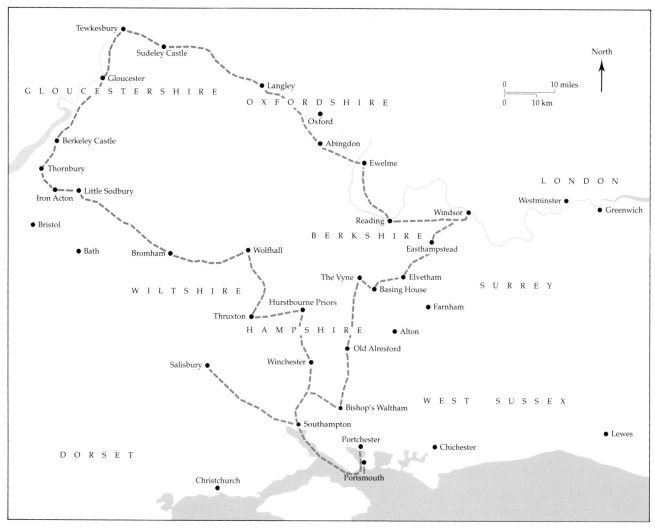

Figure 7: A map of the royal progress of 1535, on which Henry VIII and Anne Boleyn visited Acton Court and other houses of 'evangelical' gentry in the west country.

chamberlain and chancellor to Queen Catherine of Aragon;[6] and in 1520, shortly before his death, he attended the King and Queen at the Field of Cloth of Gold and the subsequent meeting with the Emperor Charles V, accompanied by two of his sons and his daughter-in-law. The youngest of his sons, Francis, followed his father at Court, but died prematurely; the eldest, Sir Anthony (despite forays like 1520) remained a country gentleman.

These manifold connections with the dynasty explain the royal favour subsequently shown to Sir Robert's grandson, and Sir Anthony's son, Nicholas, who was a young man of twenty-three when he inherited Acton Court from his father in 1532. He was a friend of Richard Rich, the betrayer of Sir Thomas More, and of Richard Cromwell, the minister's nephew, and was in the King's entourage at the Calais interview in October 1532.[7] This was the fateful occasion when Francis I met Henry VIII and Anne Boleyn and so paved the way to the King's second marriage. All this points to the fact that Nicholas, despite his grandfather's service to Queen Catherine, had followed his neighbour and uncle by marriage, Sir John Walshe, into the reformed camp. Hence the extraordinary lengths to which he went, in terms of new building work, in order to impress the King and Anne Boleyn, now Queen, during their brief stay. He had his reward for it is virtually certain that he was knighted on the occasion of the royal visit.[8]

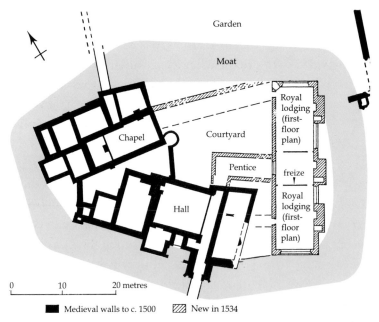

Figure 8: Plan of Acton Court, showing the east range built for the visit of Henry VIII and Anne Boleyn in 1535.

1535 is also the date which appears on the best painted version of Poyntz's portrait drawing by Holbein.[9] This would suggest that he had his portrait taken to commemorate the successful royal visit; while the very individual character of his pose announces the advanced aesthetic tastes displayed in his building works.

Archaeological excavations have revealed that the house which Nicholas inherited in 1532 was compact in plan and tightly enclosed by its surrounding moat. It consisted of three distinct ranges, thirteenth-century in origin. The south range contained the main entrance through the porch and the screens passage, with the hall and parlour/great chamber to the west, and the buttery and pantry to the east. It had been almost entirely rebuilt in the early fifteenth century, and had been refurbished by Sir Robert Poyntz. He had installed new fireplaces and floor-tiles, conceivably in honour of Henry VII's visit in 1486. He had also built an oriel window, which projected out into the moat. North-west of the hall was the first-floor chapel, attached to which were lodgings and chambers, added from the late thirteenth century onwards. To the east of the south range was the kitchen. A fourth, unexcavated range probably stood in the north-east corner of the site.

North of the house, beyond the moat, Sir Robert had created a walled garden, around which it was possible to perambulate by means of a gallery, which spanned the moat and provided direct access from the house. This was almost certainly the garden for which Nicolaus Kratzer had been commissioned to design a sundial in 1520 (VIII.1).

Fifteen years later, Nicholas Poyntz decided to demolish the medieval kitchens, and to construct a completely new two-storey east range, measuring 32.4 x 8.7 metres (106 ft x 28 ft). Like the existing medieval ranges, it was built in the local pennant sandstone, which, remarkably for such a large structure, was bedded not in mortar but in loam, and would originally have been protected externally by off-white rendering. The window surrounds and other details such as the roof finials, which would have supported heraldic beasts, were made of limestone.

The arrangement of the rooms at ground-floor level is unknown, because it was completely remodelled twenty years later. However, the first floor lay-out still survives. It consists of three large rooms 5.25 metres (17 ft 3 ins) high, together with the original roof timbers and the massive lateral oak tie-beams. The rooms at either end were lit by enormous rectangular windows in the gable walls. Each of the three rooms, which were designed to serve as royal state rooms, was provided with a fireplace and an adjacent garderobe (Figure 8).

Some of the internal decoration has also survived later alterations. The north room was panelled, and had a painted frieze with roundels, now in a poor state of preservation. The ceiling too was painted with false ribs and had applied bullions, probably gilded.[10] But the most outstanding feature is the painted frieze on the south wall of the central room, which is likely to have been executed by a French or Italian artist. It is divided into three panels. The central panel contains the bust of a female with braided hair, possibly representing one of the four seasons, while the two side panels contain 'antike' work. The wall below was panelled. Traces of ochre colouring remain on it.[11] The south room would have been hung with tapestries, some of which are mentioned in an inventory of 1532.[12] During the excavations, large quantities of moulded stucco, from a ceiling or possibly a fireplace overmantel, were found in the mid-sixteenth-century backfill of the east arm of the moat. It almost certainly came from the south room, and represents one of the earliest examples in England of this form of decoration.

No building accounts have been preserved, but the structure has been dated precisely by tree-ring analysis of the primary tiebeams and roof-timbers. This indicated that the trees were felled in 1534-5. The combination of the tree-ring date and the internal decoration leaves little room for doubt that the range was built quite specifically for the King's benefit.

The new work was linked to the older part of the house by pentices, and it was possible to walk directly from the first floor of the east range to the chapel along a covered gallery. The removal of the medieval kitchen meant that temporary kitchens had to be erected to the east of the moat, in order to cater for the extensive royal retinue. They were linked to the house by a pentice and a bridge.

In honour of the occasion, sets of ceramic plates and containers of Spanish and Italian origin were acquired. Examples of these exotic items, discarded no later than the 1540s, and possibly immediately after the visit, were discovered in the backfilled moat (VIII.4). They were accompanied by fragments of superb Venetian glass vessels, which were also probably purchased in advance of Henry's visit (VIII.3). For King Henry, a keen sportsman, one of the principal attractions of Acton Court would have lain outside in its deer-parks. Leland mentions two parks, one for red and one for fallow deer.[13] A sixteenth-century hunting stand still exists on the ridge to the east of the house, incorporated in the present Lodge Farm, though more detailed analysis of it would be required before stating that it was built in or by 1535.

The construction of the east range represented the start of a major programme of rebuilding by Sir Nicholas, which continued over the next twenty years. It included the creation of new north and west ranges, the partial rebuilding of the south range, and the infilling of the medieval moat. The mansion survived until the late seventeenth century. But after it was sold and the estate split up, it was greatly reduced in size and was converted into a farmhouse. Luckily, the one complete range which remains standing is the east range, a remarkable testament to the extravagant hospitality offered to Henry VIII and Queen Anne over a single weekend in August 1535.

R. D. Bell and K.A. Rodwell, *Acton Court* (English Heritage Archaeological Report, forthcoming)

The Renaissance Comes to Gloucestershire

As well as building a special royal apartment and decorating it with wall-paintings in the latest 'antique' taste, Sir Nicholas Poyntz also equipped it appropriately. He bought valuable Venetian glass (much of which was quickly broken), while even the earthenware was a luxury import. However, the sundial, dated 1520, shows that Poyntz's father was also advanced in his taste.

VIII.1 The Acton Court Polyhedral Sundial, 1520

This polyhedral sundial, discovered in the garden of Acton Court near the south front of the east range in 1985, is the earliest dated English example recorded and a mathematical *tour de force* of its period. It is also an early testimony to a builder's blunder. It originally consisted of four vertical dials (north, south, east and west), a horizontal dial and a reclining dial facing south. Its design is attributed to the 'deviser of the King's horologes', Nicolaus Kratzer (1487-1550), whose initials it bears (V.13-18). Similar dials appear in his MS *De Horologis* now preserved at Corpus Christi College, Oxford (MS 152). It is probable that an error by the mason led to the sundial's rejection and re-use as a building block. Although the south, north and horizontal dials are correctly set out for the latitude of Iron Acton (51°55'), the east, west and reclining dials are set out for the complement to the latitude. The inverted numerals on the east dial suggest that the three incorrect sides were properly calculated but laid out upside down. G.S.J.W.

Oolitic limestone 349 ht, 267 wdth, 349 dia

Inscr. '1520 N K'

English Heritage

G.S.J. White, 'A stone polyhedral sundial dated 1520', *Antiquaries Journal* 66 (1987), pp. 372-3

VIII.2 Photograph: Painted Frieze at Acton Court

The frieze is situated in the second of the three-room royal apartment. The decoration on the other walls of this room does not survive. The frieze is divided into three panels by balusters and capped by a *trompe l'oeil* cornice. The panels contain three different schemes of grotesque ornament executed in grey, white and ochre with touches of red and green on a black background. The centrepiece is a roundel, containing a female bust with braided hair in profile.

The painting is of very high quality and at this date is likely to have been executed by a foreign craftsman. The beasts in one of the panels may be salamanders (the badge of Francis I), which suggests a French connection. At the time, this type of design was known as 'antique work'. There are frequent references to its use in Henry VIII's palaces (e.g. *HKW* IV, p. 132). However, the Acton Court frieze appears to be the unique surviving early sixteenth-century 'antique' wall painting. R.D.B.

Foot and stem of Venetian glass ewer

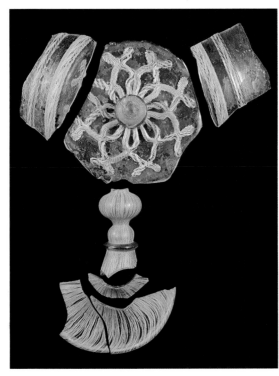

Standing cup in Venetian glass

VIII.3 Venetian Glass from Acton Court, c.1535

Three fragments of Venetian glass. The ewer handle is in *vetro a fili*, colourless soda glass with inlaid white canes. It was found in the lower fill of a drain which pre-dated the 1540s north range. At this date, the handle and the other two items are almost certainly Venetian in origin. The foot and stem is in *vetro a retorti*, colourless glass with inlaid and twisted white canes. It comes from the fill of a garderobe, beneath the 1540s west range. The standing cup is in

vetro a fili (stem) and *vetro a retorti* (body). This vessel would have possessed a cover or lid. It came from the bottom of a garderobe in the south porch and was thrown away when the south arm of the moat, filled in during the 1550s, was still open. P.C.

1. Handle from a ewer
Glass 82 lgth, 15 wdth
2. Foot and stem, probably from a goblet
Glass 62 ht, 79 dia.
3. Standing cup
Glass 130 ht, 88 dia. (foot)
A.M. Lab. no. 877619 English Heritage
H. Tait, *The Golden Age of Venetian Glass* (1979), nos. 105, 100-102, 92

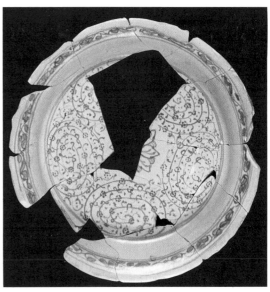

VIII.4 Glazed Earthenware from Acton Court, c.1535

Two items of glazed earthenware. The near-complete tin-glazed Spanish albarello, with an overall blue colouring (cobalt), was one of at least seven almost-identical vessels found in the excavations. They were exported to the New World and to northern Europe. It came from the bottom of the south arm of the moat, which was filled in during the 1550s. The almost-complete plate is decorated in blue over a blue-tinged tin glaze. This vessel is one of at least four from the excavation, all with similar decorative schemes, and produced at a number of centres in Liguria. It came from the infill beneath the west end of the chapel, which was re-modelled in the 1540s. A.V.

1. Blue tin-glazed albarello
Earthenware max. surviving height 235; base dia. 125; foot dia. 100
2. Glazed and decorated plate
Earthenware 192 dia., 40 ht
English Heritage
J. G. Hurst, D. S. Neal and H. J. E. Van Beuningen, *Pottery Produced and Traded in North-west Europe 1350-1650*, Rotterdam Papers VI (Rotterdam, 1987), pp. 57-9; pp. 26-30

IX The Presence Chamber: New Year, 1538

ON 1 JANUARY 1538 Henry VIII stood in his presence chamber at Greenwich to receive gifts from his family, nobility and Court. New Year's Day, not Christmas Day, was the great gift-giving day: then everyone who was anyone gave the King a present, and in return received a gift from the King of plate, whose weight was precisely graded in accordance with the rank of the recipient. This is the world of the modern corporate Christmas card: 'It is nice to receive a Christmas card from the chairman of the Board; it is even nicer to send one.'

The gift-giving ceremony took place in the presence chamber or throne room. The word 'presence' had a double significance. The throne and canopy, or chair and cloth of estate, were treated as though the King were always present; the 'presence' was also the throng of courtiers who assembled in the room to attend the King and his 'coming forth' from the privy lodgings. This happened comparatively infrequently and the presence chamber itself was used by the King only for public dining, formal receptions of ambassadors and ceremonies like the presentation of New Year gifts. Their very public nature has left a good record, however.

The drawing of 'Henry VIII Dining in the Presence Chamber' (IX.1) presents many difficulties, but it gives the only reasonably detailed picture of the domestic routine of the Tudor Court. And no doubt at all attaches to John Hussey's description of the presentation of New Year's gifts in 1538. Hussey was court agent to Viscount Lisle (VI.2), now deputy of Calais in succession to Lord Berners (II.23), and his letters are the most vivid record of Henry VIII's court in the crisis years of the Reformation.

When Hussey entered the presence chamber to present Lisle's gift, Cromwell smiled and said to the King, 'Here cometh my Lord Lisle's man.' The King made a joking answer but Hussey could not catch it. His formal reply to Hussey was kind but brief: 'I thank my lord. How doth my lord and my lady? Are they merry?' 'The King', Hussey concluded, 'stood leaning against the cupboard, receiving all things; and Mr Tuke at the end of the same cupboard, penning all things that were presented; and behind his Grace stood Mr Kingston and Sir John Russell, and beside his Grace stood the earl of Hertford and my lord privy seal. There was but a small Court.'

This, frozen in time, is the Tudor Court in the wake of the death of Henry VIII's third Queen, Jane Seymour. She had died the previous October after giving birth to the longed-for Prince Edward. It was this which accounted for both the 'small Court' and the prominence at the King's side of Jane's brother Edward, now earl of Hertford (IX.7). But the dominant force in both Court and Council, as Hussey's account makes clear, was Thomas Cromwell (IX.3), who had become lord privy seal in succession to the fallen Anne Boleyn's father. In the second rank, behind the King, were two leading courtiers: Sir William Kingston, the captain of the Guard, and Sir John Russell, gentleman of the Privy Chamber and newly appointed controller of the Household (IX.4). Sir Brian Tuke (IX.5), who was writing out a list of the gifts, was treasurer of the Chamber, and the list was a New Year's Gift Roll (IX.8). Some of these Rolls, though not that for 1538, survive. The cupboard itself was specially built and the Greenwich buildings accounts in 1532 note payments for both 'trestles and boards for the King's New Year gifts to stand upon' and 'a great hooped double stock lock for the chamber door where the King's New Year gifts was set'. This highlights the intrinsic value of the gifts. To us the fact that some were designed by Holbein would have mattered even more (IX.14-16). These items have long vanished; indeed only three items of plate from Henry VIII's Inventory survive. But the Royal Clock Salt (IX.9) alone is sufficient to give an idea of the overpowering ostentation of the collection.

IX.14 The Preliminary and Finished Designs for a Cup for Jane Seymour, by Hans Holbein

The first is a preliminary drawing; the second a worked-up version for presentation to the King. The design incorporates Queen Jane's motto, 'Bound to Obey and Serve'; the royal initials 'HI' tied by a lover's knot and, as a finial, an escutcheon for her arms imperially crowned. In the preliminary drawing the paper has been folded vertically and most of the right-hand side of the drawing has been made by off-set. The artist has made alterations: to a cameo head, the sirens' trumpets and a putto.

These are incorporated in the finished drawing (right), which is notable for the use of grey wash to give a remarkable three-dimensionality. A cup corresponding to the design was made (though probably not by Hans von Antwerpen - above, pp. 113, 114) and features in the inventories of royal plate until first pawned and then melted down by Charles I. D.S.

1. Ink on paper, 375 x 143
1848-11-25-9, British Museum
2. Ink and wash on paper, 376 x 155
Ashmolean Museum, Oxford
J. Rowlands, *The Age of Dürer and Holbein,* Exhibition catalogue: British Museum (1988), no. 205

127

IX.1 Henry VIII Dining in the Presence Chamber

This drawing shows the King dining alone, on a dais, under a cloth of estate, and served bare-headed and on bended knee. Left are the officers of the Chamber with their staves; right is a cupboard of plate with an elaborate architectural canopy. Courtiers and councillors (one to the left looking like Cromwell) attend. The numbers involved suggest that the drawing represents the King dining abroad in the presence chamber, a relatively rare occasion since he preferred to eat in the seclusion of his privy lodgings.

The authenticity of the drawing is debatable: the dress is accurate for the 1530s, but the windows look more seventeenth- than sixteenth-century. On the other hand, the rest of the architectural detail is strikingly similar to that represented in an illuminated initial in the *Valor Ecclesiasticus* of 1535. The royal arms on the cloth of estate have been reversed for engraving. D.S.

? North German School

Ink on paper, 95 x 111

1854-6-28-74, British Museum

Strong, *Renaissance Miniatures*, pl. 31

Participants in the Ceremony

When John Hussey entered the presence chamber to present Lord Lisle's New Year's gift, he saw a microcosm of the post-Reformation Court. Next to the King were two leading members of the Council, Cromwell (IX.3) and Hertford (IX.7), while behind were Russell (IX.4) and Kingston, who were councillors of the second rank and household officers. Tuke (IX.5), who was keeping note of the gifts, was an old-style bureaucrat with literary tastes.

IX.2 Henry VIII, after Holbein

This is a copy after Holbein's Privy Chamber portrait of Henry VIII. It thus represents the King as he was only a few months before the presentation of New Year's gifts to him in 1538. DS.

Oil on panel, 660 x 470

BHC2763, National Maritime Museum

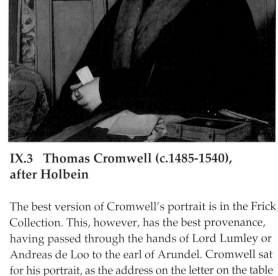

IX.3 Thomas Cromwell (c.1485-1540), after Holbein

The best version of Cromwell's portrait is in the Frick Collection. This, however, has the best provenance, having passed through the hands of Lord Lumley or Andreas de Loo to the earl of Arundel. Cromwell sat for his portrait, as the address on the letter on the table in the Frick version shows, in 1533-4, when his period as chief councillor was just beginning; the laudatory Latin inscription on this version must have been added after his execution in 1540, when he became a Protestant 'hero'. The inscription was also on the Frick version, but was removed by cleaning. D.S.

Oil on panel, 762 x 629

J. Chichester Constable; Rowlands, no. 40(a)

IX.4   Sir John Russell, later Earl of Bedford (c.1485-1555), by Hans Holbein

In the first part of Henry VIII's reign Russell was both a professional soldier (being blinded in one eye at Morlaix in 1522) and a loyal adherent of Wolsey. The combination made him an obvious choice as Wolsey's nominee to the King's Privy Chamber in 1526. After Wolsey's fall he transferred his support to Cromwell. This helped him weather Anne Boleyn's hostility, but it was only after her fall that he became controller of the Household and a councillor. Thereafter, through all his subsequent promotions - baron, lord admiral, lord privy seal and earl - he remained one of the select group who were members of both the Privy Chamber and the Privy Council. Strong suggests that his pose is designed to conceal his injured eye. D.S.

Chalks on pink-primed paper, 348 x 294
Royal Collection
Foister/Parker, no. 69.
Strong, *NPG*, I, p. 21

IX.5   Sir Brian Tuke (d.1545), after Holbein

In 1528 Tuke was occupying William Carey's (V.3) chamber at Court when news came of his death from the sweating sickness. Tuke succeeded Sir Henry Wyatt (V.5) as treasurer of the Chamber in 1528.

Under Wyatt the office had seemed about to enter the inner circle of the Privy Chamber and Council; under Tuke the treasurer became merely a functionary. Holbein captures the sitter's anxious temperament which helped bring about the decline. But his insecurities made him a good record keeper. As treasurer Tuke paid Holbein's salary when he was appointed royal painter. The original of this portrait is in the National Gallery, Washington. D.S.

Oil on panel, 790 x 650
J. Chichester Constable
Rowlands, no. 64

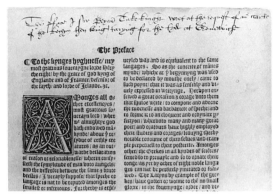

IX.6   William Thynne's 1532 Edition of Chaucer's Work

This is the first full (indeed rather too full since it contains some spurious works) printed edition of Chaucer . The editor was William Thynne, clerk of the Kitchen, but according to John Leland (below, p. 155), the preface was written by Sir Brian Tuke. Leland's claim is confirmed by the inscription in this copy: 'This preface I Sir Brian Tuke knight wrote at the request of Mr Clerk of the Kitchen, then being tarrying for the tide at Greenwich.' The preface is Tuke's only known publication. But he was also Erasmus's correspondent and the preface shows his familiarity with humanist theories of language and literature. It is also strongly nationalistic: English was becoming a great European language, Chaucer was its supreme poet, and Henry VIII, 'next God and his Apostles', Defender of its Faith. Poetry is thus put at the service of the royal supremacy, first proclaimed that same year.

In 1532 there also appeared an important edition of the *Confessio Amantis* by Chaucer's contemporary, John Gower. The editor's preface, by Thomas Berthelet, who was King's printer, argued for the usage of 'our most allowed old authors' as a model for writing good, clear English. D.S.

Printed book, 300 x 210
Clare College, Cambridge
DNB, sub William Thynne

129

IX.7 Armorial Plate of Edward Seymour, Earl of Hertford

The plate has a shield with the arms of Edward Seymour (?1506-52) and the inscription reads: THE.NOBLE.AND.VALEANT.KNIGHT.SYRRE. EDWARD.SEMER.ERLE.OF.HARTEFORD.AND. VICONTE.BEAUCHAMPE.OF.SOMERSET.AND. VNKYLL.TO.THE.RIGHT.HIGH.Z.MYGHTY. EDWARD.PRYNCE.OF.ENGLOND.DVKE.OF. CORNEWALL.ERLE.OF.CHESTER.1537.

It has hitherto been published as the Garter stall-plate of Edward Seymour, but this is impossible: Seymour was not created a knight of the Garter until 1541 and, significantly, neither the Order is mentioned in the inscription nor is the Garter depicted on the plate itself. However, it cannot have been made before October 1537 when, following upon the christening of Prince Edward on 15 October, Edward Seymour (brother of the Queen) was created earl of Hertford. As he had been installed in Greenwich Palace near the royal apartments, this plate may have been made for use at Greenwich.

The only portraits of Somerset known to survive are a posthumous miniature and the group portait of Edward VI and the pope. D.S.

English, 1537

Copper gilt, engraved and enamelled, 168 x 133

67.1113.1, British Museum

E.H. Fellowes, *The Knights of the Garter 1348-1939 with a Complete List of the Stall-Plates in St George's Chapel,* (1939), p. 79.

Strong, *NPG*, I, p. 295, II, pl. 576

The Royal Plate

Only three pieces of Henry VIII's plate survive, of which the Royal Clock Salt (IX.9) is the most ostentatious. But Holbein's designs for royal plate (IX.14-17), and Henry's own gifts (IX.10) give a good idea of the rest. The New Year's Gift Roll (IX.8) suggests the social context.

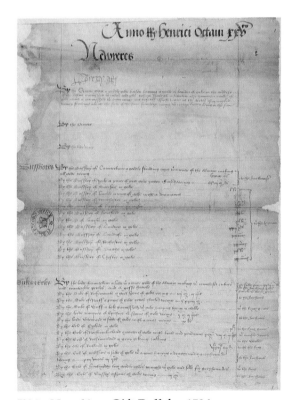

IX.8 New Year Gift Roll for 1534

The New Year's Gift Roll for 1538 is missing; that for 1534 survives. The Queen (then, of course, Anne Boleyn) gave a magnificent table fountain designed by Holbein; Cromwell 'a lair [ewer] of mother of pearl garnished with gold' and a fine towel; Seymour 'a parson [? a game] with a ball and pan of latten [brass]'; Russell 'a table [picture] of Our Lord', and Tuke, six sovereigns. D.S.

MS on paper, 425 x 310

E 101/421/13, [*LP* VII, 9], Public Record Office

Plate and Gift-Giving at Court

BY PHILIPPA GLANVILLE

In 1527, according to the chronicler Hall, Henry VIII ordered that the Greenwich banqueting and disguising houses 'with cupboard, hangings and all other things ... should stand still for three or four days, that all honest persons might see and behold the houses and riches, and thither came a great number of people'. The display of plate excited particular admiration. It consisted of 'a cupboard of seven stages [shelves] high and 13 foot long, set with standing cups; Bowls, Flagons and great pots all of fine gold: some garnished with ... stones and pearls ... another cupboard of nine stages high ... all was massy plate so silver and gilt, so high and so broad that it was a marvel to behold'.

So in 1527, as in every Tudor Court entertainment, gold glittered through every aspect of the setting. Sets of tapestries were heavy with precious metal thread; horse-trappings, masque costumes and armour were garnished with gilding or gold wire, and gilding enhanced the lead or wooden ornaments on fireplaces and ceilings. The greatest expenditure was not on these specialized uses of gold, however, but on plate and jewels. Sometimes, as in 1527, the requirement was for display; at other times, the King had to give.

The most glamorous, and the best documented, of these occasions was on 1 January.[1] At New Year every member of the Court, from the lord chancellor to the humblest servants, expected an issue of plate from the Jewel House, graded both according to their rank and to their personal

IX.9 The Royal Clock Salt

This elaborate confection, attributed to the French court goldsmith 'B', was in effect a table ornament, not a functional container for salt. It combines late-gothic and Renaissance elements, such as the cameos. The base originally contained a clock mechanism, with its dial visible within the crystal cylinder. The salt well was above the hexagonal section, and the cover was crowned with Jupiter and an eagle. The present movement and the globe finial are later restorations. One of eleven clock salts in the Royal Collection in 1550, this piece was sold in 1649/50.

The clock salt, which was presumably a gift from Francis I to Henry VIII, is one of only three pieces of plate known to have survived from Henry VIII's Jewel House. The others are the Royal Gold Cup (also French, c.1380, given away by James I in 1604 and now in the British Museum) and the gold and enamelled rock crystal bowl, which is now in the Schatzkammer of the Residenz, Munich. P.G.

French, c.1535
Silvergilt, set with precious stones, crystal and agate, 390 ht
The Worshipful Company of Goldsmiths
I. Toesca, 'The Royal Clock Salt', *Apollo* (Oct. 1969), pp. 292-7
J. Hayward, 'The Restoration of the Tudor Clock Salt', *Goldsmiths' Review* (1969-70)

IX.10 The Barber Surgeons Grace Cup

IX.11 The Boleyn Cup (Electrotype)

This standing cup, which bears the maker's mark 'HM', perhaps for Hubert Morrett, was presented by Henry VIII to the united Company of the Barber Surgeons in or shortly after 1543. The cover and foot are chased with Tudor roses, fleurs-de-lis and portcullises within scrolling foliage and the cover is surmounted by Henry's arms flanked by his supporters. The bowl, which may well replace an original wooden mazer, has been later engraved with the pre-1540 arms of the Barbers impaling the cognisance of the Surgeons, with the Tudor rose crowned. The cup is hung with bells: as Samuel Pepys recorded, the drinker has to drain the contents before shaking the bells. P.G.

With the London hallmark 1535-6, this cup has a finial of the Boleyn falcon in the form borne by Queen Anne herself. The acanthus pattern around the knop and foot, and the gadrooned stem and cover are characteristic of the 'antique' style. By Elizabeth's reign these features were considered old-fashioned, and such plate was melted down or handed on. And so it was that in 1563 this cup was given to Cirencester Parish Church by Dr Richard Masters, the royal physician; he in turn may well have received it as the Queen's New Year's gift, despite the fact that it appears in no earlier royal inventories. D.S.

Silvergilt, London Hallmark 1543-4, 267 ht

The Worshipful Company of Barbers

Information from Mr Hall, former Clerk to the Company

315 ht

St John the Baptist, Cirencester

Philippa Glanville, *Silver in Tudor and Stuart England* (1990), p. 176

standing with the King. In return they would make a gift to the King. The King's gifts were stereotyped, and their preparation was entrusted to a small group of London goldsmiths working to regular annual contracts at fixed rates. The King's greater subjects, however, were expected to be more lavish and more imaginative.

Above all, they were expected to give gold. Throughout the 1520s Cardinal Wolsey regularly gave a gold cup weighing about 60 ounces and costing well over £100. In November 1520, shortly before Edward Stafford, duke of Buckingham, fell into disgrace, he was deeply in debt and much of his plate was apparently held as security by Robert Amadas, the royal goldsmith. But his agent was instructed to borrow from Amadas, 'against Christmas', large buffet plate for his banqueting hall and altar plate for the chapel services. Moreover, the duke set out precisely his preferred design, cost and method of presentation for the New Year's gifts intended for

Henry, Catherine and the Cardinal. Henry's gold wine goblet 'of the best fashion' was to carry the motto 'with humble true heart' in French. Wolsey's cup was a little less costly (£30 rather than £36) but 'of the newest and best fashion' and again with a French motto.[2]

The 1532 New Year Gift Roll records a characteristic mixture of practicality and luxury. Most of the bishops gave money; while the earls gave principally goldsmiths' work, including a gold trencher plate and rosewater flagon, a gold dog-choke and a pair of gilt collars for greyhounds. In 1534 some enterprising court goldsmith clearly had access to a parcel of imported plate; the archbishop of Canterbury gave a 'goodly standing cup of the Almain making', weighing 79 ounces, and more German plate came in from the lord chancellor and lord chamberlain (salts set with counterfeit rubies and pearls) and from Lady Sandys. The Renaissance taste for complex and ambiguous constructions, whose ostensible function was combined with an elaborate timepiece, finds expression particularly in the later gifts to Henry from the mid-1530s. The French clock salt (IX.9), one of eleven in the Royal Collection, exemplifies this quirk, which caused the inventory clerks to struggle for definition. A 'device like a cup' given by Catherine Parr to the King was in effect a writing set, 'the cover having diverse small boxes with pictures and conclusions of arithmetic, the foot having three boxes for ink, dust and counters'.[3]

The King's return gifts, usually standing cups, sets of bowls or the simpler and less costly cruses (two-handled drinking vessels) were by no means heavy or highly decorated although his initials and those of his successive Queens, as well as their badges, were often prominent, as in the Barber Surgeons' Grace Cup (IX.10). But favoured intimates such as the duke of Suffolk (86 ounces in 1532) or Henry's bastard son, Henry Fitzroy, duke of Richmond (95 ounces in 1532), were singled out for something more substantial. Fitzroy received sets of gold cups, a gold salt supposed to be of unicorn horn, or cups 'graven with antiques' from the King, while Cardinal Wolsey gave him a gold and enamelled Garter in 1526, the year he joined the Order of the Garter.

IX.12   The Scudamore Cup

This standing cup, which originally had a cover, is made up of five separate elements, including a cast acanthus calyx and a band of engraved foliage, originally filled with black enamel. A similar band surrounds the base. The foot and bowl are deeply chased with paired scrolls and acanthus; also on foot and bowl are panels of gadroons ('bollions') on a textured background.

This cup has both the decorative elements and the shape typical of German Renaissance designs for cups published by Albrecht Altdorfer and Hans Brosamer. It is the first example of English plate to integrate Renaissance form and ornament; by contrast, the slightly earlier Howard Grace Cup (1525) retains a strong late-gothic form, to which 'antique' cast motifs have been added.   P.G.

Silvergilt (gilding renewed), London hallmark, 1529-30, 213 ht
Private Collection
J. Hayward, *Virtuoso Goldsmiths: 1540-1620* (1976), pl. 295

But Richmond felt no need to retain his father's gifts; indeed in 1534 he moved so quickly to gratify his mother-in-law, the duchess of Norfolk, that his steward had no time to enter a description or the weight of the King's standing cup 'which was sent incontinently to the duchess'.[4]

On the other hand, those of small means and relatively low status at Court stood to gain from the gift-exchange with the King: in return for a modest token they would acquire handsome plate from the Jewel House. The gilt cup received by Lucas Horenbout, King's painter, and the cruse given to Hans Holbein in 1538 (in return for a portrait of Prince Edward) were worth between £3 and £5 each, substantial acquisitions for men on salaries of about £30 a year.

Cups given by the King might be treasured because of their source. When George Talbot, earl of Shrewsbury, drew up his will in 1538, the numerous clauses detailing his plate specify no fewer than ten pieces as royal New Year gifts. For courtiers, christenings offered another occasion for a royal gift; when the Crown seized the plate of Sir Thomas Arundel in 1552, his son's baptismal gift from Henry of a salt was retained by the family. The children of the King's court painter, Lucas Horenbout, were also honoured with baptismal gifts.[5]

Other customary presentations of plate which drew heavily on the resources of the Jewel House were those to foreign ambassadors on their return home. Normally consisting of a set for a buffet, the greater the significance of the diplomatic mission, the more lavish the plate.[6]

same shape (but without cover) is the example now in the collection of the Goldsmiths' Company. The stem and foot are simpler, but the bowl, inscribed with a different Latin grace, is strikingly similar. It also bears the same hall- and maker's-marks as the Rochester Cathedral cover. H.T.

Silver gilt, 132 ht, 207 dia., London hallmarks 1528-9; 228 dia. London hallmarks 1532-3; 132 ht, 207 dia., indistinct hallmarks, possibly continental

1971.52.13, British Museum

H. Tait, 'London Huguenot Silver' in I. Scouloudi, ed., *Huguenots in Britain and their French Background: 1550-1800* (1987), pp. 89 ff., pl. 1, figs. 13, incl. an illustration of the Holbein design in Basel

IX.13 The Rochester Cathedral Silver-Gilt Tazzas and Cover

These three pieces are all that survive from a particularly grand set of secular covered tazzas. The Latin grace or inscription engraved on the inside of the rim of the bowls is the same, except for the last word on the second tazza, where an engraver's mistake has led to a meaningless contraction. The same distinctive shape, with its wide shallow bowl resting on a large ornate knop, below which extends a projecting frill and a decorated massive spreading stem and foot, can be seen in a drawing of a tazza by Holbein. The only English tazza of the

IX.14 The Preliminary and Finished Designs for a Cup for Jane Seymour, by Hans Holbein: See page 127

134

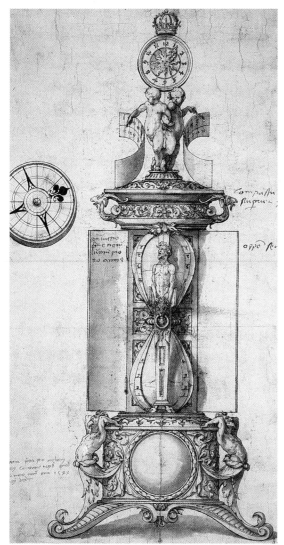

IX.15 Design for a Clock Salt, by Hans Holbein

The design is inscribed in Latin 'A New Year's gift made for Anthony Denny of the King's Bedchamber which he gave to the King on New Year's Day 1544'. Its combination of magnificence and technical ingenuity shows a shrewd appreciation of Henry's taste by one who knew him well. The central section contains an hour-glass within folding doors; above, the putti support two sundials with their hands, and a clock on their heads with a blazing sun as a pointer. To the left is a design for a compass, which fitted in the drum under the putti. Technical notes appear on the design in the hand of Nicolaus Kratzer (V.13). As in the finished drawing for the Seymour Cup, grey wash suggests the modelling with brilliant economy. The Elizabethan inventories of plate include eleven clock-salts; this was not among them. The only one to survive is (IX.9). D.S.

Ink and wash on paper, 410 x 213
1850-7-13-14, British Museum
Rowlands, *Age of Dürer and Holbein*, no. 211

IX.16 Design for the Boleyn Fountain, by Hans Holbein

This design for the table fountain presented by Anne Boleyn to Henry as her New Year's gift in 1534 incorporates her falcon badge. D.S.

Ink on paper, 171x101; Offentliche Kunstsammlung, Basel
A.J. Collins, *Jewels and Plate of Queen Elizabeth* (1955), no. 998

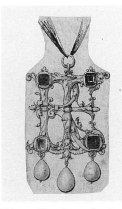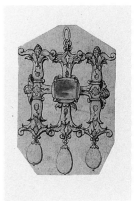

IX.17 Designs for Jewellery and Trimmings, by Hans Holbein

These two sets of designs include tassels (XI.55), a portable pillar sundial (V.16) and two ciphers: 'HI', which almost certainly stands for Henry and Jane Seymour, and 'RE'. The similarity between the latter and the initial letters in Kratzer's *Canones Horoptri* (V.14) was used to demonstrate that Holbein illuminated the manuscript for Kratzer. D.S.

Ink and coloured washes on paper
5308.123, 125, 148, 116, 117, British Museum
Rowlands, *Age of Dürer and Holbein*, no. 206

X The Gentlemen Pensioners, 1539

HENRY VIII SPENT CHRISTMAS 1539 at Greenwich. The Court was unusually full for the festivities; the arrival of a new Queen, Anne of Cleves, was also expected at any moment. The full Court provided a good moment to introduce a reform of the royal household; the imminence of a Queen, and therefore of a Queen's household, made reform something of a necessity. Fourteen years before, at Christmas 1525, another major reform of the royal household had been inaugurated in the Eltham Ordinances. Eltham was Greenwich's small sister-palace and it was chosen because the purpose of the Eltham Ordinances was retrenchment: it was a case of a small palace for a small Court. In 1539 the opposite was true. The dissolution of the monasteries had (so it seemed) made money available for everything and the Greenwich Ordinances were designed to increase the numbers and status of those resident at Court, to improve their wages and allowances and to augment the pomp and circumstance of Henry's imperial crown.

Central to this was the creation of a new royal guard. At the beginning of his reign, Henry had established a Band of Spears or Pensioners. As usual, both the name and the inspiration were French - in this case the 'Company of One Hundred Gentlemen of the King's House' instituted by Louis XI in 1474. The Pensioners were higher in rank and more heavily armed than the yeomen of the Guard and correspondingly more expensive. In the straightened financial circumstances that followed the first French war the Pensioners were disbanded, but the new revenues of the 1530s made their revival feasible. The scheme was first mooted in 1537 but not put into effect till 1539. A list of fifty was drawn up, four of whom were Cromwell's (IX.3) servants, and one each servant to Norfolk (VII.4), Suffolk (III.9) and Fitzwilliam (XII.9) (*LP* XIV ii, 783). Their first public appearance was for the reception of Anne of Cleves at Greenwich on 3 January 1540 (below, p. 138); while Sir Anthony Browne (VI.9), the master of the Horse, was their first captain. In the palace they stood in the presence chamber (the yeomen of the Guard were without in the guard chamber), and their velvet or damask doublets, heavy gold chains and formidable pole-axes impressed all.

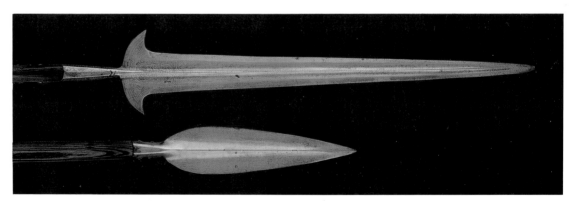

X.1 Staff Weapons of the Guards of Henry VIII

There are three pole-axes. The first (VII.1510) is very similar to the one illustrated in the portrait of William Palmer (X.2); while the second (XIV.5) has a pistol in the haft (27 of these weapons were listed in Henry VIII's Inventory). The boar-spear has the Tudor rose, formerly gilt, pounced (engraved) on both sides (95 of these were listed in the Inventory), while the two partisans are also decorated with the royal arms. The Inventory lists over a thousand partisans, gilt and trimmed with blue velvet and blue silk fringes. D.S.

Steel with wooden hafts, 2375, 1778, 180 (head), 2232, 2000, 1994 lgths
VII.1510, XIV.5, VII.881, VII.1998, VII.1972, VII.1975,
The Royal Armouries
A. V. B. Norman and G. M. Wilson, *Treasures from the Tower of London*, Exhibition catalogue (1982), no. 46
C. J. Ffoulkes, *Inventory and Survey of the Armouries of the Tower of London* 2 (1926), pp. 221, 223, 239

X.2 Sir William Palmer, attributed to Gerlach Flicke

This is the earliest portrait of a gentleman pensioner. The sitter is identified by the coat-of-arms. In the first draft list of the refounded Band of Gentleman Pensioners he appears as 'Palmer of Gloucester's son' (*LP* XIV ii, 783). The picture is tentatively dated to 1546, the last full year of Henry VIII's reign, by Flicke's movements and the style of the painting. Palmer is shown with the rich velvet doublet and coat, pole-axe and heavy gold chain that formed the insignia of the Band. He also wears a medallion around his neck and another in his cap of a mounted St George. D.S.

Gerlach Flicke, attrib., c.1546

Oil on panel, 1016 x 622

Sabin Gallery

J. L. Nevinson, 'Portraits of Gentlemen Pensioners before 1625', *Walpole Society* 34 (1958), 1-13, pp. 6, 12 and pl. II

XI The Bedchamber: the Cleves Marriage, 1540

ON 3 JANUARY 1540 Henry VIII's fourth wife, Anne of Cleves, made her formal entry into her new kingdom at a great review at Greenwich. At the foot of Shooters' Hill there was a gorgeous pavilion. Here the Queen-to-be changed into fresh garments and took some refreshment. Meantime the King rode out to meet her. First came the trumpets, then the Council-at-large, the Privy Chamber, the Lords spiritual and temporal and members of the Privy Council in order of precedence and the foreign ambassadors, and finally the marquess of Dorset carrying the sword before the King; after the King came the master of the Horse (VI.9) and the captain of the Guard with the Guard. The route was lined with knights and esquires, but first the fifty 'gentlemen called Pensioners' (above, p. 136).

But, despite the brave show, all was not well. Henry had done his best to be sure of Anne's attractiveness. A portrait of Anne (perhaps XI.2) had been rejected because it was not sufficiently revealing. Instead the King's own painter, Hans Holbein, was sent. His paintings were often said to be indistinguishable from the living flesh, but when Henry, unable to contain himself, paid his new bride a surprise visit on New Year's Day at Rochester, he was surprised and revolted. He left his gift to be presented by Sir Anthony Browne, and immediately tried to wriggle out of the marriage. But negotiations with the Cleves ambassadors in Cromwell's (IX.3) apartments in the river-front of the palace revealed no loophole and the marriage took place on 6 January in the chapel royal. The wedding night in the King's bedchamber proved no more successful than the couple's first meeting. As the King explained in graphic detail to his doctors (XI.4, 6), the marriage was unconsummated then and was to remain so. By the summer, the diplomatic situation enabled Henry to dispense with the Cleves alliance: Cromwell, the author of the marriage, was overthrown and executed - but not before he had been required to help Henry get rid of Anne.

We know almost nothing about Henry's bedchamber at Greenwich and his Inventory (below, p. 167) does not even mention the frame of the royal bed. On the other hand, it reveals a lot about the other rooms in the privy lodgings, which lay mainly in the donjon tower behind the bedchamber. This was the territory of the groom of the Stool, the King's most private servant, and his assistants. Here they organized the King's personal life and looked after his myriad possessions. Many of these were everyday objects; others reflected the King's remarkably wide range of interests. For map-making there was 'a globe of paper', 'a map made like a screen' and 'a map of England' (XI.7-15). Probably the 'great writing table of slate' was used for this purpose too. Closely linked with map-making were horology and astronomy. Several clocks were listed, including 'a hanging clock closed in glass with plummets of lead and metal', and various (sun)dials of bone and compasses (XI.16-21). Naturally there were a couple of musical instruments, including a combined virginals and regals in the withdrawing chamber (XI.22-3), and a scattering of books everywhere. The 'highest library', however, lay on the second floor in the wing projecting into the river and contained 329 books stored on and in lectern-topped desks. Several can still be identified (XI.24-9). Religion was perhaps less dominant than might have been expected, but there were several religious pictures, including 'a table with the words of Jesus', five paxes, two Latin Bibles and 'a mass book covered with black velvet' (XI.30-2). Hunting gear, on the other hand, was omni-present and there were a variety of other weapons (XI.33-9). Finally in the 'lower study being a bayne [bath]' (XI.40) there were 'seven locks great and small' which could help secure this mass of possessions (XI.41). With Henry quantity became quality, and his spending laid the foundations for future technological development.

XI.1 Henry VIII in a Surcoat Holding a Staff

An early seventeenth-century copy of the last portrait type of the King, showing him in his fifties. The key picture of this type is at Castle Howard, where the staff is inscribed with the monogram 'H' and the date '[15]42'. The 'H' has led to attribution either to Horenbout or Holbein. Rowlands rejects both artists, on the grounds that we know too much about Holbein's style and too little about Horenbout's for either to be convincing. The face is modelled on Holbein's 1537 portrait, but fleshed out a little. The furred surcoat and staff, however, point to Henry's physical decline, which seems to have accelerated after he had undergone the shame of cuckoldry by Catherine Howard. D.S.

Artist unknown. Oil on panel, 889 x 667
No. 496. National Portrait Gallery
Strong, *NPG*, I, pp. 157, 159
Rowlands, p. 236, no. R.37

Fatal Matrimony: Henry VIII and the Marriage to Anne of Cleves

BY RORY MACENTEGART

Figure 9: Anne of Cleves, by Holbein. Holbein's painting, on which this miniature is based, was attractive enough to persuade Henry VIII to agree to marry Anne. (Victoria & Albert Museum)

Henry's fourth marriage was the creation of his minister, Thomas Cromwell. In the aftermath of the death of Jane Seymour, Cromwell set his mind to finding a new Queen who would bolster his domestic position and lend weight to his foreign policy, which inclined towards friendship with the Protestant princes of Germany and northern Europe.

It was during the summer of 1538, as a Protestant German embassy arrived in London for theological and diplomatic discussions, that Cromwell first explored the possibility of a German match for Henry VIII. During private discussions with the chief ambassador, he elaborated his aims. The ambassador was suitably impressed: 'Lord Cromwell,' he wrote home, 'who is most favourably inclined to the German nation, wants very dearly that the King should wed himself with the German princes.'[1] During their conversations the ambassador could think of no suitable marital candidate among the German Protestants. But he did mention the religiously unaligned duchy of Cleves, which was connected by marriage to the Protestant leader Duke John Frederick of Saxony and possessed two eligible daughters, Anne and Amelia. Cromwell decided to follow up this possibility, and in January 1539 began preliminary enquiries on the feasibility of an Anglo-Cleves marriage.

These preliminary enquiries were well received in Germany, and soon further ambassadors were despatched from England to the Cleves court at Düsseldorf. The ambassadors confirmed the initial enthusiastic reports on the qualities of the two daughters. Henry, however, wanted some visual evidence before he would agree to accept either of them. It seems that he was sent portraits of Anne and Amelia by Barthel Bruyn (XI.2), but his ambassadors expressed no great confidence in the accuracy of the pictures. Instead, Henry's own court painter, Hans Holbein, was despatched to Cleves, and Dr Wotton pronounced the result 'most lively'. Holbein's famous, flattering, portrait of Anne clinched the matter (Figure 9). After a brief look Henry decided he wanted the thirty-four-year-old duchess to be his fourth wife. Events now proceeded apace. During October a Cleves embassy to England concluded the marriage treaty and settlement (XI.3); in November Anne departed from Düsseldorf for England; and in late December (after being delayed by appalling weather in the Channel) she arrived.

Up to this point, all had gone to plan for Cromwell. It appeared certain that by promoting the marriage he had secured an ascendancy over his rivals for many years to come.

But suddenly, just as victory appeared to be his, the grand scheme turned sour. For if Henry and Anne had looked perfect together on paper and portrait panel, in the flesh it was immediately clear that they had been dreadfully mismatched. From the moment Henry first set eyes on Anne at Rochester on New Year's Day 1540, he found her deeply unattractive: his face, according to Sir Anthony Browne, the master of the Horse (VI.9), dropped, revealing a deep 'discontentment and misliking of her person'.[2] No less horrified than Henry was Cromwell, who had confidently stayed behind at Greenwich to await the return of Henry from Rochester. As he proudly sidled up to Henry on his return and asked him how he found Anne he was shocked to receive the tart retort, 'Nothing as well as she was spoken of.' Had he known before what he knew now, the King continued, 'she should not have come within this realm'.

Henry's first reaction was to see if he could be released from the marriage by a legal technicality. There had been a precontract between Anne and the duke of Lorraine; was it still binding perhaps? The wedding was put off from the Sunday to the Tuesday as this possibility was explored. Eventually Cromwell himself, the earl of Southampton remembered (XII.9), 'repairing secretly to the King', convinced him that there was nothing in the idea. The realities of foreign policy now outweighed the King's own preferences. He could not, as he said to

XI.2: See page 142

Above:
XI.3 Anne of Cleves's Marriage Settlement

In accordance with agreements made in London between the Cleves ambassadors and Henry's Council during October and September 1539, a number of documents were exchanged on 5 January 1540 to settle the terms of the forthcoming marriage between Henry and Anne. Among them were these two documents dealing with Henry's financial settlement on Anne. The first gave her £4,377 a year; the second a further £327. Each features a miniature of Henry which appears to have been drawn by a close follower of Holbein. Indeed the similarities to Holbein's work are such that they might well have been drawn directly from miniatures of the King by the master himself. R.M.

MSS on vellum, 630 x 970

Kleve-Mark Urk. Nr. 2892, 2894 Nordrhein-Westfälsches, Hauptstaats archiv, Düsseldorf

H. Peters and H. Lahrkamp, 'Zwei Bildnisse Heinrichs VIII. auf Schenkungsurkunden fur Anna von Kleve', *Düsseldorfer Jahrbuch* 48 (1956), pp. 293-309

XI.2 Anne of Cleves

The similarity of dress and jewellery to those in Holbein's portrait of Anne of Cleves identifies the sitter; the artist is suggested by the style. Dendrochronological examination in 1974 dated the panel no earlier than 1650, so the painting was thought to be a copy. But cleaning in 1989-90 revealed a layer of fabric and glue beneath the paint, which itself is sixteenth-century in technique. This suggests a sixteenth-century original later transferred to a new panel. It is, therefore, just possible that it is one of the two paintings of Anne and her sister Amelia originally offered to the envoys of Henry VIII in 1539. They were dissatisfied with those portraits on the grounds that the high-necked bodice concealed too much of the ladies' charms. Piqued, the Cleves chancellor replied, 'Why, would you see them naked?' P.H., C.K.

Attributed to Barthel Bruyn the Elder (1493-1555)

Oil on wood panel, 520 x 385; St John's College, Oxford

Elisabeth Foucart-Walter, *Les peintures de Hans Holbein le Jeune au Louvre* (Paris, 1985)

Cromwell, risk 'making a ruffle in the world: that is to mean, to drive her brother [the duke of Cleves] into the hands of the emperor and the French king's hands, being now together'. Henry submitted to the inevitable with a bad grace.

At eight o'clock in the morning of 6 January 1540, Henry and Anne were married by Archbishop Cranmer in the chapel royal at Greenwich. The lavish celebrations which followed the wedding went off in great style, but when Henry and Anne retired alone to the bedchamber the fireworks stopped. Though Henry did his best, he found himself unable to stir that great body of his to any degree of activity. When Cromwell nervously poked his head into the King's privy chamber the following morning and asked how Henry now liked his Queen, he received the grave reply, 'As ye know. I liked her before not well, but now I like much worse.' 'For', he continued solemnly, 'I have felt her belly, and her breasts, and thereby, as I can judge, she should be no maid which struck me so to the heart when I felt them, that I had neither will nor courage to proceed any further in other matters.'

Things scarcely improved over the following months. Though Henry continued to sleep with Anne from night to night, that was all he did. He would come to bed in the evening, kiss her and take her by the hand, say 'good night, sweet heart', and promptly fall asleep; in the morning he would kiss her again, bid her 'farewell, darling', and depart. For her part, Anne remained blissfully unaware of what was going on. When asked some months later by a group of her ladies whether she was still a virgin, she innocently reproached them, 'How can I be a maid, and sleep every night with the King?' When one of the ladies replied that 'there must be more than that', Anne proceeded to describe Henry's bedchamber performances and asked, 'Is this not enough?' The awkward silence which followed was finally broken by the worldly-wise countess of Rutland: 'Madam,' she assured Anne, 'there must be more than this, or it will be long before we have a duke of York.'

Though Anne could continue happily in her innocence, able to tell her ladies-in-waiting that

'I am contented with this, for I know no more', Henry found the lack of a sexual dimension to the marriage intolerable. To his closest physician, Dr Butts (XI.4), he protested his own virility, assuring him that since the wedding he had had two wet dreams and thought himself able 'to do the act with others but not with her'. The problem was Anne's physical attributes: in Henry's 'misliking of her body for the hanging of her breasts and the looseness of her flesh'.

For Thomas Cromwell, it had all gone horribly wrong. Far from providing a springboard with which to overleap his enemies, the Cleves marriage put him badly on the defensive. During the opening months of 1540 his enemies began to attack. They conducted their campaign on two fronts. First, they subverted the Cleves marriage; then they set directly about over-throwing Cromwell. As their instrument of subversion they employed the seductive wiles of Catherine Howard, the flighty niece of Cromwell's deadly enemy, the duke of Norfolk. Bishop Gardiner (Norfolk's ally) arranged for Henry and Catherine to meet at banquets at Winchester Palace in Southwark; the dowager Duchess Agnes (Norfolk's step-mother) groomed Catherine on her new role.[3] Quickly Henry was hooked. Now the attack on Cromwell could come out into the open. He fought back in kind. The result was a vicious faction fight that reached its climax in the summer of 1540. The issue seems to have been forced when the anti-Cromwell faction concocted an indictment of treason against the minister and presented it to the King. The charges were too serious to ignore: either the accusers or the accused must fall. But whom to choose? It was a close-run thing. But Cromwell's promotion of the Cleves marriage had tipped the balance of the King's trust away from him when he needed it most. On 10 June he was arrested at the Council board and thrown in the Tower; on 28 July he was executed.

On 8 July Anne's marriage was annulled. She had professed to the end that she considered Henry 'to be her true lord and husband', but in vain. However, the financial terms exacted from Henry were generous, which suggests that Anne's innocence was limited to matters sexual.

XI.4 Sir William Butts, MD

A near-contemporary copy, probably executed for a junior branch of the family, of Holbein's original portrait of c.1540-43, now in the Isabella Stuart Gardner Museum, Boston. The portrait is related to Holbein's representation of Butts in his cartoon for the group portrait of 'Henry VIII and the Barber Surgeons'.

In the group portrait Butts appears in a place of honour second on Henry's right as one of the King's physicians. In this capacity he was a key figure in the protection and patronage of the 'New' religion at Court. Unlike his hard-line conservative colleague as royal physician, Dr John Chamber (XI.6), Butts would have heard Henry VIII's account of his failure to consummate the Cleves marriage with no pleasure. He was one of the first physicians to make a distinguished lay, rather than a clerical career. D.S.

Unknown artist after Hans Holbein
Oil on panel, 470 x 375
No. 210. National Portrait Gallery
Strong, *NPG*, I, pp. 33-4
Rowlands, p. 149, no. 80

XI.5   The Barbers Instrument Case

The enamelled royal arms, together with the engraved figures of SS George and Thomas Becket on the back, suggest that this was Henry VIII's gift to a royal surgeon, like Thomas Vicary with whom the case is traditionally associated. It must have been made before 1525 when the greyhound supporter of the royal arms was replaced by the lion. The arms of the Barbers Company and the cognizance of the Fellowship of Surgeons appear separately, together with cast figures of SS Cosmas and Damian, patrons of the Fellowship. In 1540 the Company and the Fellowship united under the royal auspices, and Holbein was commissioned to paint his great group portrait to commemorate the event and eternalize Henry VIII's interest in medicine.

The Renaissance motifs such as dolphins and floral scrolls on the side panels are the earliest surviving example of Renaissance ornament on a piece of English silver. The surgical instruments it once contained do not survive. P.G.

English c.1520-25
Silver, parcelgilt and enamel, with wood and leather lining and with original leather case, 180 ht
The Worshipful Company of Barbers
P. Glanville, *Silver in Tudor and Early Stuart England* (1990), fig. 214

XI.6   The Annulment of the Cleves Marriage

These are the 'letters testimonial', sent to inform Henry VIII of the judgment of the united Convocations of Canterbury and York on the nullity of his fourth marriage, and signed by those present. The process took three days, from start to finish. On 6 July the King issued a commission, empowering his clergy to rule on his marriage; on the morning of the 7th, the Convocations met in the Chapter House of Westminster Abbey and delegated the hearing of evidence to a committee; in the afternoon representatives of the committee went to Whitehall and, between 1 and 6 o'clock, took depositions from most of the witnesses; on the 8th the committee discussed the depositions and at 3 p.m. the full Convocations ruled the marriage invalid on the grounds of the precontract to the duke of Lorraine, inadequate consent and non-consummation. On the 9th the letters testimonial transmitting this verdict to Henry were drawn up and sent. Among the 158 signatories were Cranmer, who had celebrated the marriage; Nicholas Wotton, who had negotiated it; and, in his capacity as dean of St Stephen's, Westminster, Dr John Chamber, to whom (in his other capacity as royal physician) Henry had confided the reasons for his inability to consummate the marriage. D.S.

MS on vellum, 480 x 460
E30/1470 [*LP* XV, 860] Public Record Office

Henry VIII and Mapmaking

BY PETER BARBER

Figure 10: Sir Thomas Elyot, author of the *Boke Named the Governour*, by Holbein. The *Boke* placed a high value on map-making as a necessary accomplishment for gentlemen. (Royal Collection)

The international crisis of 1538-40, which was the background to the Cleves marriage, also saw maps for the first time being fully enrolled into the service of the English state.[1] The young Henry VIII, like most of his contemporaries, had regarded them primarily as cultural artifacts: props in Court pageants, status and power symbols and as what today would be called educational aids.[2]

The maps depicted the universe, the world or England, Ireland and Scotland, often in a generalized or schematic way, so as to convey certain basic concepts or to give room to the all-important historical, biblical, zoological and ethnographical illustrations for which the map provided a spatial framework. In other words, even in the increasingly common printed and manuscript copies of Ptolemy's *Geographia,* with 'modern' and 'ancient' maps of the world and its regions, what was on offer was not so much geography, in our sense of the word, as cosmography.[3] As the other side of the coin, there were exceedingly few English local, regional or administrative maps.[4]

In his early years as King, Henry, Eurocentric and his head rather too full of chivalric ideals,[5] was unaware that maps could play a vital practical role in the conduct of government. He allowed Sebastian Cabot to transfer his services to Spain in 1512, apparently oblivious to the possibility that his cartographic knowledge might later have been turned against England.[6] Furthermore, no maps seem to have been generated in 1513-20 during the English occupation of Tournai - in contrast to the profuse mapping that accompanied the occupation of Boulogne after 1544.[7] In 1509, the practical use of maps seems to have been confined to some lawyers, perhaps influenced by their Flemish counterparts, who were beginning to draft and consult sketch maps and plans to clarify legal disputes,[8] and to some merchants in the larger ports who were familiar with the nautical charts that Mediterranean seamen had been using since about 1300. Their captains and crews, however, still generally viewed charts with incomprehension and contempt, preferring the traditional chartless northern method of navigation.[9]

There were the beginnings of a change in attitude towards maps at Court from the early 1520s. Henry seems then to have commissioned map-like paintings of his early successes in France (V.10-11) and Cardinal Wolsey used at least one plan while preparing for the Field of Cloth of Gold.[10] The impetus probably came from Nicolaus Kratzer, the King's astronomer since 1519 (V.13), and other members of the Court circle who shared Thomas More's intellectual, though not his religious, enthusiasms.[11]

Southern Germany, Kratzer's home area, had been the scene of daring cartographical innovation since the late fifteenth century, and the emphasis on direct observation, measurement and practical utility, be it in depicting towns, provinces, routes or battles, foreshadowed later developments in England.[12] In 1524, Kratzer himself flirted with the idea of utilizing his travels with Henry's peripatetic Court to map England afresh.[13] More's brother-in-law, John Rastell (d.1536), was an early propagandist for the practical potential of maps, mathematics, measurement and the 'new geography'.[14] Holbein, another southern German, was providentially available to give attractive shape to these enthusiasms. The influence of these men and their ideas on the King seems to have grown in the early 1520s when Henry's Court, ornamented with More as councillor attendant, was perhaps at its most self-consciously intellectual.

At any rate, it was at the festivities in Greenwich in 1527 (*per se* a conventional enough occasion for a cartographic display) that the three men, assisted by the King's painter, the Neapolitan, Vincenzo Volpe, are first known to have publicly displayed the new style of

XI.7 Pictorial Map of the North Coast of Kent

This colourful roll, devoid of cartographic finesse, illustrates the least developed type of practical map, or 'plat', made for official purposes. Almost certainly produced locally on the basis of a pilot's information, it was intended to illustrate the area's state of vulnerability and preparedness for an armed confrontation with France. The nature of the shore, and its suitability for landings, is indicated, as are existing precautions against invasion, such as beacons, church towers and a barrier of ships at Whitstable. The map may also have been intended to persuade Henry to select Faversham as a port of departure for France: notes give soundings for,

and the ship-bearing capacity of, the Medway and what is probably a powder mill with a crane for loading is also shown. Though associated in the past with the crisis of 1514, there is no reason, on stylistic grounds, why the roll should not date from the crises of 1519 or even 1538-40. P.B.

Anonymous, early 16th cent.

Ink and gouache(?) on paper, 410 x 77

Cotton Roll XIII.12. British Library

S. Tyacke and J. Huddy, *Christopher Saxton and Tudor Mapmaking* (1980), pp. 11-12 (9), reproduced opposite p. 16

P. M. Barber, 'Maps and Monarchs in England, 1485-1625' in D. Buisseret, ed., *Maps and Monarchs in Early Modern Europe* (forthcoming)

XI.8 Dover Harbour in 1532

Dover bay, England's traditional lifeline to Calais, was prey to tide-borne shingle which by the 1520s had destroyed the earliest harbour. Late in 1532, the townsmen, probably aware that the King had commissioned Volpe some two years earlier to prepare a map of Rye and Hastings, paid him 22 shillings for what was almost certainly this 'plat' for presentation to Henry. It is the earliest surviving 'plat' that can be linked to a governmental or quasi-governmental project. Hardly recognizable as a plan to modern eyes,

it fulfils its function by using an artificial perspective to show the second, inner harbour in the Dour valley that the burgesses rather unrealistically wished to see created. In its failure to distinguish existing from proposed and its lack of concern for accurate measurement it is typical of the earlier pictorial plats created by artists. P.B.

[Vincenzo Volpe] Watercolour on vellum, 525 x 1345

Cotton MS Augustus I i, 19. British Library; *HKW* IV, pp. 731-2

A. Macdonald, 'Plans of Dover Harbour in the Sixteenth Century', *Archaeologia Cantiana* 49 (1937), pp. 110-12

XI.9 Dover 1538

This magnificent plat was executed following Henry's urgent visit to Dover in early September 1538 and his demand for a 'plat of the works' to be produced within a fortnight. It shows the progress made with scouring the bottom of the harbour, with the works to protect it from shingle and to defend it against invasion. Its execution can probably be attributed to the capable surveyor of Calais, Sir Richard Lee, through comparison with his later plan of Edinburgh (BL, Cotton MS Augustus I ii, 56), rather than to his Dover counterpart, John Thompson,

the overseer of the works, as previously thought. Although the plat is pictorial, the pink used for the sea shows some development towards symbolism; proposed is distinguished from existing in words and the annotations also reveal some, albeit clumsy, concern for measurement (e.g. 'the length of the groyne stondyng forthe from the long or south east Jette is lx feetes'). P.B.

[Sir Richard Lee (?) 1538]

Ink and watercolour on paper, 780 x 1900

Cotton MS Augustus I i, 22, 23. British Library; *HKW* IV, pp. 744-5

A. Macdonald, 'Plans of Dover Harbour', pl. 1, pp. 111-14

maps. The realism and accuracy of a painting of the siege of Thérouanne by the English in 1513, based on a pictorial plan taken on the spot (V.11), and a relatively detailed modern map of the world (V.12) amazed onlookers: their amazement testimony enough to the novelty of such things.[15] The cartographic revolution in England, however, centred not around such grand maps but around the far humbler 'plat', as utilitarian maps and plans came to be called.

In the course of the 1520s, Macchiavelli and Castiglione, for the first time in modern literature, emphasized the military utility of maps (by then a reflection of Italian and German practice).[16] But in 1531, in *The Boke Named the Governour*, Thomas Elyot (Figure 10), another, if semi-detached, member of the Court intellectual circle, elaborated further on the ways in which 'figures' could be of use to princes, emphasizing particularly that 'in visiting his own dominions [the governor] shall set them out in figure, in such wise that at his eye shall appear to

XI.10   Castles in the Downs, 1539

In February 1539 Henry ordered the creation of three castles in the Downs, at Deal, Sandown and Walmer. As recommended by Elyot in *The Boke Named the Governour* (1531), plats were utilized in their creation. The bird's-eye view of the 'Castle in the Downes' (right) is an early study for Deal, the largest of the three, while the drawing of 'A Castle for the Downes' is a show drawing of the prototype for Walmer and Sandown. Richard Benese, the surveyor, Christopher Dickenson, the master mason, and William Clement, the master carpenter, had previously only had experience of palace building as is betrayed in the details of the bird's-eye view. They learned quickly, however, and the show drawing, like the resulting castles, are influenced by contemporary ideas of fortification and combine offence and defence very skilfully.   P.B.

Inscr. 'Castle in the Downes'; 'A Castle for the Downes'

Drawing office of Richard Benese, ChristopherDickenson and William Clements, 1539

Ink and watercolour on paper 555 x 476; 592 x 471

Cotton MS Augustus I i, 20-21, British Library

HKW IV, pp. 455-65 and particularly p. 464

him where he shall employ his study and treasure, as well for the safeguard of his country as for the commodity and honour thereof'.[17]

Even here Elyot was by then partly reflecting practice. There had been abortive calls for surveys of the English coasts in 1519 (which may have generated a few plats (XI.7) and again in 1533, while from at least 1530 plats of strategic towns such as Rye and Dover (XI.8-9) had been commissioned, sometimes by the King himself, as a means of illustrating solutions to their problems.[18] Very gradually a corps of mainly native-born military engineers and platmakers, quite distinct from the earlier artist-cartographers, emerged from widely varying backgrounds: mariners, gunners and particularly masons, like John Rogers and Sir Richard Lee. Most seem to have been self-trained.[19] While they generally appear to have derived their graphic style from Flanders, they readily experimented for themselves.[20] Lee, the leading figure in the group, was closely associated with Cromwell. [21]

It was the windfall of wealth from dissolved monasteries at a time of severe international crisis in 1538-9 that provided the final impulse to the integration of maps with government. While in Greenwich in the autumn and winter of 1538-9, Henry and Cromwell ordered and financed a cartographic survey of the shores of the kingdom.[22]

Despite their superficially pictorial nature and the occasional cartographic awkwardness,

148

XI.11 Chart of Zeegat van Texel and the Zuiderzee, 1539

In September 1539 Henry was tempted by the idea of minimizing the possible difficulties with Charles V and Francis I of a long land journey from Cleves and a crossing from Calais to Dover by bringing Anne of Cleves to England by sea directly from Harderwijk in Guelderland. There were no available charts and so two experienced shipmasters, John Aborough and Richard Couche, were secretly sent to the Zuiderzee to survey the route. They produced a written rutter (now in Hatfield House) and, indicative of growing map-consciousness, this rough chart: the earliest surviving English examples of either type of

navigational aid. The chart, oriented to the east, is not drawn to scale, and devotes most space to the areas of greatest navigational difficulty. On 10 October the Great Admiral of England, Sir William Fitzwilliam, reported that Henry was 'marvellously inflamed' with the 'plat which John Aborough and Couche have brought home ... supposing many things to be done theron' (*LP* XIV ii, 309). P.B.

[John Aborough, September 1539]

Ink on paper, 315 x 415

Cotton MS Augustus I ii, 29, British Library

Alwyn Ruddock, 'The Earliest Original English Seaman's Rutter and Pilot's Chart', *Journal of the Institute of Navigation* 14 (1961), pp. 409-31

XI.12 Chart showing Anne of Cleves's Projected Passage to England, 1539

This hitherto little-noticed map, oriented to the east and showing the North Sea between England and the Netherlands, was an example of the 'many things' to which Henry VIII was inspired by Aborough's sketch-map (XI.11). It must have been created in the first three weeks of October 1539 to convince the ambassadors from Cleves of the viability of sending Anne of Cleves to London by sea from Harderwijk in Guelderland. It shows how Anne was to be smuggled out of the Zuiderzee to the royal flagship, depicted with the royal and other banners flying. Other ships are shown blockading the coast south of Zierikzee.

The depiction of the Zuiderzee is a direct copy of John Aborough's rough sketch (XI.11), providing the sole surviving example of how the great series of Henrician coastal plats were compiled, probably at Court, from sketches made on the spot. Another sketch plat must have provided the information for the mouth of the Thames. The ambassadors, fearful of a long voyage in winter, were not impressed, and by 25 October 1539 Henry had agreed to bring Anne to England from Calais. P.B.

Anonymous [partly after John Aborough], early October 1539

Ink and watercolour on paper, 465 x 645

Cotton MS Augustus I ii, 64, British Library

P. M. Barber, 'Monarchs, Ministers and Maps'

hydrography and marine science. Much of the geographical and ethnographical content stemmed from Rotz's own direct experience and from information about earlier Portuguese voyages. The Chart of South-East Asia (fos. 9v-10) is especially noteworthy. The Rajah's procession and the house on stilts, placed in Malaya, actually relate to observation in Ticou in Sumatra in 1529-30, while the depiction of land, also known as 'Java-La-Grande', beyond the strait to the south of (i.e. above) 'Lytil Java' has long been cited as evidence for an early Portuguese discovery of Australia. Rotz had begun the atlas while in French employ, but Henry's love of such charts was well-known. He would, no doubt, have echoed Sir Thomas Elyot, who could 'not tell what more pleasure should happen to a gentle wit than to behold in his house everything that within all the world is contained'. P.B.

XI.13   The Rotz Atlas, 1542

Jean Rotz, an experienced mariner of Scottish descent from Dieppe and recently appointed royal hydrographer to Henry VIII, sought to anchor himself in the royal favour through this atlas, dedicated to the King (fos. 1v-2), which he claimed embraced all

Jean Rotz, *The Boke of Idrography*, 1542
Ink and watercolour on vellum, 570 x 730
Royal MS 20 E IX, fos. 1v-2 (photo), 9v-10. British Library
Helen Wallis, ed., *The Maps and Text of the 'Boke of Idrography'
presented by Jean Rotz to Henry VIII*, Roxburghe Club (Oxford, 1981).
P. M. Barber, 'Monarchs, Ministers and Maps'

the resulting plats were ideally adapted to their purpose of locating and suggesting means of defending weak points. The British Library's surviving examples bear fragmentary yet impressive witness to what was arguably the greatest exercise in the mapping of England before the Ordnance Survey (which itself had similar origins in military necessity).

Nor was this all. Foreigners, like Jean Rotz (XI.13) were soon lured to England to map its shores and plan its defences.[23] Plans were used in autumn 1539 to ensure the passage of Anne of Cleves to England (XI.11-12),[24] to control the building of coastal forts (XI.10),[25] and later to create settlements in the pale of Calais,[26] to depict the extent of sanctuaries in English towns,[27] and in diplomatic negotiations with France.[28] Under this incessant pressure, and given the ample funds that were, briefly, available, cartographic experiments were made: the first English large-scale maps drawn to an explicit scale, of places such as Boulogne and Portsmouth, were created.[29]

By the time of Henry's death, maps had become accepted as the King's eyes in distant regions. Nor was there a greater cartographic enthusiast and connoisseur, nor a greater friend and recruiter of able mapmakers.[30] Amidst the state papers in his private library in Whitehall, there were drawers full of 'plats' and plentiful instruments for their creation as well as utilization.[31] Draughtsmen regularly came from Greenwich to make neat vellum copies of Henry's own sketch maps and engineers were called from France to explain their plats in person.[32] His privy gallery was filled with grander maps displaying his (XI.15) and his allies' kingdoms, his territorial omniscience, his victories and his claims.[33]

In barely twenty years and in large part in response to his wishes, maps had become an indispensible tool of English government.

Tuæ celsitudinis deditissimus seruus
Iohannes Mallardus

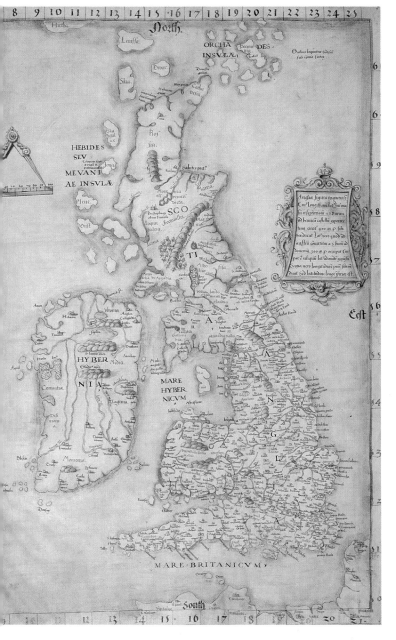

um te certo scirem nihil æque per om
nia desiderare R α illustrißime,
atq, res diuinas quam amplißime cum vbiq, terra
rum, tum vero florentißima anglia tua propagari,
non abre mihi visus sum facturus, si ab hoc potißimu
scripti genere ad celsitudinem tuam scribere incipe
rem quod et gloriam Regis illius cælestis et
gregis tui salutem quam maxime promoueret.
neque enim quicquam habet vel magnificentius,
vel regalius ista sublimitas tua quam vt ad exē
plum magni illius pastoris, te tuaque omnia

XI.14   Jean Mallard, Le Premier Livre de la Cosmographie en Rethorique Francoyse, c.1539

Another Frenchman in Henry's service was Jean Mallard. This manuscript, written and decorated in his own hand, contains a French verse cosmography covering the Atlantic coasts and the western coast of South America. An earlier copy of the work had been offered to Francis I. It is prefaced by a circular world map, promised to Francis but produced for Henry. In the preface Mallard successfully petitioned Henry for a position of court poet in England (XI.31-2). J.M.B

Illuminated MS on vellum, 265 x 185

Royal MS 20 B XII, British Library

Helen Wallis, ed., *The Boke of Idrography presented by Jean Rotz to Henry VIII*, pp. 10-11, 62-3

XI.15   Map of England

This is the sort of show 'Mappe of England' that is recorded as hanging in the galleries of several of Henry's palaces (including Greenwich - BL, Harley MS 1419A, fo. 58) by the end of his reign. Though its coastlines derive from the 'Gough Map' of about 1360, now in the Bodleian Library, it is much influenced by Renaissance geographical ideas. Thus it is the earliest surviving map of Britain to be graduated for latitude and longitude and to be drawn on a projection: that devised for Ptolemaic maps in the late fifteenth century by Nicolaus Germanus. It has many new place names which are generally well fixed, including, probably for the first time, and very suggestive of royal connections, Hampton Court. A link with Nicolaus Kratzer, who had talked of creating a new Ptolemaic map of England in 1524, cannot be excluded.

Another scheme for mapping Britain was one of the many ideas running through the too-fertile brain of John Leland. In his 'New Yeares gyfte' he mentioned a project for a map of Britain engraved in silver or brass - evidently for printing. The scheme was not realized until the middle of Elizabeth's reign. P.B.

Inscr. 'Angliae figura'. Scale: c. 1: 3,000,000

Anonymous, c. 1534-46

Ink and colours on vellum 635 x 420

Cotton MS Augustus I i, 9. British Library

G.R. Crone, *Early Maps of the British Isles AD 1000 - AD 1579*, Royal Geographical Society Reproductions of Early Maps, 17 (1961), pp. 8, 22-3

Henry VIII's Technological Tastes

As a boy, Henry VIII showed 'remarkable docility for mathematics', and the taste remained with him: he discussed astronomy with More (II.21) and patronized Kratzer (V.13). He had a multitude of scientific instruments, especially clocks, but only two survive (XI.16-17).

XI.16 Astrolabe made for King Henry VIII

The maker, Sebastian Le Seney, came from Normandy in 1537 and was employed in the King's service at a salary of 20s 8d a quarter. There can be no doubt that this instrument was made for the King. Prominently placed on the back of the astrolabe are the engraved initials, 'H R', on either side of the crowned royal coat-of-arms incorrectly engraved in the first quarter. On the obverse, the 'rete' and the 'label' are probably not original; the latter bears the inscription: 'ROY. HENRY. PAR.LA.GRASE.DE. DEIV [sic]'. The 'alidade' (on the reverse) has been repaired and now contains only the last part of the Garter motto: 'QVI MAL Y PENCE [sic]'. H.T.

Inscr. on reverse: BASTIEN LE SENEY FACIT Gilt brass 85 dia.
Reg. no. 78, 111, 113. British Museum
Gunther, *The Astrolabes of the World*, 2 vols. (Oxford, 1932, repr. 1976)

XI.17 Clock supposedly given by Henry VIII to Anne Boleyn

The clock case, which, like the movement, is sixteenth-century though modified, is Renaissance in form, with corner pilasters and a pierced frieze of grotesque-work with busts in roundels. At the sides are arched doors engraved with the royal arms, while on the pierced top, which encloses a bell, is a lion finial holding a shield of the royal arms. The two weights are engraved with the letters 'H' and 'A' with lovers' knots, and two mottoes: 'Diev et Mon Droit' (Henry's), and 'The Most Happy' (Anne's).

In the later eighteenth century the clock was in the collection of Horace Walpole at Strawberry Hill. Walpole, who pioneered the revival of interest in the Tudor period, certainly believed (or chose to believe) that the clock had been given to Anne Boleyn by Henry VIII. It is unclear whether we should do the same. D.S.

Clock: gilt metal, partly 16th cent., 255 x 109 x 107
Bracket: gilt wood, mid-18th cent., 276 x 178 x 182
Weights: lead sheathed in gilt copper, 197 ht; 178 ht; 32 dia.
Royal Collection
Cedric Jagger, *Royal Clocks* (1983), pp. 232-9

XI.18 Watch, c.1600

A very fine verge watch with movement of brass, steel and blued steel set between plates separated by casket-shaped pillars and contained in a gilt brass case with engraved and *à jour* decoration representing men in armour and mythological figures. On the side of the case is a hunting frieze, and on the central medallion on the back is engraved the figure of a huntsman with the letters 'M R S', flanked by two seated figures and griffins. The underside of the silver compass-plate bears an engraved picture of a river scene, with a walled town on the bank. It has been suggested by Hugh Tait that the circular medallion which hangs around Henry VIII's neck in most of the Holbein-type portraits is in fact the engraved back of such a watch. W.H.

Prob. French, c.1600

Brass, gilt brass, steel, blued steel, 67 ht, 88 dia.

F 230, Museum of the History of Science, Oxford

F. R. Maddison and A. J. Turner, *Museum of the History of Science, Catalogue 2, Watches* (Oxford, 1973), pp. 9-10, item W1

XI.19 Portable Clock

The initials of the maker's name could be the 'I' and the 'Z' carved individually on the outside of two of the pillars. The movement is in a gilt-brass tambour case, with a hinged, pierced cover, decorated with animal and human figures, including boar-hunting scenes around the side. At this time intricate astronomical and automaton clocks were made for the European courts and rich merchants. The other development was towards miniaturization, as in this example which in size is between a clock and a watch. W.H.

Prob. German, c.1550

Iron, brass, gilt brass, 25 ht, 60 dia.

B 1, Museum of the History of Science, Oxford

A. Turner, ed., *Time: Catalogue of the Images of Time Exhibition in Amsterdam* (Amsterdam: Foundation 'Tijd voor Tijd', 1990), p. 117

XI.20 Table Clock

The movement of steel and brass is enclosed in an engraved drum-shaped canister case of gilt brass with no hinges. It has a verge escapement, probably originally with a dumb-bell foliot, but now with a balance wheel to which weights have been added at diametrically opposite points on the rim. There is a 24-hour dial (numbered I-XII (twice) and 1-24), with touch pins and a single iron (steel) hand. W.H.

Prob. French, c.1550

Iron, brass, gilt brass, 44 ht, 62 dia.

153, Museum of the History of Science, Oxford

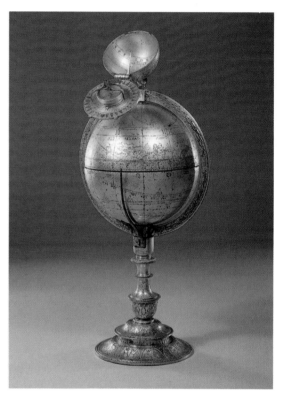

XI.21 Globe Clock

This is a composite instrument made up of two genuine sixteenth-century instruments, a globe clock and a scaphe or cup sundial (52 mm diameter), put together during the present century - a practice not frowned upon by an earlier generation of collectors.

Time is indicated by a fixed pointer of blued steel in front of the revolving gilt copper globe. Three hour-scales are engraved on the globe; also engraved are the ecliptic, with illustrations and names of the twelve signs of the Zodiac, the Equator, the Tropics, and the Arctic and Antartic Circles. W.H.

Prob. French, c.1550

Brass, gilt copper, gilt brass, blued steel, 285 ht, globe 105 dia.

G 379, Museum of the History of Science, Oxford

K. Maurice, *Die Deutsche Raderuhr*, 2 vols. (Munchen, 1976), I, pp. 57-67, 147-51, II, plates 249-63

Henry VIII's Music

Henry VIII is deservedly famous as both a musical performer and as a patron. But his abilities as a composer have been over-rated: he did not compose 'Greensleeves' and 'Pastime with Good Company' is probably an arrangement (XI.23).

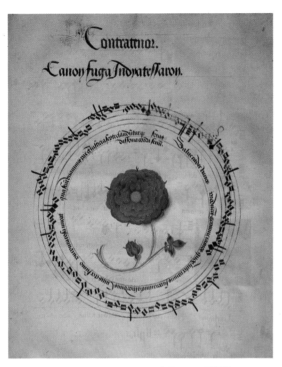

XI.22   Canon in Honour of Henry VIII, 1516

XI.23   'Henry VIII's Manuscript'

Each of the two voices of this perpetual canon is written round a finely painted Tudor rose. These bassus and contratenor parts, set at the musical interval of a fourth apart ('In diatessaron'), are intended for two singers each, making a double canon. The canon is the first musical entry in a presentation volume elaborately contrived to honour Henry VIII. Its text, celebrating the union of the houses of York and Lancaster, also appears on a banner decorating the elaborate illuminated title-page, where heraldic reference is made to the marriage of Henry and Catherine of Aragon.

The music in the rest of the volume consists of four- and five-part motets markedly Flemish in style and is laid out in the more conventional form of a choir-book. The first of these pieces sets a longer text from the title-page, again in honour of the united houses of York and Lancaster. Its composer, 'Mr Sampson', has been identified as Richard Sampson, an accomplished diplomat, at this time Wolsey's vicar-general in the diocese of Tournai and later bishop of Chichester. The remaining works are in praise of the Virgin Mary, perhaps as an oblique tribute to the birth in 1516 of Princess Mary, the first of Henry's children to live. A.S.

Media 490 x 725 [open]

Royal MS 11 E XI, fos. 2v-3. British Library

This manuscript is the principal evidence for Henry VIII's activities as a composer, containing (beside work by other composers) twenty vocal pieces for three or four voices, and thirteen three- or four-part instrumental works, ascribed to him. Only one other of his pieces has survived, a three-part motet 'Quam pulchra es', his only known sacred work. Henry VIII's most famous composition, the song 'Pastime with good company', by 'The King Henry VIII', uses a popular melody which was first printed in 1529. However, it seems likely that Henry's version, together with most of the other pieces and the manuscript itself, is earlier and dates from the second decade of the century, when the King was young and Court life characterized by the celebrations and entertainments with which some of the pieces can be linked. Though this volume has for long been known as 'Henry VIII's manuscript', it was never in the King's possession, but must rather have been made for someone close to the Court - possibly Sir Henry Guildford, controller of the Household and master of the Revels. A.S.

MS on paper 325 x 510 [open]

Additional MS 31,922, fos. 14v-15. British Library

John Stevens, ed., *Music at the Court of Henry VIII: Musica Britannica*, 18 (1969)

Greenwich and Henry VIII's Royal Library

BY JAMES CARLEY

Henry VIII was the first English king to write, publish and print a book: the attack on Luther known as the *Assertio septem sacramentorum*. Henry was also the first king fully to be at home with books. Earlier kings had of course been literate. From the days of the Anglo-Saxons they had possessed books; while the Lancastrians had actually been learned. But it is only under Edward IV (1461-83) that the king's books start to turn into a royal library, with a continuous history both as an institution and a collection. Edward's books, however huge and cheerfully illuminated, were those of a man who wished 'to be read to, not to read'.[1] Henry VIII was different. An illumination in his psalter, itself small and easy to hold (XI.31), shows him reading; while the innumerable marginalia in his books (for he was a compulsive annotator) show that they were read (below, p. 161).

Yet this bookman-King was also responsible for the destruction of the monastic libraries. John Bale, who approved of the dissolution, thought 'the loss of our libraries ... a most horrible infamy'.[2] The dissolution was, at the same time, as both Bale and his mentor John Leland recognized, an opportunity to enrich the Royal Collection with the cream of the monastic libraries and turn it into a 'national' library. The library at Greenwich Palace has an important and hitherto neglected part to play in this story of high hopes not entirely deceived.

Edward IV's collection had been taken over by Henry VII, who had added other books of a similar type and lodged them in his new palace of Richmond. And it was to Richmond that the post of royal librarian, established in 1492 and held successively by two denizened Frenchmen, Quentin Poulet and Gilles Duwes, was at first attached.[3] Under Henry VIII, to judge from a partial list compiled in 1535,[4] the Richmond collection became more or less frozen; instead, the King built up his own in his favourite palace of Greenwich.

In 1519 Henry VIII undertook important building works at Greenwich, and added a wing projecting north into the Thames to the tall donjon block that contained his private apartments (above, p. 22). On the second floor of the new wing was the 'highest library'. At Henry's death the library was furnished with seven 'desks', or combined lecterns and bookshelves (Figure 11), and a table. In the desks and under the table were 329 books, bound variously in red velvet and in leather.[5] This was the usual way to store books before wall shelves were introduced in the later sixteenth century. Indeed, in both size and arrangement the Greenwich library was very similar to the contemporary library of Margaret of Austria, regent of the Netherlands.[6]

In 1519, the year the Greenwich library was built, Henry VIII was showing a new, and rather short-lived commitment to business. But his most devoted application to study came with his decision to have his first marriage dissolved. The King worked directly with his advisers to trawl theological and legal authorities, and his determination to make the search exhaustive led to the first major transfers from the monastic to the royal libraries. It also, of course, determined the kind of books culled.[7] In 1533 Henry at last got his divorce; three years later the dissolution of the monasteries began. Monastic books were now Henry's for the asking but the direct interest which motivated his acquisitions during the divorce had gone.

Higher arguments were needed. They were supplied largely by John Leland, the early Tudor antiquary. In 1534, armed with a royal commission, he had begun a systematic search of the monastic libraries to find materials to advance the cause of British history, on the one hand, and true religion, on the other.[8] The dissolution altered his priorities. In his New Year gift to King Henry of 1546 (XI.24), he surveyed his achievements and set out his plans. 'First', he claimed,

'I have conserved many good authors, the which otherwise had been like to have perished ... Of the which part remain in the most magnificent libraries of your royal palaces.'[9] In his *Antiphilarchia* he named the libraries in receipt of ancient books as Whitehall, Hampton Court and Greenwich.[10] The first two were the palaces, seized from Wolsey, which eventually displaced Greenwich in Henry's favour. Whitehall became the main library, though the library, like the palace, was very much a working one. Its contents are known thanks to an inventory drawn up in 1542.[11] The library was then in the charge of Sir Anthony Denny as keeper of the palace; while William Tyldesley, the royal librarian since 1535, was Denny's subordinate as a member of the wardrobe of the Beds (XI.25). The books were arranged in three alphabetical series and numbered. The numbers (to 910 and to 1450) were also inscribed in arabic figures in the volumes. Royal books with such numbers certainly come from Whitehall; books without equally certainly do not.[12] No such system applied, however, at the libraries of Hampton Court or Greenwich and we know about their contents only after they had been broken up. In 1549 a new royal librarian, Bartholomew Traheron, was appointed. As part of the general retrenchment that followed Henry VIII's death, he was authorized to transfer books to Whitehall.[13] There followed a weeding out of duplicates. Several were acquired by Sir Thomas Pope, and later given to the library of Trinity College, Oxford, which he founded in 1555 (XI.26-8). His donation consisted of ninety-nine volumes: seventy-three printed books and twenty-six manuscripts. Fifteen printed books bear a heavily erased inscription 'ex Hampton Court', and twenty-seven a similarly erased 'ex Greenwich'. The Greenwich books are typical of libraries of the period: there is a standard mix of up-to-date humanist editions of the Fathers, older scholastic texts, biblical commentaries (XI.26-7), contemporary theologians and philosopers, some ancient historians, and finally a single work in Greek (XI.28).

For the manuscripts given by Pope, things are less clear-cut, since they contain no 'ex libris'. Nevertheless there are several indications that they too came from the royal collection: eight bear

Figure 11: This woodcut, from the *The Ship of Fools*, shows a bibliomane seated at the sort of lectern-top desk that was used to store books in Henry VIII's library at Greenwich.

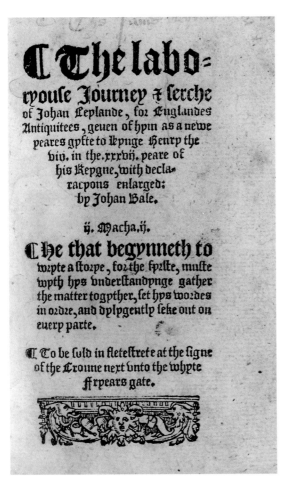

XI.24   John Bale, The laboryouse Journey and Serche of Johan Lelande for Englandes Antiquitees, London, 1549

Leland was a giver of New Year gifts. In 1534, when he was just beginning his antiquarian journeys through England, he gave Henry VIII 'two books of stories', which, as they are noted as being 'with the King's grace', Henry may actually have read (*LP* VII, 9). In 1546, when his travels were over and he was starting to digest his materials, he presented the 'New Yeares gyfte' to Henry VIII, which, three years later, was edited for publication by his disciple, John Bale. The 'New Yeares gyfte' described Leland's achievements to date, in travelling every inch of the country and saving many ex-monastic manuscripts (above, p. 155), and outlined his projects for the future. He had already completed a dictionary of English

writers; there was to follow a description of England, with a map engraved in silver or brass (evidently for printing), a history of the antiquities of Britain, a peerage, and finally a description of Henry VIII's palaces. All proved abortive, as Leland went mad in 1550. But his notes provided both a mine and an inspiration for future generations of scholars. D.S.

Printed book, 137 x 186 [open]

G.2931. British Library

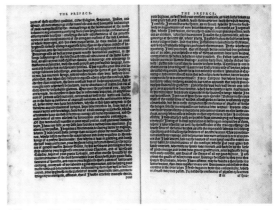

XI.25   Sir Thomas Elyot, The Dictionary, London, Thomas Berthelet, 1538

Elyot's *Dictionary*, modelled in part on Ambrogio Calepino's *Dictionarium*, was the first Latin-English dictionary to be based on humanist ideals of classical scholarship. According to Elyot's account in his preface, the King was informed by the triumvirate of Sir Anthony Denny, gentleman of the Privy Chamber, William Tyldesley, the royal librarian, and Cromwell himself, about Elyot's project. Henry VIII thereupon offered both advice and access to his library. The result so dissatisfied Elyot with the thoroughness of his researches hitherto that he stopped the press and added an appendix for the first part of the alphabet which had already been set. This is Elyot's presentation copy to Cromwell, with a complimentary letter in Elyot's beautiful italic hand. It was probably one of the handful of books 'had into the King's library' after the minister's fall in 1540. J.C., D.S.

Printed book, 295 x 395 [open]

C.18.m.2, sig. A ii(v)-iii. British Library

brief descriptions in a hand very similar to that of the cataloguer of the main Whitehall collection;[14] another has the monogram 'TC', which otherwise turns up exclusively in ex-monastic manuscripts acquired for the royal library;[15] finally one (Clement of Llanthony, *Concordia evangelistarum*) is probably one of the Lincolnshire monastic manuscripts marked down for transfer to the royal library around 1530.[16] Bearing in mind the provenance of the printed books, it seems reasonable to ascribe most of the manuscripts to Greenwich also.

We can go further. In 1604 Charles Howard, earl of Nottingham, gave twelve medieval

XI.26 A. Broikwy, In Quatuor Evangelia Enarrationes, Coloniae, apud Petrum Quentell, 1539

This volume, bound in white buckskin, and bearing the deleted 'ex grenewych' inscription, was probably supplied to Henry VIII by Thomas Berthelet, the King's printer, in c.1545. Although it was originally thought that Berthelet had his own binding shop, H. M. Nixon has since shown that books printed by Berthelet were actually sent out to different London binders. Among these was the binder of the volume shown here,

who has been called the 'Greenwich Binder' by Nixon. The characteristic features of the work of the 'Greenwich binder' seem to be that his royal shield is made up of small tools, and that the edges of the leaves of books bound by him bear the following inscription, in gilt: 'Rex in aeternum vive' (May the King live forever). These features are also found on (XI.27). It should be emphasized that the 'Greenwich binder was not a palace binder', still less that all books at Greenwich were bound by him (see for instance XI.28). This volume, along with (XI.27-8), and a further twenty-four books, was acquired by Sir Thomas Pope, an Oxfordshire lawyer and middle-ranking government official, and given to Trinity College, his newly endowed Oxford foundation, in 1555. A.C.

Printed book, 2o 337 x 210 x 55

Old Library, I.7.5. Trinity College, Oxford

Nixon, 'Early English Gold-tooled Bookbindings', pp. 300-302

Fine Bindings 1500-1700 from Oxford Libraries: catalogue of an exhibition (Oxford, 1968, repr. 1987), p. 38, no. 62.

R. Gameson and A. Coates, *The Old Library, Trinity College, Oxford* (Oxford, 1988), pp. 50-51, no. 2 (plate 16a)

XI.27 Theophylact, Archbishop of Achrida, Enarrationes in Quatuor Evangelica, Basel, no printer named, 1540

The binding of this book, which Henry VIII must have acquired between 1540 and 1547, is also the work of the 'Greenwich Binder'. In addition to the crown motif on (XI.26), the binding is decorated with the H R monogram, the Tudor rose, the fleur-de-lis and the portcullis. A.C.

Printed book, 2o 323 x 210 x 75

Old Library I.10.11 Trinity College, Oxford

Gameson & Coates, *The Old Library, Trinity College, Oxford*, p. 51, no. 3

manuscripts and several printed books to Oxford. Once again the signs of Henrician ownership are clear: one manuscript seems to be annotated by the King;[17] two bear the 'TC' monogram;[18] most are bound in a characteristic black velvet binding; one, however, is the work of the 'King Henry's Binder',[19] as are thirteen of the printed books.[20] The printed books are standard editions of the Fathers, and so precisely the kind of material to become redundant when the Henrician collections were being consolidated. Finally, several of the manuscripts contain annotations in the hand of John Leland.[21] Equally importantly, none has a Whitehall inventory number. Here then is another clutch of de-acquisitioned books from Hampton Court or Greenwich. The conclusion, therefore, is fairly radical. We are dealing, not with one royal library, Whitehall, as historians have tended to assume, but with at least three. And of these Greenwich was probably the next to Whitehall in importance for printed books, while as far as manuscripts were concerned, its contents were likely to have been at once more varied and magnificent. Henry the bookman put his mark more widely than we thought.

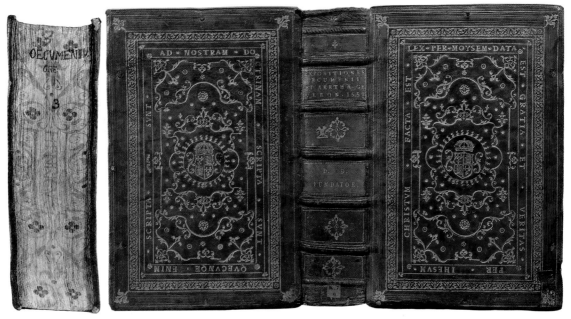

XI.28 Oecumenius, Expositiones ex Diversis Sanctorum Patrum Commentariis ab Oecumenio et Aretha Collectae, Verona, apud Sephanum & fratres Sabios, 1532

The binding of this volume, in brown calf, has been identified by Nixon as the work of the 'King Edward and Queen Mary Binder'. The characteristic features of this bindery are the royal shield, all on one tool, and the inscriptions: on the upper cover, 'lex per moysem data est gratia et veritas per ihesum christum facta est'; on the lower, 'ad nostram doctrinam scripta sunt quecunque enim scripta sunt'.

Both make typically 'evangelical' points: the first contrasts the law of Moses with the saving grace of Christ; the second emphasizes the authority of Scripture itself. On the edges of the leaves is a floral frame surrounding the words 'Rex', on the upper edge, and 'Henricus', on the fore-edge. A.S.

Printed book, 2o 456 x 232 x 96

Old Library K 7 9. Trinity College, Oxford

Nixon, 'Early English Gold-tooled Bookbindings', pp. 295-8

Gameson & Coates, *The Old Library, Trinity College, Oxford*, pp. 51, no. 4 (plate 16b)

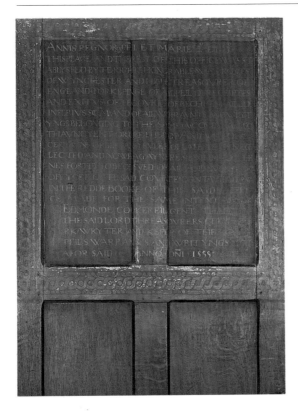

XI.29 Ambry or Cupboard Doors, with Gilt Guilloche Design, 1555

The doors bear the inscription that in 1555 the lord treasurer caused this place and the rest of the office to be fitted out with presses for keeping the records of the Exchequer.

Cupboards with even more elaborately decorated doors lined the walls of Constable Montmorency's library at the château d'Ecouen. Similar arrangements were probably to be found in Henry VIII's libraries and treasure chambers. Our modern method of storing books, by fitted shelving mounted round the walls of a room, did not become usual till the end of the sixteenth century, when books themselves were far more plentiful and the need for compact storage correspondingly greater. D.S.

Oak with gilt decoration

2140 x 777

Public Record Office

Elizabeth Hallam, 'Nine Centuries of Keeping the Public Records', in *The Records of the Nation*, ed. Peter Spufford and G. H. Martin (Woodbridge, 1990), 23-42, p. 31

The Religion of Henry VIII

BY DIARMAID MACCULLOCH

It is easy to mock Henry VIII. How can we take seriously the religion of a man whose theological outlook came to resemble a magpie's nest; who built his palace at Nonsuch squarely over a village church and churchyard, and whose bowling alley at Hampton Court was lit by church windows from an Oxfordshire abbey? Henry's lurches in religious policy can all too easily be linked with with his diplomatic priority of the moment: evangelical to please German Lutheran princes and to gain the attention of the devious King Francis of France; Catholic to conciliate the affronted piety of Emperor Charles V. Yet to regard all this as mere selfishness or cynical diplomacy would be to underestimate Henry, even though his store of selfishness and cynicism could hardly be surpassed. Throughout his career he not only read theology but wrote it, turning to it from the pleasures of war and sport for long periods particularly at personal crises: his estrangement from Catherine of Aragon, the death of Jane Seymour, his betrayal and humiliation by Catherine Howard. Indeed, the greatest crisis of his life, the struggle for his first divorce, was made all the more difficult and far-reaching in its effects because he refused to regard the issue as anything other than a confrontation between himself and an angry God: the same confrontation which forced Luther into an equally cataclysmic struggle with the traditional Church.

In his early years, Henry seemed the predictable product of an ostentatiously pious family. His father spent lavishly on works of piety to give his soul especially speedy passage through purgatory, while his formidable grandmother, Lady Margaret Beaufort, was persuaded by her chaplain John Fisher to divert most of her pious energy less conventionally into institutions promoting humanist scholarship. The young king followed both these influences. He heard mass several times a day at the variety of altars littering his palaces; went on pilgrimage to Our Lady of Walsingham; paid fitful but fruitful attention to his tutors; read widely and enjoyed being flattered by humanist scholars who liked to think of themselves as equipped to change the world by their learning. Yet there were early signs of individuality. Henry VII had established his embarrassingly shaky royal title by force and large-scale intimidation, but his son took the divine inspiration of his kingship very seriously. The elder Henry had not let his piety stand in the way of curbs on the jurisdiction of the Church authorities; now, in a renewed series of clashes which quickly followed the reconciliation of his accession, the young Henry said openly that the Church's pretensions encroached on his God-given royal dignity. To begin with, his wrath fell only on the Church at home. On the international stage, the pope had no more loyal ally, who fought the schismatic king of France in the name of papal obedience in 1512, and who in 1521 defended the Holy Father against Martin Luther in the *Assertio Septem Sacramentorum*. As a result, Henry could rejoice in the unique royal title of Defender of the Faith: a description which he felt justified in using all his life.

The great change came during the 1520s in Henry's dawning obsession with God's wrathful judgment on his marriage to Catherine of Aragon. We cannot be certain where the idea came from, but it seems independent of his fierce love for Anne Boleyn. If he had no surviving lawful son, it was a sign that he should never have married his deceased brother's wife - the Bible forbade it, and no pope could dispense the prohibition. No argument could shift him, nor would he be tempted by any strategy for gaining a divorce which would offer a less direct challenge to papal power. Instead he threw his energy into the direction of a theological campaign to prove his point. Perhaps he was so immovable because his new conviction involved admitting that he had unwittingly done wrong: Henry always liked to be in the right, and he built up a large psychological investment in having admitted his mistake.

But another mistake emerged to unsettle the King's view of himself and his rightness before God. As Pope Clement haplessly strove to avoid a decision on the divorce which would bring down the fury of Catherine's nephew, the Holy Roman Emperor Charles V, Henry was driven to see the papacy, which he had supported so steadfastly, as standing in the way of God's condemnation of his marriage. Now he must rebuild his mental world out of the ruins of certainties which had satisfied Europe for centuries, with no coherent guidelines apart from the conviction that God had singled him out by virtue of his coronation to guide his realm into all truth. In this privileged situation, he might gather to himself anything from the flotsam of the theological upheavals taking place on the continent. The results were unpredictable; confused observers at the time, and have continued to confuse ever since.

Through the 1530s and 1540s, Henry was open to influence: from reformers in whom (however temporarily) he placed love and trust, such as Anne Boleyn, Thomas Cromwell and Thomas Cranmer, or from conservatives who exploited his sudden revulsions from the changes he had unleashed. Access to the King was all-important, so that it was vital that, in his last months, Henry was normally surrounded by courtiers with a determination to push England into religious reform, and that his last wife, Catherine Parr, shared these sympathies as she determined the education of his son. These influences have been well charted in recent years to make more sense of the twists of Henrician policy. Yet on some issues the King made up or changed his own mind in accepting or rejecting religious change. The idea of purgatory, central to the old faith, lost its grip on him, so that in his personal revisions of official doctrine drafted in 1537 and published in 1543, he reduced purgatory's ancient power over human destiny to the vaguest of assertions. The suspicion of clerical pretension which had marked even his youthful piety was now greatly strengthened by his clashes over the divorce and break with Rome. This coloured his view of the sacraments, so that he downgraded the importance of extreme unction and of individual confession to a priest, and rejected the full traditional mystique of priestly ordination. The rather complacent annotations to his personal psalter also reveal that he remained proud of his achievement in destroying shrines and sacred images (XI.31).

Alongside this was the King who remained on crucial questions a conservative to his dying day. He never accepted the central Protestant doctrine of justification by faith, despite all efforts to persuade him. He cherished his beautiful personal rosary (XI.30); maintained the mass in all its

XI.30 Henry VIII's Rosary

The rosary consists of a ring from which hang a cross, ten Ave beads, and a large bead for Pater Noster. It is richly carved throughout and the Pater bead is hinged, with two more biblical scenes carved inside.
The attribution to Henry VIII comes from the royal arms carved in the Pater bead and the iconography of the decoration. On one side of the cross are Christ and the four Evangelists; on the other, the four Latin Fathers; while the beads are carved with the Apostles, Sentences of the Creed, Prophets and Sybils, and scenes from the Old and New Testaments. The whole typifies the eclectic mixture of Henry VIII's religion. D.S.

Boxwood 580 lgth: Chatsworth Collection
Treasures from Chatsworth, International Exhibitions Foundation (1979- 80), no. 184

BEATVS vir qui non abiit in confilio impiorum, & in via peccatorum non ftetit, & in cathedra pe= ftilentiæ non fedit.

XI.31 Henry VIII's Psalter

The manuscript Latin psalter used personally by Henry towards the end of his life was written and illuminated for him by a Frenchman, Jean Mallard, who is variously described as, among other things, his poet, orator and scribe. Mallard, an accomplished scribe and illuminator as well as a man of letters, had for a time been court poet to Francis I but lost the

position when Clément Marot, a former holder of the post, returned to France in 1537 after a period of exile. Although Mallard was still in France in 1538, when Francis paid him for work on a Book of Hours, he soon migrated to England. His salary is recorded in the royal accounts in June 1539 and again the two following years, after which he seems to have returned to France.

The manuscript, in Mallard's characteristic Roman script, is illustrated with seven miniatures, in five of which Henry himself is portrayed in his favourite character of King David p. 162). Latin marginal notes in the King's hand appear throughout the book, some of them very revealing. Most striking is the remark 'a hard saying' beside Psalm 37 v. 25: 'I have been young and now am old yet have I not seen the righteous forsaken, nor his seed begging bread.' J.M.B

Jean Mallard, c. 1540

Illuminated MS on vellum 205 x 140

Royal MS 2 A XVI. British Library

Pamela Tudor-Craig, 'Henry VIII and King David', in D. Williams, ed., *Early Tudor England: Proceedings of the 1987 Harlaxton Symposium* (Woodbridge, 1989), pp. 195-205

XI.32 Jean Mallard, Paraphrastica in Precationem Dominicam Elegia

Mallard used an italic script for this Latin verse paraphrase of the Lord's Prayer. The little manuscript, with its decorative initial letter and binding of white velvet (now only partially preserved), is typical of the kind of book which might be offered to the king as a New Year gift. J.M.B

Illuminated MS on vellum, 155 x 145

Royal MS 7 D XIII. British Library

ancient Latin splendour, and left instructions for a generous supply of requiems to guide his soul through a purgatory which his doctrinal statements had done much to weaken. Henry was at his most intransigent on the subject of marriage - understandably, since this had lain at the heart of his recurrent personal crises. Not only did he insist (against the facts of scripture and Church history) that marriage was one of the basic scriptural sacraments like baptism and the eucharist, but he also upheld the ancient ban on clerical marriage, additionally refusing to release from their vows of celibacy the monks and nuns whose lives he had shattered.

What united these diverse strands? Apparently the conviction of his unique relationship with God as his anointed deputy on earth, a conviction that seemed real enough to be shared by his devoted but not uncritical admirer Archbishop Cranmer, and by much of the political establishment. Increasingly Henry identified himself with the Old Testament hero-king David. His illuminated psalter fuses the Old Testament king and the Tudor King into one (XI.31).

The Sports of Kings

BY SIMON THURLEY

Henry VIII is seen, and rightly, as a great sporting King. During his lifetime foreign ambassadors described him jousting and playing tennis and he is known to have been in the hunting saddle until his very last years. His father, Henry VII, although not known for his sporting achievements, was also a keen tennis player and evidently enjoyed hunting. But his son clearly far outshone him in both interest and achievement. This was not merely a matter of the difference of age, for in the early years of the sixteenth century there was a perceptible change in attitude towards sport in the English Court.

A revival of interest in physical exercise began in fifteenth-century Italy, and was given its classic expression by Castiglione in his *Book of the Courtier* of 1527. Hitherto, the sole justification for sport had been to prepare a man for the serious business of war; indeed the two were scarcely separate. Castiglione continued to pay lip-service to this. But the emphasis shifts from the game of war to the social game. Sporting prowess was now valued because it inculcated physical grace and offered the opportunity for competitive display.[1] English theoreticians, while taking up Castiglione's ideal of the courtly amateur sportsman, gave it a characteristically practical interpretation by emphasizing the health-giving properties of exercise. 'By exercise, which is a vehement motion,' Sir Thomas Elyot wrote in *The Boke Named the Governour* of 1531, 'the health of man is preserved and his strength increased'. Andrew Boorde went further and in *A Compendyous Regyment or a Dyetary of Health* (c.1542) recommended a straightforward work-out, complete with weights. First thing in the morning, before hearing mass, a man should 'moderately exercise' his body with some labour 'or playing at the tennis or casting a bowl, or peising [holding or swinging] weights or plummets of lead in your hands'.[2] To these streams of theorizing, native and foreign, must be added simple fact. The Court included large numbers of active young men with a lot of time on their hands. When the royal household was essentially a war band, which it was until the fifteenth century, frequent warfare gave their energies a productive outlet. When the household became a court, and when peace became the rule rather than war, an alternative was needed.[3] It was found in organized sport. Then as now, of course, upper-class sport demanded expensive equipment. As in other fields, the court of Burgundy led the way and in the late fifteenth century made ample architectural provision for sporting events. Both tiltyards, tennis courts and bowling alleys were common features of their palaces.

There is no evidence to show that the Yorkist kings followed the Burgundian example. Instead it was left to Henry VII to build the first complex of recreational buildings at an English royal palace. This was at Richmond where they were described in 1501 by a herald at the marriage of Prince Arthur with Catherine of Aragon: 'In the lower end of this garden be pleasant galleries, and houses of pleasure to disport in, at chess, tables [draughts], dice, cards, bils [billiards]; bowling alleys, butts for archers, and goodly tennis plays [courts] as well to use the said plays and disports as to behold them so disporting.'[4] The emphasis on provision for spectators is noteworthy, for watch was all Henry VII did with the rougher sports, in particular jousting. With Henry VIII the King himself became a participant. His education had included vigorous participation in 'all such convenient sports and exercises as behoveth his estate to have experience in',[5] and when he became King in 1509 the Court was launched into a continual round of sport. Hunting and jousting were the most popular and frequent sports of the King's youth, although he also engaged in indoor games like tennis and bowls. After 1528 jousting suffered a sudden eclipse, and, though jousts continued, after 1530 the King never participated again.[6]

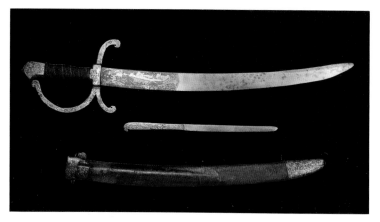

XI.33 Henry VIII's Wood-knife and Byknife

The etched decoration on the wood-knife, or hunting sword, includes arabesques, scenes of boar hunts (on the quillons), the closing stages of the siege of Boulogne in 1544 on one side of the blade and a Latin inscription commemorating the capture of the town on the other. The handle of the companion by knife is damascened in gold.

The wood-knife is probably one of the pair listed in Henry VIII's Inventory as two 'long woodknives ... of Dego his making'. 'Dego' can be identified as the Spanish swordsmith and damascener, Diego de Caias, who in 1542 was expelled from France, where he had been working for the Dauphin. Probably by March, and certainly by October, 1543 he had entered Henry VIII's service. The Inventory also includes three daggers and an arming sword made by him. He is the only swordsmith to be mentioned by name. D.S.

Diego de Caias, c.1545

Steel etched and gilt sword: 654 lgth woodknife: 308 lgth

Royal Collection

Claude Blair, 'A Royal Swordsmith and Damascener: Diego de Caias', *Metropolitan Museum Journal*, 3 (1970), pp. 149-98

XI.34 Henry VIII's (?) Dagger

The blade is single edged and etched near the hilt with roses, pomegranates and foliage, the quillons are acorn-shaped and made in one with a shell-guard. The grip is modern. The royal badges and the quality of the workmanship make it likely that this was a personal weapon of the King; at any rate it must date from the first two decades of the reign since the pomegranate was the badge of Catherine of Aragon. D.S.

English, early 16th cent.

Steel etched 465 lgth

X.39. Royal Armouries

XI.35 Henry VIII's Hawking Equipment

The hood is made of leather with a cover of patterned red silk or velvet, embroidered with gold thread and edged with gold chain-work. There is an opening at the front to allow the beak to protrude; at the back there is a split for ease of fitting, with draw-strings to either side. The glove is made of brown doe-skin reinforced with grey and embroidered with rows of silver-gilt thread.

Together with the stirrups (XI.36), the glove and hood formed part of the Ashmolean Museum's foundation collection. The collection was given to the University of Oxford in 1683 by Elias Ashmole but derived largely from the museum of the Tradescants, father and son, at Lambeth. The catalogue of the Musaeum Tradescantianum, published in 1656, includes entries for 'Henry the 8 his Stirrups, Haukes-Hoods, Gloves', and for 'Henry 8, hawking-glove, hawks-hood, dogs-coller'. 'Foure hauks hoodes' and 'one hawkeing glove of Henry ye 8th' were sold under the Commonwealth from among the possessions of Charles I. The younger Tradescant was not himself the buyer at the sale but he may subsequently have acquired the hawking equipment for his museum. A.McG.

Leather and embroidered silk, 38 x 64, 285 x 130

1685 B 228. Ashmolean Museum, Oxford

Arthur MacGregor, ed., *The Late King's Goods. Collections, Possessions and Patronage of Charles I in the Light of the Commonwealth Sale Inventories* (London and Oxford, 1989), p. 407, fig. 113

THE BEDCHAMBER: THE CLEVES MARRIAGE, 1540

This was due partly to his increasing age and partly to the fact that the rough-and-tumble of the tiltyard was replaced by more sophisticated sports. Hunting of course remained the staple, especially during the progress which in essence was no more than an extended hunting party (above, p. 118). For the rest, from 1530 indoor sports gained the ascendancy and Henry created areas set aside for indoor recreations at his principal greater houses. Hampton Court, Greenwich and Whitehall all had special areas set aside for recreation,[7] and many other palaces had recreational buildings. The greatest recreational complex was at Whitehall where four tennis courts, two bowling alleys and a cockpit were provided in addition to a large tiltyard and a park stocked for hunting.[8]

The King's works at Greenwich reflect his changing attitudes to sport. In the early part of the reign almost all the works at Greenwich were connected with the King's recreations of tilting, hunting and revelling. Among his first works was the building of new stables.[9] Two were erected: the stable for the King's coursers beside the old stables, and one for the King's stud mares in the park. The first substantial buildings other than these were 'the towers and a house which shall be set over the green before the tilt behind the manor of Greenwich'.[10] These were the two tiltyard towers prominent in all views of the palace (Figure 4). The towers were linked by the tiltyard gallery, in which tilting equipment was kept at ground-floor level.[11] This arrangement of towers and gallery provided the maximum space for viewing the tournaments and could also be utilized for other sorts of entertainment. The most famous of these was in 1527, when Henry entertained the French ambassadors at Greenwich and the complex was extended by the addition of two new halls (above, pp. 64-66).

After 1530, when the King's sporting interests turned from the tiltyard, an area of Greenwich Palace was, together with areas in other palaces, developed as a recreation centre. The tennis court (or play) at Greenwich was a modest affair: it was timber-framed and was approached by a gallery which was probably used for viewing.[12] Its windows were protected by wire frames, and its floor tiled.[13] Repair accounts refer to its being sited near the Friars' yard, and connected to the queen's privy stair by lodgings.[14] In addition to the tennis play a cockpit was constructed with special coops for the King's prizefighters. The palace keeper was instructed to look after them.[15] There was also a bowling alley situated beneath the queen's long gallery, a building which connected the main palace to the tiltyard gallery.[16] The most extraordinary sporting addition to the palace was, however, the king's hawk mews. The young King had had 'no affection' for hawking, despite the efforts of one of his Privy Chamber, Sir William Tyler (V.14), 'to show your Highness

XI.36 Henry VIII's Stirrups

The stirrups vary slightly in size and construction and do not form a matching pair. By long tradition these are equated with the stirrups mentioned in a

royal warrant of 1635 (PRO, LC 5/134, 91) instructing William Smithsby, keeper of the Hampton Court wardrobe, to 'deliver to John Treidescant king Henry the Eight his Cap, his stirrups, Henry the 7th his gloves and Combcase'. They belong to a general type that has been variously ascribed to Germany and Spain, but most recently Guy Wilson has suggested that these examples might have emanated from the Royal Armour Workshop at Greenwich. A.McG

Tinned iron 156 x 158

1685 B 449-50. Ashmolean Museum, Oxford

C. Ffoulkes, *European Arms and Armour in the University of Oxford* (Oxford, 1912), p. 55, no. 158, pl. 16

G.M. Wilson in A. MacGregor ed., *Tradescant's Rareties* (Oxford, 1983) pp. 186-8, no. 84, figs. 41-2

of the high pleasure he findeth in his hawks'. No doubt Henry then found it too sedentary. But when he reached 'father Tyler's' age, he more than made up for his earlier neglect. For at Greenwich the new mews was situated directly adjacent to the king's lodgings and was called the cage. Only one room separated the cage from the Queen's bedchamber.

The accounts describe, in some detail its perches and lattice windows.[17] At his death, there were masses of hawking equipment in his private apartments and two examples survive (XI.35).

Finally, with the King's increasing corpulence, hunting itself had to be made an altogether gentler activity. The long progress was abandoned from 1543, and the facilities improved in the 'suburban' palaces round London. At Greenwich the mounting blocks in the park were raised higher 'that the King's grace may not only get upon his horse easily but light down upon the same', and bridges were built in Woolwich marshes for Henry 'to ride over the ditches a-hawking and a-hunting safely'. The good sportsman had gone to seed at last.[18]

XI.37 An Archer's Bracer

This archer's bracer or wrist-guard was laced to the wrist by thongs passing through the sixteen small holes. It protected the hand grasping the bow from being chafed by the bow-string whenever an arrow was released. The ornament in relief on the other side, which retains some of the original gilding but not the colouring, includes oak leaves and acorns below an inscription, 'Jesus helpe', on either side of the emblem of the crowned Tudor rose. The prominence of this badge and the high quality of the workmanship indicate that the bracer belonged to a person of rank in the royal service, for use in archery as a sport at the Tudor Court. H.T.

English, early 16th cent., Cuir-bouilli, 125 lgth
Reg. no. 1922, 1-10, 1. British Museum
C. J. Longman and H. Walrond, *Archery* (1894), p. 161, fig. 110
O.M. Dalton, 'A Late-Medieval Bracer in the British Museum', *The Antiquaries Journal* 11 (1922), pp. 208-10, with two line-drawings

XI.38 Henry VIII's (?) Crossbow

This crossbow, made almost certainly during the reign of Henry VIII, may well have been for the use of the King himself. This is suggested by the etched

royal arms of England, as adopted by Henry around 1527, on the bow, and the etched strapwork pattern, also found on the bow, which is very similar to the pattern on a Greenwich armour of about 1540 made for Henry and now at Windsor Castle. The similarity of the design suggests that the same pattern book, if not the same artist, was used for the decoration, which in turn might imply that both items were made for the same owner. Only seven crossbows are listed in Henry VIII's Inventory, and this may be one of them. It is definitely one of only a handful of Tudor crossbows to survive. R.W-S.

Bow: steel etched and gilt 750 lgth
Stock: pear wood inlaid. 463 span
Reg. no.: 39-65tz Glasgow Museums and Art Galleries
William Reid, 'A Royal Crossbow in the Scott Collection', *The Scottish Art Review* 7 (1959), pp.10-13, 29-30

XI.39 Henry VIII's Handgun

This gun is remarkable both for its mechanical sophistication and its decoration. It is breech loaded with a re-usable steel cartridge (the 'chamber') through a hinged breech-block which anticipates the nineteenth-century Snider action. On and around the breech are engraved St George, the Tudor rose and the monogram 'HR'. The barrel is fluted like a columm, with a capital-like muzzle. The breech-block is incised with the date 1537 and stamped with a maker's mark which may be that of William Hunt, who in 1538 was appointed keeper of the King's handguns. The gun originally had a cheek pad, which means that it may be the piece listed in his Inventory as 'one chamber piece in a stock of wood lined in the cheek with velvet'. D.S.

Steel and wood 975 lgth
XII.1 Royal Armouries
J. W. Reid, *The Lore of Arms* (1976), pp. 114-15

Henry VIII's Inventory

On 28 January 1547 Henry VIII died in his great new palace of Whitehall. The following
September orders were given for an Inventory of his possessions, the equivalent to a probate
inventory for a lesser mortal, to be drawn up. The resulting lists take up two huge volumes:
the 'first part of the inventory of the jewels, plate, stuff, ordnance, munitions and other goods
belonging to our late sovereign lord King Henry the Eight' is now Society of Antiquaries
MS 129; the 'second part' (itself so unwieldy that it has been subdivided into two separate
volumes) is in the British Library as Harley MS 1419 A and B. Between them, the two parts offer
a complete record of forty years of unprecedented acquisitiveness. They also provide the basis
for studying a King who not only accumulated but innovated. We have drawn heavily on them
in our specialized studies of Henry's musical tastes, of his armour, weapons, tapestries,
plate and books. Indeed it is hardly too much to say that Henry VIII's Inventory is the key
document of his reign, and the basis for the King's most compelling claims to greatness.
That is how we have used the Inventory so far; now we employ it more sentimentally, to give a
snapshot of his privy lodgings at Greenwich at the moment of his death. Here were possessions
of no great value, but only the detritus of everyday life, left after one visit and to be picked up
at the next.

Henry visited Greenwich on 22 December 1546, probably as a brief stop-over on a river trip
from Whitehall. He returned to Whitehall and never left it. There was no next visit to Greenwich.

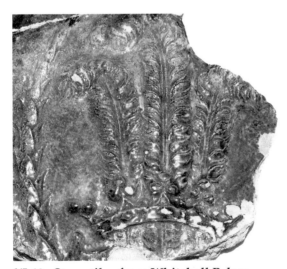

XI.40　Stove tiles from Whitehall Palace

In central and north-western Europe the use of
ceramic wood-burning stoves for interior heating
was widespread from the thirteenth century. By the
fourteenth century these stoves had developed into
structures made up of individual decorated tiles,
a tradition which continued well into the nineteenth
century. Stove tiles of this type first appear in
England in the fifteenth century, and from the early
sixteenth century there are several significant groups
which have been excavated, especially in the city of
London. The Whitehall stove tile group is the largest
found to date and has yet to be published in the
forthcoming east side Whitehall excavation report.

The tiles have a rectangular face and a convex back,
semi-circular in plan, which forms a partly enclosed
chamber for channelling the hot fumes. Each tile is
edged with flanges, which can either be covered
with fillets, grout or 'L'-shaped side members.
The decoration of the tiles indicates that they were
specially commissioned for the King. They have the
royal arms and the monogram 'H R' on each panel.
The corner members, decorated with running
grotesques, also have tablets embossed with the
same monogram.

Unfortunately the contextual information from
the 1930s excavations at Whitehall is very poor.
But enough exists to state that the tiles were found in
the area of the King's privy gallery, and in the direct
vicinity of the 'bain' or bathing room. This suggests
that the stove may have heated the King's ground-
floor bathroom. The use of stoves in royal palaces of
the period is not uncommon. Several travellers
mention the stove in Queen Elizabeth's bathroom at
Hampton Court, and stove tiles were recovered
during the Greenwich Palace excavations. S.T.

English Heritage/Historic Royal Palaces Agency
D. Gaimster, 'A survey of Cologne-type stove-tiles found in
Britain', in Ingebord Unger with a contribution from David
Gaimster, *Kölner Ofenkacheln, Die Bestande des Museums für
Angewandte Kunst und des Kölnischen Stadtmuseums* (Kölnisches
Stadtmuseum, 1988)

XI.41   The Beddington Lock

This lock was formerly at Beddington Place, Surrey. This became a royal manor in 1539 when its former owner, Sir Nicholas Carew (V.6), was attainted and executed for treason. The lock has two independent keyholes for two different keys. These operate two separate bolts which can be united by inserting a pin allowing both to be operated by a single key. The lower keyhole is covered with a cast-iron slide of the royal arms. The lock was almost certainly made by Henry Romains, the royal locksmith. Locks of this form were transported from one building to another and the locks on the private apartments were part of a suit with Henry himself holding the master-key. P.G.

Wrought-iron 225 x 344
M397-1921. Victoria and Albert Museum
Claude Blair, 'The Most Superb of All Royal Locks', *Apollo* (December 1966), pp. 493-4

XI.42   German Diptych Sundial

Diptych dials are so called because they consisted of two leaves; here the upper leaf is missing. On the lower leaf are engraved hour-lines for a horizontal dial for use with a string gnomon, and a geometrical pattern. Of the compass, only the bowl remains.

This instrument was found in the Thames. It appears to be one of the earliest known examples, and is also relatively crude when compared with the fine Nuremberg instruments of the mid-1500s and early 1600s (XI.43). Similar dials are frequently mentioned in Henry VIII's Inventory. W.H.

Prob. Nuremberg, c.1500
Ivory, 67 x 46 x 8; compass bowl 20 dia.
210, Museum of the History of Science, Oxford
P. Gouk, *The Ivory Sundials of Nuremberg* (Cambridge: Whipple Museum of the History of Science, 1988), p. 135, item 59, fig. 131

XI.43   Diptych Sundial

This elegant instrument is designed to tell the time by night as well as by day: the lid has a nocturnal dial (for telling the time by the Pole Star at night) of gilt brass with punched numerals, calibrated by named months, and a universal equinoctial dial. When opened, the instrument reveals three dials and a magnetic compass of which only the bowl remains. W.H.

Prob. German, dated 1539, corrected from 1529
Ivory, gilt brass and brass, 112 x 93 x 14; compass bowl 30 dia.
G 182, Museum of the History of Science, Oxford
A.J. Turner, 'Sun-dials: History and Classification', *History of Science*, vol. 27 (1989), pp.303-318

XI.44   Fireshovel and Andirons

This fireshovel was excavated from a house in Pottergate, Norwich. It must date from before 1507, as the house was destroyed in a fire that year. Hearth equipment, of a similar though vastly more elaborate type, was in use in Henry's palaces. The andirons now at Knole, and bearing the badges and ciphers of Henry and Anne Boleyn, have been identfed as the work of the royal smith, Henry Romains (XI.41). D.S.

Iron 352 lgth
SF149N/1364. Norwich Castle Museum
Excavation report in *East Anglian Archaeology* 26

XI.45 Willoughby de Broke Coffer

This coffer, covered in black cut-velvet, is probably seventeenth- or even eighteenth- century. But the drop front, and the tills or drawers lined with yellow fabric have changed little since Tudor times. In particular, the book-binder's leather which faces the front of the drawers is strikingly similar to that which is used in the Edward VI State Paper Chest in the Victoria and Albert Museum. Because the Tudor Court was so mobile, everything had to be portable, and, for preference, to have its own case. D.S.

Wood, covered and lined 686 x 457 x 356: Warwickshire Museum
Sheelah Ruggles-Brise, 'Some Royal Coffers', *Connoisseur* 129 (August 1952), pp.19-24

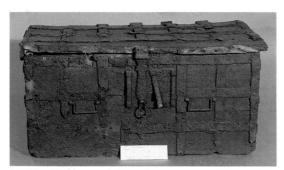

XI.46 Coffer and Chest

Two chests: a 'forcer' or strong-box and a 'standard' or travelling chest completely covered in boiled leather and bound with iron straps. The 'standard' has two handles and two locks. The top is a solid piece of oak, shaped into a slight curve; the inside is lined with cloth. This has been taken to mean that the chest was intended to hold clothes and linen. But in July 1533 'three great trussing coffers' were covered in leather and lined in 'Bristol red' cloth for 'the King's plate in the privy chamber' at Greenwich. In view of its strength and defensive capacity such would seem a more likely use for this chest as well. D.S.

1. 'Forcer' or Strong-Box
Wood covered with shaved hide 152 x 114 x 76
10.47. Museum of Leathercraft, Northampton
2. Chest
Wood, covered in cuir bouilli and iron bound
457 x 1219 x 508

E 27/case 5. Public Record Office
Celia Jenning, *Early Chests in Wood and Iron* (HMSO, 1974), no. VII
J. W. Kirby, 'Building Works at Placentia, 1532-3',
Transactions of the Greenwich and Lewisham Antiquarian Society 5 (1957) 22-50, p. 47

XI.47 Dog Collar

There were several collars in the Inventory, including '65 lyams [leashes for hounds] and collars' in the closet next to the privy chamber at Greenwich (Harley MS 1419 A, fo. 55v). A Henry VIII 'dogs-collar' appears in the original Tradescant Museum catalogue, but does not appear to survive in the Ashmolean (XI.35). D. S.

German, 15th or 16th cent.
Iron with original leather lining 530 lgth
No. 5. Leeds Castle Foundation
C. R. Beard,'Dog-Collars', *Connoisseur* (March 1940), 102-6, no. II

XI.48 Inkwell

Inkwells must have been a mainstay of the Horners' craft, since they feature on the Company's arms. Cattle horns become soft when heated and can be moulded into different shapes. Such work was smelly and not greatly profitable.

Ink for writing on parchment or paper was originally made from soot, water and gum. This mixture thickened easily and clogged the quill pen (usually goose). Improved writing inks, consisting of tannic or gallic acid obtained from tree bark and iron salt, were introduced by the seventeenth century.

Henry's Inventory shows ample provision for writing, despite the King's ambivalent attitude to that activity. There were several well-furnished writing desks, but the only one to survive is the magnificently decorated specimen in the Victoria and Albert Museum. R.W.

Horn, 16th cent., 50 ht

4895. Museum of London

XI.49 Tennis Ball

This ball was found lobbed up into the hammer beam roof of Westminster Hall during repairs there in the 1920s. Real (or royal) tennis was originally played with the hand, but racquets were introduced around 1500. In the closet next to the privy chamber the Inventory notes '7 racquets for the tennis' (Harley MS 1419 A, fo. 54v). R.W.

16th cent. type

Dog leather, with a core of packed hair, 50 dia.

A23502. Museum of London

XI.50 Hawk's Bell

Hawk's bells were attached to the bird's legs by leather thongs called bewits. The hawk (usually a falcon for a King) remained hooded, to keep it restrained, on the handler's wrist until the hunted bird flew. When it caught the prey the hawk could be traced by the sound of its bells. A box in the closet next to the privy chamber contained a complete set of hawking equipment: '30 hawk's hoods of divers sorts, 12 pair of hawk's bells small and great, and a falconer's glove' (Harley MS 1419 A, fo. 54v). R.W.

Copper alloy, 15th-16th cent., 16 dia.

80. 447/9. Museum of London

XI.51 Jettons or Counters

Jettons from Tournai and Nuremberg are the commonest sixteenth-century examples found in England. Horizontal lines were marked on a board, table or cloth, and the jettons acquired a numerical value according to their place on the counter. In the Inventory, 'counters of tin' appear as part of the usual equipment of writing desks. R.W.

Copper alloy, 16th cent., 25 dia.

80. 279/2, 406/31,33,35. Museum of London

XI.52 Scissors

Recorded in archaeological excavations in the City of London from mid-fourteenth-century contexts, scissors were associated with trade, and shears with domestic use. By the early sixteenth century scissors were in more general usage. Holbein includes scissors in his portraits of the astronomer Nicolaus Kratzer, 1528, and George Gize, merchant, 1532, while in the Inventory they are another regular part of writing desk equipment, for example: 'a desk covered with printer's leather furnished with boxes with counters of tin and having a pair of scissors, a pair of compasses, a pen knife and a pointel [a stylus or pencil] cased in metal' (Harley MS 1419 A, fo. 54v). R.W.

Iron, 16th cent., 135 lgth

10911. Museum of London

XI.53 Pouch with Head-Comb

Combs were made of wood, ivory, bone and horn, and often finely carved. Several comb-cases are mentioned in the Inventory, both with and without their contents. R.W.

Bone, 16th cent. 95 ht

A3826. Museum of London

XI.54 Purses

Purses, for holding money and other small objects, were worn attached to the belt, by both men and women. A purse with a decorative flap of very similar design to (1.) was found on the *Mary Rose*, which sank in 1545.

Purses or pouches were also used for holding documents and there were larger, all- purpose leather bags known as stock bags. In the closet next to the privy chamber, for instance, the Inventory lists 'a stock bag with divers leather purses having in them pieces in ure [current coin] of gold and silver' (Harley MS 1419 A, fo. 55). R.W.

1. Leather, 16th cent. ht: 133 and 150

A3686, A2261. Museum of London

2. Goatskin

Front of purse

484.56, 945.61 Museum of Leathercraft, Northampton

3. Document pouch

E 101/499/21. Public Record Office

XI.55 Lace and Tassel

The tassel is made of large and small silk buttons and cords.

Laces worn with mantles had a tassel at each end (see for example the effigies of Henry VII and Elizabeth of York, Westminster Abbey, 1512-17: II.11-12). This lace, by contrast, was perhaps tied to a

personal weapon, such as a sword or dagger (see portrait of Edward, Prince of Wales, attributed to William Scrots, c.1546).

There were a few tassels and laces in the Inventory, including 'a lace for the mantle of the Garter of silk and gold' (this would have been the kind of tassel Holbein designed IX.17) and, more humbly, 'a tassel of hair to make clean combs' (Harley MS 1419 A, fos. 58v, 60). Tassels were also hung on tennis nets, to see whether the ball went under or over. R.W.

Silk with metal purl, 16th cent. 860 lgth

A14655. Museum of London

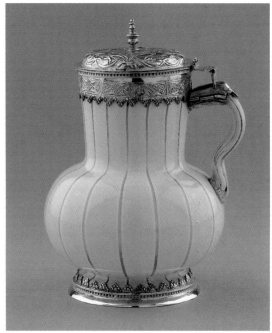

XI.56 Two Silver-Mounted 'Venetian' Glass Jugs

The simpler of the two jugs is made of *vetro a fili*, opaque-white canes embedded in a 'gather' of clear *cristallo* glass; the more complex jug, of *vetro a retorti*, blue and white glass with twisted white glass canes. These two examples can be precisely dated by their silver mounts to the London hallmarking year, 1548-9. The form of the jugs is English, not Venetian, so it seems likely that they were made by the Muranese glass-blowers, who were recorded as being in England in September 1549. The jugs are the only glass surviving from mid-sixteenth-century England (the glass of the Parr Pot being a later copy). Henry VIII's Inventory lists thirty-eight items of glass in the lower study at Greenwich (BL, Harley MS 1419A, fo. 62). H.T.

Glass with silver mounts: 150 ht; 150 ht

AF 3133, 1987-72-2 British Museum

H. Tait, *The Golden Age of Venetian Glass* (1979), p. 65, no. 81, col. pl. 11

XII Henry VIII and the Navy

WHEN HENRY VIII signed the treaty of Greenwich with Scotland in 1543, the Scots ambassadors presented him with Elder's map of the two kingdoms. Three years earlier, James V had circumnavigated Scotland in the *Great Michael*. These events seem to have transformed Henry VIII's strategic understanding of Scotland. When the Scots, having repudiated the treaty of Greenwich, returned to the Auld Alliance with France in late 1543, Henry did not send an army against them but a navy. That he was able to do so was a tribute to one of his most important achievements: the creation of a navy and a naval organization.

Henry VIII: the Real Founder of the Navy?

BY DAVID LOADES

Henry VIII may not have founded the king's navy, but he certainly transformed it. Although he inherited from his father two formidable carracks, the *Regent* and the *Sovereign*, he had in 1509 only a handful of other ships. During the thirty-eight years of his reign he built forty-six ships and thirteen small galleys called row-barges; he purchased twenty-six ships and took thirteen others as prizes.[1] At his death in 1547 he owned about seventy vessels of all sizes, over fifty of which were serviceable, and deployed them at all seasons from Berwick to the Isle of Man. His father had built a small dockyard at Portsmouth, and hired a storehouse at Greenwich. Henry built new dockyards at Deptford and Woolwich, expanded that at Portsmouth, and added workshops, storehouses and fortified anchorages. In 1509 the King's ships were managed by a single clerk, as they had been intermittently for centuries. By 1547 there was a council 'for marine causes', presided over by the vice-admiral, and consisting of a treasurer, surveyor and rigger, clerk controller, master of the Naval Ordnance, and clerk.[2] In place of one middle-ranking officer, who doubled as a junior member of the royal household, there was a staff of highly paid professionals, controlling considerable plant and the beginnings of a permanent workforce. In 1509 the navy was what it had always been (when it existed at all) - a small core of royal ships, to which were added in time of war hired merchantmen, both English and foreign, in which soldiers and small guns were placed for the purpose of grappling and boarding enemy ships. By 1547 the navy was a standing force, with a regular schedule of repair and maintenance, and normal operational functions in peacetime. Extra ships were still hired for war, but now constituted no more than half the total, and were used mainly as auxiliaries because they were not designed to carry the heavy, port-firing guns which had become the standard equipment of royal warships.

This dramatic transformation was largely the work of the King himself. He was deeply interested in both ships and guns, building rapidly and expensively upon the foundations which his father had laid down. Henry VII had employed French gun-founders, and had caused forges to be established in Ashdown Forest early in his reign,[3] but his interest had waned with the increasing peace and security of his later years. Henry VIII set up his own foundry at Houndsditch in 1511, and was soon experimenting energetically with new types and calibres of gun, both bronze and iron. For serious business he at first ordered in large quantities from abroad, particularly Mechlin, but by the end of his reign England could produce most of the guns that it needed,[4] and later in the century was to be an exporter of high quality products which were much sought after. Observers frequently commented upon the King's keen interest in the range and accuracy of new weapons,

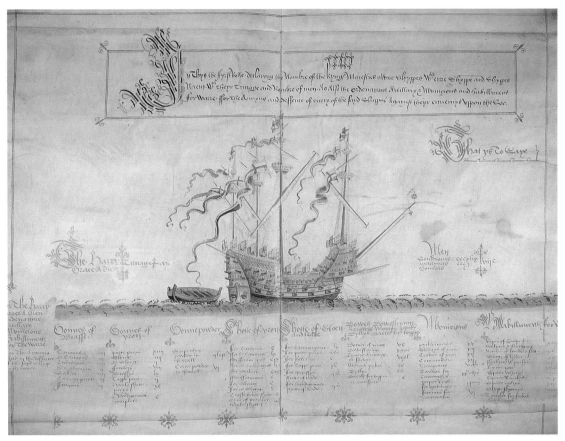

Figure 12: *Great Harry* in 1546, from Anthony Anthony's rolls.

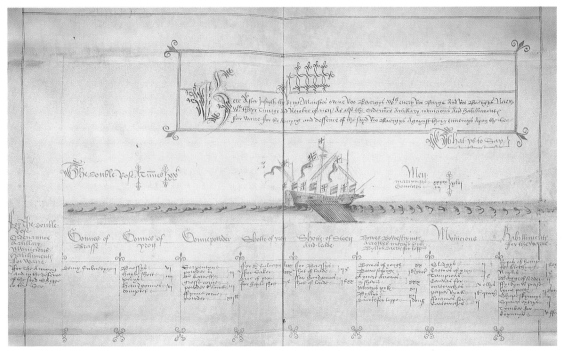

Figure 13: *Rose Slype* in 1546, from Anthony Anthony's rolls.

The *Great Harry* (1,000 tons) and the tiny row-barge *Rose Slype* (20 tons) were the biggest and smallest ships in Henry VIII's navy as recorded in Anthony Anthony's three rolls. Anthony's rolls reveal the extent to which Henry's navy of forty-six ships had been re-equipped by 1546 with new muzzle-loading bronze guns, rather than traditional breech-loading iron guns. R.C.D.B. (Pepys MS 2991, fols. 2-3, 98-9, Magdalene College, Cambridge)

rightly seeing this as a part of his general enthusiasm for the arts of war. It is not known who invented the gun-port. Before 1509 there is some evidence that the Portuguese carracks operating in the Indian Ocean carried a small number of heavy guns mounted in the waist. Venetian and Genoese war-galleys also mounted a single heavy gun in the prow, in place of the previous ram; but without the gun-port, side-firing guns could only be mounted at or above deck level, which greatly restricted the number and weight of the armament which could be carried.[5] The invention of the port itself is by tradition ascribed to a Breton shipwright named Descharges, in about 1500; but the first ships known to have mounted side-firing guns below the main deck level were the *Mary Rose* and the *Peter Pomegranate*, laid down in 1509 and launched in 1510.[6] Whether it was one of Henry's shipwrights, or the King himself, who had the bright idea of adapting ports for this purpose is not known, but it was certainly an English innovation. Thereafter all new royal ships of any size incorporated this feature, and older ships such as the *Regent* and the *Sovereign* were modified. It would appear, however, that there were distinct limits to the King's tactical intelligence and originality because, having made this breakthrough in warship design, it was to be another thirty years before the synchronized broadside began to be used. Apart from the effect upon enemy morale, the most immediate consequence of the adoption of the gun-port was the abandonment of the traditional clinker method of shipbuilding (which depended upon the strength of the ship's skin) in favour of the carvel method (which depended upon the strength of the frame).

Henry wanted not only effective warships, but Great Ships, worthy of his honour and his pretensions to international status. It greatly irked him at the time of his accession that his relatively poverty-stricken brother-in-law, James IV of Scotland, actually had a larger ship than he did - the French-built *Great Michael*. His reply was the *Henry Grâce à Dieu*, laid down on 4 December 1512, and 'hallowed' at Erith on the Thames on 13 June 1514.[7] This gigantic vessel probably displaced 1,000 tons (although some estimates made her half as big again), and the cost of her building, with the three small barques designed to attend upon her, was £8,708 5s 3d. Whether her firepower was commensurate with her bulk may be doubted, but she was praised for her sailing qualities, and continued in service (being twice rebuilt) until destroyed by accidental fire in 1553.
The *Great Harry*, as she was usually known, was remarkable mainly for her size and the splendour of her ornamentation, but another vessel was launched about a year later which was altogether more interesting from a technical point of view, and equally the result of Henry's direct involvement. This was the galleasse correctly called the *Princess Mary*, but nearly always referred to simply as the *Great Galley*.[8] She seems to have displaced between 600 and 800 tons, to have

XII.1 Insignia of the High Almoner, c.1513

This toy-like ship found at Billingsgate in 1981 was made in the image of the three-masted ship which Wolsey built in 1512 and subsequently gave to

Henry VIII's war effort. At the same time Wolsey had the ship reproduced on the official seal of the Royal Almonry. Thereafter it was used on all documents connected with the Royal Maundy. Wolsey's tenure as the King's Almoner or High Almoner lasted from 1509 to 1514, but this ship remains the emblem of the Royal Almonry. The little 'E' visible on the ship stands for 'Elymonysarii' or Almonry. R.C.D.B.

Black metal, 35 x 56
A.G.Pilson Collection
D.J.P. Baldwin, *Chapel Royal, Ancient and Modern* (1990), pp. 42, 161, 376-8

XII.2 Model of Mary Rose (1512-45)

This model by Bassett-Lowke illustrates the latest knowledge about the form of the *Mary Rose* at the time of her loss on 19 July 1545. Since her rediscovery in 1967, much information has been derived from systematic archaeological studies. Comparison with the drawing contained in the Anthony Anthony Roll reveals much about the faults of that depiction, but excavation confirmed the extent to which Henry's navy had been re-equipped with muzzle-loading bronze guns instead of breech-loading iron guns. The rig is conjectural, based on various documentary sources. R.C.D.B.

6150 x 5950

Scale 1:48.

National Maritime Museum

M.Rule, *Mary Rose: the excavation and raising of Henry VIII's flagship*, (1983)

carried four masts, and to have been propelled either by sail or by 120 oars. An impressed Italian observer described her as being three times the size of a first-class Venetian galley. Another contemporary account, written for the benefit of Louise of Savoy, the Queen Mother of France, declared that she carried 207 pieces of artillery, of which 70 were brass, and 800-1,000 fighting men.[9] The latter figure may well be doubted, as it was substantially more than the equivalent number for the *Great Harry*, but the precision of the gun count carries conviction. There is no means of knowing the size of the individual guns, but as she was a flush decked ship, built without castles, they must have been mounted on a single gundeck, above the rowers. On the whole galleys and galleasses did not do well in northern waters, but the *Great Galley* remained in service for many years, until she was eventually rebuilt as a sailing ship sometime before 1540. The Venetian Sebastian Giustinian, who was in London at the time of the launching, reported that the weight of the *Galley*'s guns 'would be too much for the strongest castle',[10] but there was never any suggestion that she was cumbersome or unserviceable for that reason.

The naming ceremony was carried out by the Queen on 29 October 1515, one of the earliest occasions on which a royal lady can be associated with such an event. The entire Court was in attendance, and Henry put on a characteristic performance. Dressed in a sailor's coat and trousers of cloth of gold, he acted as pilot, hugely enjoying himself, and blowing upon a gold captain's whistle 'nearly as loud as a trumpet'. After the ceremony the bishop of Durham celebrated mass on board, and the whole company dined.[11] The King did not make a habit of attending launching ceremonies thereafter, but his interest in ships did not wane. In 1518 he specially commissioned a small barque for his own use. She was called the *Katherine Pleasaunce*, and her cabins were panelled and furnished for the King and Queen's use. This prototype royal yacht was used to convey the royal couple to France in 1520 for Henry's meeting with Francis I at the Field of Cloth of Gold. Later in his reign, in 1541, it was reported that he was sending to Italy for three shipwrights skilled in the building of galleys, but the writer did not believe that he would use them, because he was already building small galleys to his own design.[12] These were the thirteen row-barges already mentioned, propelled by 20 oars and displacing 20-30 tons. Each carried a small number of guns, and they

XII.3 Engraving of the Embarkation of Henry VIII from Dover, 1520 (Detail)

This engraving represents Henry VIII's embarkation from Dover on 30 May 1520, when *Great Bark*, *Less Bark*, *Katherine Pleasaunce*, *Mary* and *John* and two row-barges were used. The largest of those ships was the *Great Bark* at 500 tons, but Henry actually sailed on the specially built *Katherine Pleasaunce*.

Henry's largest ships were not used on that occasion because Dover harbour was too silted up to permit their entry. This suggests the features of the latest and largest ships in Henry's navy and a new fort were chosen by Volpe (XI.8) in order to appeal to Henry's sense of occasion, and pride. R.C.D.B.

Engraving; 830 x 1380

National Maritime Museum

C.S. Laird Clowes, *Sailing Ships, Their History and Development, Part II* (1948), p. 18

M. Oppenheim, *History of the Royal Navy* (1896), pp. 43-58

seem to have been designed for scouting, and to protect the sailing ships from attack by hostile galleys when the former were becalmed. They saw good service against the French in the 1540s, and the best testimony to their effectiveness is that the French copied them. One true galley was built in England at this time, the *Galley Subtle* launched in 1544. This may well have been designed by one of Henry's Italian recruits, because English shipwrights had no skill in such matters. The *Galley Subtle* even had to be commanded in action by a Spanish captain who communicated with his crew through an interpreter, because no suitable English officer could be found.[13] The King went to Portsmouth on several occasions, and actually witnessed the tragic loss of the *Mary Rose* on 19 July 1545. Deptford, Woolwich and other anchorages nearer to London saw him more often, and on one occasion he dined on board the *Great Harry* while she lay at Rye for some routine maintenance work.

Henry had no direct experience of sea fighting, and the longest voyage he ever made was across the Channel to Calais, but in this as in other respects, he knew how to pick effective men to serve him. The earl of Oxford, the lord admiral whom he inherited from his father, was an aristocratic sinecurist of the old school, but when Oxford died in 1512 he was replaced by Sir Edward Howard. Howard was equally an aristocrat, being a son of the earl of Surrey, but he was also one of the King's 'minions' and a warlike man of action. Howard had already distinguished himself in the previous year by defeating the notorious Scottish adventurer Sir Andrew Barton, and capturing his ships. After less than a year in office he was killed in a rash attack on the French galleys near Brest, and was succeeded by his brother, Sir Thomas.[14] Thomas, soon to be earl of Surrey, and after 1525 duke of Norfolk, remained in effective charge of the navy until 1536. In 1525 he was succeeded as titular admiral by the King's young son, Henry Fitzroy, duke of Richmond, but by continuing as vice-admiral Norfolk ensured that an experienced commander was involved in naval policy during an unusually long interval of peace. When Richmond died in July 1536 another experienced man was appointed, William Fitzwilliam, earl of Southampton. Fitzwilliam's seafaring had been limited, but he had several ships of his own, and was familiar with the problems of managing them. After the brief tenures of John, Lord Russell and Edward Seymour, earl of Hertford (1540-42), in January 1543 John Dudley, Viscount Lisle became Henry's last, and in many ways most effective, lord admiral. Dudley was a soldier rather than a seaman, but he had some experience of sea-command, and was supported as vice-admiral by Sir Francis Bryan, who had more.[15] Dudley took his naval duties very seriously. It was during his tenure of office that the Council for Marine Causes was established, which gave England a decisive edge over both France and Spain in terms of naval organization, and the orders which he issued to the fleet in August 1545 show him to have been familiar with the latest Spanish tactics. For the first time an English war fleet was organized in squadrons, and expected to maintain some sort of formation in battle, instead of simply sailing into a mêlée of ship against ship.[16] In the event lack of wind handed the initiative to the French galleys, and when the conditions changed the dramatic sinking of the *Mary Rose* distracted attention from the remainder of the action, but Dudley can probably claim the credit for advancing the tactical use of gunfire well beyond the haphazard state still envisaged in the previous set of battle orders, which had been issued in 1530.

The lord admirals contined to be aristocratic councillors first, soldiers second, and seamen third (if at all), but the officers who served under them, men like William Woodhouse, William Gonson and Robert Legge, were men thoroughly versed in the affairs of the sea, and the King had more access to good advice in this aspect of his government than he had in many others. Moreover, the evidence suggests that Henry, prompted by his own personal interest, listened to that advice. Nevertheless his aims were limited, and his priorities gave little scope for the wider perspectives of maritime enterprise. The King did not look much beyond fighting the French in the Channel or the North Sea, and 'wafting' his merchants to Denmark or the Netherlands. Henry VII had briefly but effectively encouraged the Bristol merchants to venture across the Atlantic, and the aspirations stimulated by that experience lingered on in verses by John Rastell, the author of *A New Interlude of the Four Elements* (above, p. 146).[17] But the King was not to be drawn. English merchants traded to the Indies from Seville, and in 1527 (according to one Spanish source)

XII.4 The Encampment of the English Forces near Portsmouth, 19 July 1545

Basire's engraving shows where the French fleet of 225 ships carrying 30,000 troops under Claude d'Annebault's command waited off St Helens to land and re-embark troops on the Isle of Wight.

Four French galleys are shown engaging the English 'Van' and the *Great Harry* early on 19 July 1545. Within an hour these light airs changed so that wind and tide moving in opposition made life difficult for the French.

Thereafter Henry VIII, who had had the mortification of watching the *Mary Rose* sink almost in front of him off Southsea Castle, would see his pinnaces and row-barges drive off the threat from the French galleys and save the English fleet from being drawn into a close fight. R.C.D.B.

620 x 1895

National Maritime Museum

A. McKee, *King Henry VII's Mary Rose* (1973), pp. 8-12, 47-70

M.Rule, *Mary Rose* (1983), pp. 30-38

Henry sent a ship of his own there, but if so the initiative was not followed up.[18] He probably was behind the voyage of John Rut to Newfoundland in the same year, but the ambitious promptings of Robert Thorne and Roger Barlow went substantially unheeded. English merchants continued to go to Spain, in spite of increasing political difficulties, and English factors can be found as far east as Chios, but this was all the fruit of private initiative in which the King had no part. Like most English kings, Henry was keenly aware of the need to encourage the merchant marine, if only to guarantee himself a supply of military auxiliaries, and he maintained his father's navigation acts, but took no other significant steps in that direction. It was later claimed that the fishing fleet to Iceland (a training ground for mariners) had declined from 149 sail in 1528 to 43 in 1547.[19]

Henry was probably more interested in the enterprise of Robert Reneger of Southampton than he was in humdrum feats of legitimate commerce. In March 1545 Reneger seized (without any substantial pretext) the *San Salvador*, inward bound from the Indies, and relieved her of a cargo worth over seven million marevedis. There was a major diplomatic storm, but Reneger was not punished, and the money was not returned. Not surprisingly, Anglo-Spanish trade became even more difficult.[20] However, if the King's idea of supporting his merchants was sometimes eccentric, in other ways he was orthodox enough. More mundane piracy was suppressed with vigour, and the difficulties of securing conviction through the Admiralty courts were circumvented by a statute of 1538. Maritime law was based on Roman law, which required either confession or eyewitness proof, so piracy was brought under the jurisdiction of the common law, which required only the verdict of a jury. The lord admiral's involvement was preserved by making him an *ex officio* member of each commission of oyer and terminer established to hear such cases.[21] As the reign advanced patrols against pirates became increasingly frequent, although it was not always the King's ships which were used. The great annual cloth fleet to Antwerp was always provided with an armed escort (at the merchants' expense), and there are even references to fisheries protection. In spite of his lack of general interest in maritime enterprise, Henry's military priorities produced other incidental benefits for the seafaring community. In 1543 seamen were exempted from service in the army, and in 1545 the standard wage was raised from 5s to 6s 8d a month, in order to stimulate recruitment. In 1513 the Guild of the Most Glorious Trinity of Deptford (later known as Trinity House) was established 'for the reformation of the navy lately much decayed by the admission of young men without experience'. The Guild provided a system of instruction and licensing for pilots. Later, by a statute of 1566 it was also given responsibility for 'sea marks', such as buoys and lights.[22] A similar guild was established at Newcastle-on-Tyne in 1536. Concern about the provision of safe and convenient anchorages for his warships prompted the King to commission a survey of Dover harbour in 1532, and to spend large sums of money on harbour works there.[23] In the same year an Act of Parliament endeavoured to protect Plymouth, Dartmouth, Teignmouth, Falmouth and Fowey from the effects of gravel silting. Very few merchant ships displaced more than two hundred tons, and it was the King's Great Ships which presented the main problems of docking and inshore navigation. It was this consideration, rather than any more general intellectual curiosity, which led to the appointment of the Frenchman Jean Rotz as the first Hydrographer Royal in 1542, and to the careful surveys which were made of the Thames estuary.

Henry's interest and commitment, together with the knowledge which that commitment produced, put naval policy, armament and organization upon a new footing, but the limitations of his political vision prevented the development of any new strategy of sea power. The King had learned the lessons taught by Fortescue, and by the Libel of English Policy, but a 'blue water' strategy had to await the generation of Hawkins and Drake.

The Strategic Context

Henry VIII grasped the potential of his navy to suppress piracy, to attack French ports and shipping, and to support a land campaign in France. A narrow seas deployment could help counter the naval threat of the Auld Alliance of France and Scotland, and threaten the sea-lanes linking Charles V's realms of Spain, the Netherlands and the Empire.

XII.5 World Chart by Girolamo Verrazano, 1529 (revised to 1540)

In 1527 Girolamo Verrazano gave Henry VIII a chart like this one which was to hang in the long gallery at Whitehall Palace until 1698.

It revealed that the three Verrazano brothers operating out of Dieppe under the patronage of Francis I had surveyed a significant part of North America during 1523. Henry's interest in Dieppois charts grew after 1533 when Francis I secured a change in papal interpretation of the treaty of Tordesillas - to the effect that Spain and Portugal had no inherent rights over lands not discovered before Christmas 1492. Henry knew that Pope Clement VII had so ruled in the light of another of Girolamo Verrazano's charts presented to the Vatican in 1529.

Henry first committed warships to American exploration in 1527 assigning John Rut the *Samson* and his new warship *Mary Guildford* to sail to Newfoundland. In 1536 Hore used the *Trinity* and *Mynion* to sail to Cape Breton Island at the mouth of the St Lawrence River. R.C.D.B.

Ink and watercolour on vellum, 720 x 1080

G201:1/15MS, National Maritime Museum

D.B. Quinn, R.A. Skelton, W. Cumming, *The Discovery of North America* (1971), pp. 70-84.

M. Destombes, 'Nautical Charts Attributed to Verrazano (1525-1528)', *Imago Mundi*, X1 (1954), pp. 57-66

XII.6 Astronomicum Caesareum, 1540

One of just seventeen hand printed and finished copies of Apianus's book was presented to Henry VIII in 1540, because of his known interest in mathematics and astronomy. Its mysterious title page and contents reveal contemporary excitement about astronomy in European universities and among navigators exploring the Southern Hemisphere.

Peter Apianus, appointed Professor of Mathematics at Ingolstadt in 1527, was the first to publish an outline treatise on determining longitude by lunar distances, and the first to publish sine tables. However such books were expensive and difficult to use except for the scholar and astronomer. Simplification was required before such useful knowledge could be exploited by English navigators at sea. R.C.D.B.

Printed book; 460 x 665

C1352, National Maritime Museum

O. Gingerich, 'Apianus's Astronomicum Caesareum', *Journal of History of Astronomy*, 2 (1971), pp.168-77

Equipping the Ships

The provision of guns and powder to Henry's navy was the duty of the Ordnance Office at the Tower of London. While Henry's location of new dockyard facilities at Deptford, Woolwich and Erith made their job easier, the cost and difficulty of victualling led in 1546 to reformed control through the Navy Board. The administrative skills and shrewdness of the then lord admiral, John Dudley, Viscount Lisle, also played an important part in the change.

XII.7   Falconette, early 16th century

Two such wrought-iron guns were trawled up in Pevensey Bay and presented to Hastings Museum in June 1907. They represent an early sixteenth-century type of iron gun probably made in the Weald of Sussex. Such anti-personnel guns, known generically as 'serpentines', were made in great numbers by Wealden ironmasters for Henry VIII's navy. Originally they were secured on to a swivel mount or a two-wheeled elm carriage. Into the breach at one end of the gun were fitted, alternately, two containers with charges of 'serpentine powder', and a flint or stone shot. Similar guns were used in the war of 1512-13, but this gun was probably lost in the course of the inconclusive battle off Newhaven and Beachy Head on 15 August 1545. R.C.D.B.

Wrought iron; 1960 x 150

Hastings Museum

Sussex Daily News, 7 June 1907

XII.8   Henry VIII's Tidal Almanack for 1546

On folio 7 of this volume Samuel Pepys wrote 'that this appear'd to SP to have been K Hen 8th's own Book'. It must have been compiled during 1545 for the following year's tides, but also contains a fine manuscript chart of Europe from the Baltic to Gibraltar. It was a remarkable achievement because its woodcut maps made possible a means of finding the time of high water anywhere in northern Europe, for even the simplest minded seaman. It also contained a perpetual lunar calendar and other useful navigational information. The events that determined the outcome of the battles off Portsmouth and then Newhaven in 1545 showed the importance of such almanacks. R.C.D.B.

Printed book and manuscript chart; 87 x 108

MS. NVT40, National Maritime Museum

D. Howse, *Sir Francis Drake's Nautical Almanack* (1980)

E.G.R. Taylor, *Haven Finding Art* (1971), pp. 170-71

The Commanders

The office of lord admiral was, like the other great offices of state, held largely for prestige and profit. This allowed for a very active admiral, like Sir Edward Howard (1513); a complete sinecurist, like Henry VIII's bastard son, the duke of Richmond (1525-36), and men more experienced as soldiers than sailors like the earls of Surrey and Southampton (XII.9). This left effective executive command in the hands of vice admirals, like Sir George Carew (XII.10).

XII.9 Portrait of William Fitzwilliam, Earl of Southampton (d.1542), by Holbein

XII.10 Portrait of Sir George Carew (d.1545), by Holbein

A friend of Henry VIII from childhood, William Fitzwilliam served in both the royal household and at sea. He was wounded in combat at Brest in 1513. Ambassador to France in 1521, he became treasurer of the Household in 1525, lord admiral in 1536 and was created earl of Southampton in 1537. As lord admiral, he organized the reception of Anne of Cleves, looking after her in Calais from 11 to 27 December 1539. He reported on her in glowing terms to Henry, so much so that his half-brother, Sir Anthony Browne, feared for his future after the collapse of the marriage. But Fitzwilliam survived by turning against Cromwell, whom he succeeded as lord privy seal while Russell obtained the admiralty. In the painted version of this portrait, a naval scene appears in the background. R.C.D.B., D.S.

Sir George Carew was the hapless commander of *Mary Rose* when she sank on 19 July 1545. The day before, Henry had shared his naval strategy with Viscount Lisle, the Lord High Admiral and Sir George Carew before placing a gold whistle and chain around Sir George as a mark of his promotion to Vice-Admiral. Later, under sail Sir George seems to have lost control of the crew of *Mary Rose*, as too many men gathered on one side. However, it was ultimately his failure to reassert control over his men and to seal the gun-ports which proved fatal. His final remarks to his uncle Sir Gawen Carew, captain of the nearby *Matthew*, were: 'I have the sort of Knaves I cannot rule.' R.C.D.B.

319 x 235

Royal Collection

M.Rule, *Mary Rose* (1983), pp. 37-9

Foister/Parker, no. 76

388 x 274

Royal Collection

Foister/Parker, no. 66

Notes to the Essays

ABBREVIATIONS

BL	British Library
CSP Ven.	*Calendar of State Paper, Venetian*, ed. R. Brown, 9 vols. (1864-98)
DNB	*Dictionary of National Biography*
Foister/Parker	S. Foister, *Drawings by Holbein from the Royal Library Windsor Castle* (1983)
HKW	H.M. Colvin et al., *The History of the King's Works*, 6 vols. (1951-82).
History of Parliament	S.T. Bindoff, ed., *The History of Parliament: The House of Commons, 1509-58*, 3 vols. (1983)
LP	*Letters and Papers, Foreign and Domestic, of the Reign of Henry VIII, 1509-47*, ed. J.S. Brewer, J. Gairdner and R.H. Brodie, 21 vols. and addenda (1862-1932)
More: NPG	J.B. Trapp and H.S. Herbrüggen, *'The Kings's Good Servant', Sir Thomas More, 1477/8-1535*, Exhibition catalogue: National Portrait Gallery (1977).
PRO	Public Record Office
Rowlands	J. Rowlands, *Holbein: The Paintings of Hans Holbein the Younger* (Oxford, 1985)
Strong, *NPG*	R. Strong, *National Portrait Gallery: Tudor and Jacobean Portraits*, 2 vols. (1969)
Strong, *Renaissance Miniature*	R. Strong, *The English Renaissance Miniature* (1983)

The place of publication of all books, unless otherwise noted, is London.

Early Tudor London by Rosemary Weinstein

1. Ida Darlington and James Howgego, *Printed Maps of London, c.1553-1850* (1964), pp. 6-8.
2. PRO, E 36/218 (I.4).
3. Thomas Platter, *Travels of England* (1599)
4. Bodleian, MS Douce 363, fos. 52v-53 (I.5)
5. C. A. Sneyd, ed., *A Relation, or Rather a True Account of the Island of England ... about the year 1500*, Camden Society 1st series 37 (1847).
6. Darlington and Howgego, *Printed Maps*, p. 6.
7. George Cavendish, *The Life and Death of Cardinal Wolsey*, ed. R. S. Sylvester, Early English Text Society (1959), pp. 66-7.
8. Tony Dyson, *The Medieval London Waterfront*, Annual Archaeology Lecture: Museum of London (1989), pp. l4-15.
9. John Schofield and Tony Dyson, *Archaeology of the City of London* (1980), p. 52.
10. Dyson, *Medieval Waterfront*, p. 9.
11. Ibid. p. 8.

Greenwich Palace by Simon Thurley

1. *HKW* II, pp. 949-50; P. W. Dixon, *Excavations at Greenwich Palace, 1970-1* (1972), p. 7; *HKW* IV, pp. 97-8.
2. W. Lambarde, *Perambulation of Kent*, ed. R. Church (Bath, 1970), p. 390.
3. S. Bentley, ed., *Excerpta Historica* (London, 1831), p. 116.
4. BL, Additional MS 59899 fos. 4v, 24, 63.
5. BL, Additional MS 59899 fos. 62v, 63, 68, 79.
6. As shown in Figure 1 and the 1693 plan.
7. The privy kitchen is mentioned in Henry's Chamber accounts: PRO, E36/214 fo. 150v. It was fully excavated: Dixon, *Excavations*, pp. 18-19.
8. N[ottingham] U[niversity] L[ibrary], MS Ne.01, fo. 34.
9. Mentioned in Henry VII's Chamber accounts: PRO, E36/214, fo. 147.
10. Excavation has shown that Wyngaerde's drawing of the river front (unlike Figure 1) is inaccurate.
11. Bodleian, Rawlinson MS D 775, fo. 27.
12. 'The gallary betwen the dynyng chamber and the grett chamber': NUL, MS Ne.01, fo. 42.
13. 'goinge up the stayres to the great chamber': PRO, E351/3218.
14. *HKW* IV, p. 111.
15. The presence chamber was 'next the waterside': Bodleian, Rawlinson MS D 781, fo. 13v.
16. 'in the gallary betwene the pallet chamber and the chappell': BL, Additional MS 10109, fo. 74v, also see PRO, E351/3208. Cavendish, in his *Life of Wolsey* confirms this: ed. R. S. Sylvester, Early English Text Society (1959), p. 98.
17. 'a brecke walle bytwen the kyngs privy chambre and the beede chamber' NUL, MS Ne.01, fo. 33.
18. W. Douglas Simpson, 'The Building accounts of Tattershall Castle,

1434-1472', *Lincoln Record Society* 55 (1960); M. W. Thompson, 'Tattershall Castle', *Archaeological Journal* 131 (1974), pp. 317-21; M. W. Thompson, Tattershall Castle (National Trust, 1977).
19. W. Douglas Simpson, 'Buckden Palace', *Journal of the British Archaeological Association*, 3rd series 2 (1937), pp. 121-30.
20. R. Allen Brown, *English Castles*, (London, 1976), pp. 39-41; M. W. Thompson, *The Decline of the Castle* (Cambridge, 1987), pp. 28-9.
21. P. Murray, *The Architecture of the Italian Renaissance*, (London, 1969), pp. 63-93.
22. 'Thomas Forster towards the fynisshing of the chapel at Greenwytche': PRO, E36/216, fo. 114. Also see PRO, E36/216, fo. 34; *LP* III i, 483.
23. PRO, E36/216, fo. 34.
24. *LP* III i, 483.
25. Below, p. 155.
26. Dixon, *Excavations*, pp. 16-17.
27. Bodleian, Rawlinson MS D 776, fo. 26; PRO, E351/3209. As originally built, the turret at the junction of the north range and the south east angle of the donjon was a porch leading into the ground floor of the north range. Later a newel was inserted, the entrance to the north range blocked and the courtyard door narrowed (Dixon, *Excavations*, p. 17). It is clear from Henrician accounts that a stair existed in this position as early as 1533 and so the alteration is ascribed to Henry VIII.
28. For the existence of the gallery see Dixon, *Excavations*, p. 16.
29. Bodleian, Rawlinson MS D 776, fo. 37v.
30. Bodleian, Rawlinson MS D 780, fo. 37.
31. Bodleian, Rawlinson MS D 777, fo. 169v.
32. Bodleian, Rawlinson MS D 780, fo. 33.
33. BL, Harley MS 1419A, fo. 58.
34. BL, Harley MS 1419A, fo. 62v, 61.
35. 'repayryng of vi panes in study betweyne the said bedde chambre and raying chambre': Bodleian, Rawlinson MS D 775, fo. 44v.
36. 'galerys betwene the said raying [chamber] and the quenes chambers': Bodleian, Rawlinson MS D 776, fo. 24.
37. Bodleian, Rawlinson MS D 777, fo. 167.
38. Bodleian, Rawlinson MS D 775, fos. 32, 77v.
39. Bodleian, Rawlinson MS D 776, fo. 41; MS Film 308, fo. 17. The stair to the garden led down from her privy chamber: Bodleian, Rawlinson MS D 775, fo. 62.
40. *HKW* II, pp. 949-50; *HKW* III, p. 195.
41. 'the gallery betwexte the quenes chamber and the clossyt at the frears' and 'the galory goyng frome the kyngs privy chambr to the frears': NUL, MS Ne.02, fo. 34v.
42. The roof to the west of the king's privy chamber was over 'the gallery entring into the kyngs and quenes bedchamber': PRO, E101/504/2, fo. 36v.
43. See notes 30-3 above.
44. *HKW* III, p. 195.
45. PRO, E101/504/2, fos. 25, 29, 30v, 33v, 34.
46. BL, Additional MS 10109, fo. 84.
47. Bodleian, Rawlinson MS D 781, fo. 34v; BL, Additional MS

10109, fo. 51.
48. Bodleian, Rawlinson MS D 781, fo. 13v. Also see PRO, E101/504/2, fo.33v.
49. Bodleian, Rawlinson MS D 780, fo. 25v.
50. Ibid, fo. 28.
51. A roundel is referred to in 1533: Bodleian, Rawlinson MS D 775, fo. 52v.
52. Bodleian, Rawlinson MS D 775 fos. 26v, 34v; 780, fos. 32v, 36v; 781, fo. 15.

Stained Glass in Henry VIII's Palaces by Hilary Wayment

1. H. C. Wayment, 'Twenty-four Vidimuses for Cardinal Wolsey', *Master Drawings* 23/24 (1985-6), pp. 503-17.
2. Id., 'The foreign Glass at Hengrave Hall and St James's, Bury St Edmunds'; *Journal of the British Society of Master Glass Painters* 18 (1986-7), pp. 166-79.
3. *HKW* III, p. 262.
4. *HKW* III, pp. 398-9.
5. Arthur Oswald, 'The Glazing of the Savoy Hospital', *Journal of the British Society of Master Glass Painters* 11 (1954-5), pp. 224-32.
6. H. C. Wayment, 'The Stained Glass of the Chapel of the Vyne', *National Trust Studies* 1980 (1979), pp. 35-47.
7. Id., 'The East Window of St Margaret's, Westminster', *The Antiquaries Journal* 61 (1981), pp. 292-301. One of the tracery angels seems to imply a knowledge of Heemskerk's St Luke Painting the Virgin (1532): M.J. Friedlander, *Early Netherlandish Painting* XIII (Leyden and Brussels 1975), n. 183 pl. 92.
8. Ian Nairn and Nikolaus Pevsner, *Surrey* (Harmondsworth 1971), p. 479.
9. David Starkey, 'Ightham Mote: Architecture and Politics in Early Tudor England', *Archaeologia* 102 (1983) 153-63, pp. 154-5.
10. *Victoria County History*, *Berkshire* (1972), p.95: in this case the whole field of the window consisted of heraldic quarries.
11. H. G. Wayment, 'Wolsey and Stained Glass', in S.J. Gunn and P.G. Lindley, *Cardinal Wolsey: Church, State and Art* (Cambridge, forthcoming).
12. *LP* VII, 250.
13. Bodleian, Rawlinson MS D 776, fo. 18.
14. Example in King's College Chapel, Cambridge: H.G. Wayment, *King's College Chapel, Cambridge, the Side-Chapel Glass*, (Cambridge 1988), pp. 123-4 (with refs to other examples) and pl.7d.
15. E.g. the shield of sixteen quarterings (c. 1580) for Henry Hastings, 3rd earl of Huntingdon, in the Oliver King Chapel of St George's Chapel, Windsor.
16. Oswald Barron in H. Avray Tipping, *The Story of Montacute and its House* (1933), pp. 292-301.
17. M. H. Caviness et al., *Stained Glass before 1700 in American Collections: Mid-Atlantic and Southeastern Seaboard States*, Corpus Vitrearum Checklist II (Washington 1987), pp. 162-7.

Henry VIII and the Founding of the Greenwich Armouries by Karen Watts

1. It is, however, very likely that the Black Prince's helm at Canturbury Cathedral, King Henry V's helm at Westminster Abbey, the Warwick Shaffron at the Royal Armouries (VI 446) and a number of other pieces are of English origin. Many Italianate helmets in English churches may also have an English provenance: G.F.Laking, *A Record of European Armour and Arms through Seven Centuries* (1926) II, pp. 88-94; V, pp, 154-273.
2. The agreement was negotiated by Sir Richard Jermingham in Milan on 16 March 1511: BL, Stowe MS 146, fo.134.
3. PRO, E 36/1, fo. 52. The list of the equipment is reproduced by C. J. Ffoulkes, *The Armourer and his Craft*, (1912), pp 27-8.
4. Royal Armouries, HM Tower of London, VI 6-12. George Lovekyn mentions the bard in an inventory in May 1519. This is quoted in Claude Blair, 'The Emperor Maximilian's Gift of Armour to King Henry VIII and the Silvered and Engraved Armour at the Tower of London', *Archeologia* 99 (1965).
5. Dr. Helmut Nickel identified this mark with the armourer Martin van Royne: H. Nickel, S. W. Pyhrr, L. Tarassuk, *The Art of Chivalry* (New York, 1982).
6. The indenture is quoted by Blair 'Emperor Maximilian's Gift', p. 27.
7. Blair, 'Emperor Maximilian's Gift', p. 36.
8. Royal Armouries, HM Tower of London, IV 22.
9. Waffensammlung, Kunsthistorisches Museum, Vienna, A.109.
10. *Catalogue for the Exhibition of Armour Made in the Royal Workshops at Greenwich* (1951), p. 57 ff.
11. Royal Armouries, HM Tower of London, II 6.
12. *Exhibition of Armour* p. 57.
13. W.Reid, *Guildhall Miscellany* 2 (1966), p. 331; O. P. G. Hogg, *The Royal Arsenal*, (1963) I, pp. 103-5.

The Early Tudor Tournament by Steven Gunn

1. Maurice Keen, *Chivalry* (1984), pp. 83-101; Richard Barber and Juliet Barker, *Tournaments: Jousts, Chivalry and Pageants in the Middle Ages* (Woodbridge, 1989), pp. 13-27.
2. James Gairdner, ed., *Memorials of King Henry the Seventh* (Rolls Series, 1858), p. 122; Edward Hall, [*The Chronicle*] (1809), pp. 707-8.
3. J.J. Scarisbrick, *Henry VIII* (1968), pp. 484-5.
4. Hall, *Chronicle*, p. 514; Sydney Anglo, ed., *The Great Tournament Roll of Westminster* (2 vols., Oxford, 1968) I, pp. 138, 141.
5. Sydney Anglo, 'Archives of the English Tournament: Score Cheques and Lists', *Journal of the Society of Archivists* 2 (1961), pp. 153-62.
6. Steven Gunn, *Charles Brandon, Duke of Suffolk* c.1484-1545 (Oxford, 1988), pp. 9-10, 33-4, 68.
7. Gunn, *Charles Brandon*, pp. 67-8.
8. Hall, *Chronicle*, p. 591.
9. Sydney Anglo, *Spectacle, Pageantry, and Early Tudor Policy* (Oxford, 1969), pp. 108-23.
10. Joycelyne Russell, *The Field of Cloth of Gold* (1969), pp. 105-41.
11. Rawdon Brown et al., eds., *Calendar of State Papers, Venetian* (9 vols., 1862-98), IV 105.
12. Anglo, *Spectacle, Pageantry and Early Tudor Policy*, pp. 120-1.

The Banqueting and Disguising Houses of 1527 by Simon Thurley

1. *CSP Ven* IV, p. 61.
2. E. Hall, [*The Chronicle*] (1809), p. 847.
3. The best accounts are in PRO, E 36/227, fos. 1-36v (*LP* IV ii, 3097). Also see BL, Egerton MS 2605, fos. 1-14; PRO, SP1/41, fos. 235-74; PRO, SP2/C. fos 323-55v. These have been fully discussed in S. Anglo, 'La Salle de Banquet et le Théâtre construits à Greenwich pour les fêtes franco-anglaises de 1527', in *Le Lieu* théâtral *à la Renaissance*, ed. J. Jacjuot, (Paris, 1964), pp. 273-99; S. Anglo, *Spectacle, Pageantry and Early Tudor Policy* (Oxford, 1969), pp. 209-25.
4. PRO, E36/227, fo. 26v.
5. Now in the Staatliche Museen, Berlin-Dahlem. Reproduced in E.W. Ives, *Anne Boleyn*, (Oxford, 1966), pl. 24.
6. Reproduced in J. Summerson, *Architecture in Britain 1530-1830*, 7th edition (Harmondsworth 1983), pp. 32-3.
7. Both are also reproduced in C. Lloyd and S. Thurley, *Henry VIII: Images of a Tudor King* (Oxford, 1990), pls. 38, 40-1.
8. PRO, SP2/C. fo. 323.
9. Bodleian, Rawlinson MS D 776, fo. 80v.
10. *HKW* IV, p. 109.

Nicolaus Kratzer: The King's Astronomer and Renaissance Instrument-Maker by Willem Hackman

1. J.B. Trapp and H.S. Herbrüggen, 'The King's Good Servant', *Sir Thomas More 1447/8-1535* (London: National Portrait Gallery exhibition catalogue, 1977), p. 96, item 187.
2. J.D. North, 'Nicolaus Kratzer - 'The King's Astronomer', Science and History' in *Studies in Honor of Edward Rosen* (Studia Copernicana XVI, 1978), pp. 210, 223, 205-234.
3. *LP* III ii, p. 1535; XIV ii, p. 311; IV ii, p.1596
4. E.F. Rogers, *The Correspondence of Sir Thomas More* (Princeton,1947), pp. 249-250.
5. Anthony Wood, *History and Antiquities of the Colleges and Halls in the University of Oxford*, ed J. Gutch (1796), vol. II ii, p. 834.
6. Corpus Christi College, Oxford, MS 152, fo.l(v); P. Pattenden, *Sundials at an Oxford College* (Oxford: Roman Books, 1979), pp. 20, 88, notes 25 and 26.
7. 'Nicolaus Kratzer' pp. 216-7.
8. Pattenden, *Sundials*, p. 15, figure 1.
9. Pattenden, *Sundials*, Appendix II, pp. 73-76.
10. Sir Roy Strong, *The Renaissance Garden in England* (1979), p. 38.
11. G.S.J. White, 'An Early Renaissance Stone Polyhedral Sundial Found at Iron Acton Court, Near Bristol' *Antiquarian Horology*, 16 (1986), pp. 139-144, and his 'A Stone Polyhedral Sundial Dated 1520, Attributed to Nicholas Kratzer and Found at Iron Acton Court, near Bristol', *The Antiquaries Journal*, 67 (1987), pp. 372-3.
12. Paul Ganz, *The Paintings of Hans Holbein* (1950), p. 233.
13. R. Foster and P. Tudor-Craig, *The Secret Life of Paintings* (1986), pp. 75-95.

14. G.L.E. Turner, 'Mathematical Instrument-making in London in the Sixteenth Century', in S. Tyacke, ed., *English Map-Making 1500-1650* (1983), pp. 93-106.
15. F. Maddison, 'Medieval Scientific Instruments and the Development of Navigational Instruments in the XVth and XVIth Centuries'(Agrupamento de estudos de Cartografia antiga XXX Seccao de Coimbra), *Revista da Universidade de Coimbra*, 24 (1969), p. 42.

A Diplomatic Revolution? Anglo-French Relations and the Treaties of 1527 by Charles Giry-Deloison

1. T.Rymer, *Foedera, conventiones, literae...*(hereafter *Foedera*), 10 vols., 3ed. (The Hague, 1739-45) VI ii, pp.88-91; J. Dumont, *Corps Universel Diplomatique...*, 8 vols. (The Hague, 1725-1731) IV i, pp.476-82. LP IV ii, 3080, 3105.
2. *LP* III iii, 2292 and *Journal de Louise de Savoie*, J.-F. Michaud and J.-J.-F. Poujoulat eds., Nouvelle collection de Mémoires pour servir à l'histoire de France (Paris, 1838) V, p. 92.
3. *LP* I i 5.
4. *LP* I i 5.
5. J.J. Scarisbrick, *Henry VIII* (1968), pp. 40-64.
6. C.G. Cruickshank, *Army Royal. An Account of Henry VIII's Invasion of France, 1513* (Oxford, 1969) and id., *The English Occupation of Tournai 1513-1519* (Oxford, 1971); S.J. Gunn, 'The French Wars of Henry VIII' in J. Black, ed., *The Origins of War in Early Modern Europe* (Edinburgh, 1987) pp. 28-47.
7. C[alendar of] S[tate] P[apers,] Sp[anish], ed. G.A. Bergenrot et al., 13 vols. (1862-1954), III i (1525-6), 33, 64, 73; *LP* IV i, 1212, 1301.
8. 'La France anglaise' au Moyen Age (Paris, 1988), actes du 111 Congrès national des Sociétés savantes, Poitiers, 1986.
9. c.f. Scarisbrick, *Henry VIII*, S. Doran, *England and Europe 1485-1603* (1986), P. Gwyn, *The King's Cardinal: The rise and fall of Thomas Wolsey* (1990) and S.J. Gunn, 'Wolsey's foreign policy and the domestic crisis of 1527-28 in S.J. Gunn and P. Lindley eds., *Cardinal Wolsey: Church, State and Art* (forthcoming), pp. 149-77.
10. *CSP Sp.* II (1509-25), 672, and see G. Jacqueton, *La politique extérieure de Louise de Savoie. Relations diplomatiques de la France et de l'Angleterre pendant la captivité de Francois 1er, 1525-1526*, Paris, 1892), pp. 46-97.
11. *CSP Sp.* III i (1525-6), 7; E. Hall, [*The Chronicle*] (1809), p. 706; Jacqueton, *Politique extérieure*, pp. 300-304.
12. Hall, *Chronicle*, p. 693.
13. *CSP Sp.* III i (1525-6), 46.
14. *CSP Sp.* III i (1525-6), 119.
15. *CSP Sp.* III i (1525-6), 160.
16. G.W. Bernard, *War, taxation and rebellion in early Tudor England: Henry VIII, Wolsey and the Amicable Grant of 1525* (Brighton, 1986), pp. 125-129 and P. Gwyn *The King's Cardinal*, pp. 401-403.
17. *LP* IV i, 1243, 1263, 1266, 1295; Hall, *Chronicle*, pp. 696-702.
18. Hall, *Chronicle*, pp. 698, 700-701.
19. E.W. Ives, *Anne Boleyn* (Oxford, 1986), pp. 77-110.
20. *Ordonnances de François 1er*, 8 vols. (Paris, 1902-1972) IV, 418.
21. *Foedera* VI ii, pp. 21-25; Jacqueton, *Politique extérieure*, pp. 134-47.
22. *Foedera* VI ii, pp. 25-29; Jacqueton, *Politique extérieure*, pp. 136-140.
23. *Foedera* VI ii, pp. 30-31.
24. *Foedera* VI ii, pp. 31-32.
25. *Foedera* VI ii, pp. 29-30.
26. *LP* IV ii, 3143, 3144, 3145, 3271.
27. *LP* IV ii, 3138.
28. *LP* IV ii, 3254.
29. *LP* IV ii, 3337.
30. J. Dumont, *Corps diplomatique* IV i, pp. 487-496.
31. *Foedera* VI ii, p. 91.
32. *LP* IV iii, 5515.
33. J. Dumont, *Corps diplomatique* IV ii, pp. 1-6.
34. *CSP Ven.* IV (1527-33), 491; *LP* IV iii, 5785.
35. Margaret of Savoy was regent of the Netherlands, Charles V's aunt and Louise of Savoy's sister-in-law.
36. J. Dumont, *Corps diplomatique* IV, pp. 7-17, and see R. Scheurer, 'Les relations franco-anglaises pendant la négociation de la paix de Dames (juillet 1527-août 1529)' in P.M. Smith and I.D. McFarlane, eds., *Literature and the Arts in the Reign of Francis I. Essays presented to C.A. Mayer* (Lexington, 1985), pp. 142-162.
37. *LP* XVIII, 361, 440; XVIII i 754; *CSP Sp.* VI ii (1542-3), 163, 164.
38. *LP* XIX i, 921.

Illuminated Manuscripts and the Development of the Portrait Miniature by Janet Backhouse

1. Lorne Campbell and Susan Foister, 'Gerard, Lucas and Susanna Horenbout', *Burlington Magazine* 128 (1986), 719-27, p. 722.
2. J.B. Trapp and Joseph Schulte Herbriggen, 'The King's Good Servant': Sir Thomas More, 1477/8-1535 (1977), no. 117.
3. All the documentary evidence for the careers of the Horenbouts is given in Campbell and Foister, 'Gerard, Lucas and Susanna Horenbout'.
4. See Erna Auerbach, *Tudor Artists* (1954), pp. 446; id., 'Notes on Flemish miniaturists in England', *Burlington Magazine* 96 (1954), pp. 51-3.
5. See in particular T.H. Colding, *Aspects of Miniature Painting* (Copenhagen, 1953).
6. R. Bayne-Powell, *Catalogue of portrait miniatures in the Fitzwilliam Museum, Cambridge* (Cambridge, 1985), p. 12930.
7. The most convenient source for most of these miniatures is Roy Strong, *Artists of the Tudor Court* (1983), pp. 35-44.
8. See G. Lebel, 'British-French artistic relations', *Gazette des Beaux-Arts* 1 (Paris, 1948), pp. 272-3; *CSP Ven.* III (1520-26), 1451.
9. *LP* IV ii, 3169.
10. Discussed in more detail in Janet Backhouse, 'Illuminated manuscripts and the early development of the portrait miniature', in Daniel Williams, ed., *Early Tudor England: Proceedings of the 1987 Harlaxton Symposium* (Woodbridge, 1989), 1-17, pp. 13-16.
11. For an outstanding example, see the portrait of the duke of Bedford in the Bedford Hours, reproduced in Janet Backhouse, *The Bedford Hours*, (1990), pl. 43 and frontispiece (enlarged).
12. V.J. Murrell, *The way howe to lymne: Tudor miniatures observed* (1983).

Music at the Court of Henry VIII by Peter Holman

1. Oliver Strunk ed., *Source Readings in Music History* (1952, 2nd ed. 1981) II, The Renaissance, pp. 93-4.
2. E.D. Mackerness, *A Social History of English Music* (1964), pp. 49-50.
3. Rawdon Brown, ed., *Four Years at the Court of Henry VIII* (1854) I, p. 86; John Stevens, *Music and Poetry in the Early Tudor Court* (Cambridge, 1961, 2nd Oct. 1979), pp. 275-6.
4. John Stevens, ed., *Music at the Court of Henry VIII*, Musica Britannica, 18 (1961, 2nd ed. 1969), pp. 101-2.
5. Iain Fenlon, 'Instrumental Music, Songs and Verse from Sixteenth-Century Winchester: British Library Additional MS 60577' in id. ed., *Music in Mediaeval and Early Modern Europe: Patronage, Sources and Texts* (Cambridge, 1981), pp. 93-116; Judith Blezzard, 'A New Source of Tudor Music', *The Musical Times* 122 (August 1981), pp. 532-35.
6. Sydney Anglo, *Spectacle, Pageantry, and Early Tudor Policy* (Oxford, 1969); Suzanne R. Westfall, *Patrons and Performance: Early Tudor Household Revels* (Oxford, 1990), pp. 13-62; for the Chapel Royal in general, see David Baldwin, *The Chapel Royal, Ancient and Modern* (1990).
7. Rawdon Brown, *Four Years I*, pp. 78-9.
8. Louise Litterick, 'The Manuscript Royal 20. A. XVI of the British Library', (Ph.D. diss., New York University, 1976); Smeaton's authorship of (VII.7) is proposed in Edward Lowinsky, 'MS 1070 of the Royal College of Music in London', *Proceedings of the Royal Musical Association* 96 (1969-70), pp. 1-28, and id., 'A Music Book for Anne Boleyn', John G. Rowe and William H. Stockdale eds., *Florilegium historiale: Essays Presented to Wallace K. Ferguson* (Toronto and Buffalo, 1971), pp. 160-235; it is disputed in Anthony M. Cummings, 'The Transmission of Some Josquin Motets', *Journal of the Royal Musical Association* 115/1 (1990), p. 9, fn. 25.
9. Edmund Bowles, '"Haut et Bas": the Grouping of Musical Instruments in the Middle Ages', *Musica Disciplina* 8 (1954), pp. 115-40.
10. Henry Cart De Lafontaine, *The King's Musick* (1909, revised ed. 1973), pp. 7-8; for Van Wilder, see Jane A. Bernstein, 'Philip Van Wilder and the Netherlandish Chanson in England', *Musica Disciplina* 33 (1979), pp. 55-75; David Humphreys, 'Philip Van Wilder: a Study of his Work and his Sources', *Soundings* 9 (1979-80), pp. 13-36
11. For the alta capella, see Keith Polk, 'Wind Bands of Mediaeval Flemish Cities', *Brass and Woodwind Quarterly* 1 (1968), pp. 93-113; id., 'Municipal Wind Music in Flanders in the Late Middle Ages', *Brass and Woodwind Quarterly* 2 (1969), pp. 1-15; id., 'The Trombone, the Slide Trumpet and the Ensemble Tradition of the Early Renaissance', *Early Music* 17 (1989), pp. 389-97.
12. David Lasocki, 'Professional Recorder Playing in England 1500-1740, 1: 1500-1640', *Early Music* 10 (1982), pp. 23-26; Peter Holman,

'The English Royal Violin Consort in the Sixteenth Century', *Proceedings of the Royal Musical Association* 109 (1982-83), pp. 39-59; Ian Woodfield, *The Early History of the Viol* (Cambridge, 1984), pp. 206-9.

13. Roger Prior, 'Jewish Musicians at the Tudor Court', *Musical Quarterly* 69 (1983), pp. 253-65.

14. For the Bassanos as instrument makers, see David Lasocki, 'The Anglo-Venetian Bassano Family as Instrument Makers and Repairers', *The Galpin Society Journal* 38 (1985), pp. 112-32; Giulio M. Ongaro, 'Sixteenth-century Venetian Wind Instrument Makers and their Clients', *Early Music* 13 (1985), pp. 391-7; David Lasocki, 'The Bassanos: Anglo- Venetian and Venetian', *Early Music* 14 (1986), pp. 558-60; Beryl Kenyon de Pascual, 'Bassano Instruments in Spain?', *The Galpin Society Journal* 40 (1987), pp. 74-5.

15. John Harley, 'Music at the English Court in the Eighteenth and Nineteenth Centuries', *Music & Letters* 50 (1969), pp. 332-49.

Anne Boleyn as Patron by Maria Dowling

1. E. W. Ives, *Anne Boleyn* (Oxford, 1986), chapter 13, 'Art, Image and Taste'.

2. Maria Dowling, ed.,'William Latymer's Chronickille of Anne Bulleyne', *Camden Miscellany* 30 (1990), p. 63.

3. Maria Dowling and Joy Shakespeare, eds., 'The Recollections of Rose Hickman', *Bulletin of the Institute of Historical Research* 55 (1982), p. 97.

4. Ives, *Anne Boleyn*, pp. 317-8, 289-92, 293-5.

5. BL, Royal MS 20 B XVII, dedicatory epistle.

6. BL, Additional MS 17, 492, 'Devonshire MS'.

7. Quoted in Edmond Bapst, *Deux Gentilshommes-poètes de la cour de Henry VIII* (Paris, 1891), p. 27.

8. BL, Royal MS 16 E XIII (V.11).

9. Latymer, 'Chronickille', p. 56; Nicolas Bourbon, *Nugae* (Lyons, 1538), passim.

10. BL, Sloane MS 1207, Alwaye's petition; Latymer, 'Chronickille', p. 56.

11. John Bruce and Thomas Perowne, eds., *Correspondence of Matthew Parker*, Parker Society (Cambridge, 1853), no. 3.

12. John Foxe, *Acts and Monuments*, ed. S.R. Cattley, 8 vols. (1837) IV, pp. 657-8; Ives, *Anne Boleyn*, p. 163 and n.

13. George Wyatt, *Extracts from the Life of tne Virtuous, Christian and Renowned Queen Anne Boleigne*, ed. R. Triphook, (1817), pp. 16-17, Anne Gainsford's account; J. G. Nichols, ed., *Narratives of the Days of the Reformation*, Camden Society (1859), pp. 52-7, John Louthe's account.

14. William Marshall, *The Form and Manner of Subvention or Helping for Poor People, Devised and Practised in the City of Ypres in Flanders* (1535), dedicatory preface.

15. Foxe, *Acts and Monuments* V, p. 132, letter of Tyndale to Frith.

16. PRO, SP1/102, fo. 125 (*LP* X, 371), confession of Tristram Revell.

17. Calendar of State Papers, Spanish, ed. G.A. Bergenroth et al., 13 vols. (1862-19540), V ii (1536-8), 85, Chapuys to Charles V, April 1536.

18. Latymer, 'Chronickille', pp. 39, 41-3 for sixteenth-century praise of Anne as a reformer.

Goldsmiths and their Work at the Court of Henry VIII by Hugh Tait

1. R. A. Crichton, *Cambridge Plate*, Exhibition catalogue: Fitzwilliam Museum (Cambridge, 1975); P. Glanville, *Silver in Tudor and Early Stuart England* (1990), fig. 64.

2. J. Pope-Hennessy, *Cellini*, 1988.

3. H. Tait, 'London Huguenot Silver' in I. Scouloudi, ed., *Huguenots in Britain and their French Background* (1987), pp. 90-1.

4. H. Tait, 'The girdle prayer-book or 'tablett': an important class of Renaissance jewellery at the court of Henry VIII', *Jewellery Studies* 2 (1985), pp. 29-58, figs. 1- 26.

The Royal Visit to Acton Court in 1535 by Robert Bell

1. *LP* VIII, 989.

2. *Calendar of Close Rolls, Edward III* XII (1364-8), pp.61-2.

3. BL, Sloane MS 3424, fo. 7(v).

4. J. Gairdner, *History of the Life and Reign of Richard III* (rev. ed. 1898), pp.363-9, n.viii.

5. J. Leland *De Rebus Britannicis Collectanea* (1774) IV, pp.186, 198-9.

6. *LP* Addenda I i, 165, 177.

7. *Historical Manuscript Commission, Marquis of Bath* IV, p. 2.

8. *LP* VIII, 149/37; IX, 914/22.

9. Susan Foister, *Drawings by Holbein from the Royal Library Windsor Castle* (1983), p. 42.

10. See *HKW* IV, p.104 for a description of the decorating of the King's privy chamber at Greenwich in 1533 with a fret ceiling, embellished with 'bullions'.

11. Ibid. p.27. The timbers in the hall roofs at Greenwich and the Tower of London were painted with yellow ochre.

12. East Sussex RO, SAS G21/26.

13. L. T. Smith, ed., *Itinerary of John Leland* (1910) V, p.99.

Plate and Gift-Giving at Court by Philippa Glanville

1. A. J. Collins, *Jewels and Plate of Queen Elizabeth: The Inventory of 1574* (1955), espec. pp. 101-110, is the basic treatment.

2. H. Ellis, *Original Letters Illustrative of English History*, 3rd series, 4 vols (1846) II, pp. 220-2.

3. J. Hayward, *Virtuoso Goldsmiths and the Triumph of Mannerism, 1540-1620* (1976); P. Glanville, *Silver in Tudor and Early Stuart England* (1990), chapter 1.

4. 'Inventory of Henry Fitzroy, Duke of Richmond', *Camden Miscellany* 3, Camden Society 61 (1855), pp. 1-13.

5. S. Foister and L. Campbell, 'Gerard, Lucas and Susan Horenbout', *Burlington Magazine* 128 (1986), pp. 719-27; F. Broadhurst, ed., 'Will of George Talbot, earl of Shrewsbury, 1538', *Derbyshire Archaeological and Natural History Society Journal* 31 (1909), pp. 73-88.

6. E.g., Finot, *Inventaire sommaire des archives départmentales*, Nord 8 (Lille, 1895), p. 178; West Inventory, 1534: PROB 2/488.

Fatal Matrimony by Rory MacEntegart

1. Hessisches Staatsarchiv, Marburg, PA 2575, fo. 251v: 'herr Crumellus, welcher zum hochsten der Teutschen Nation genaigt ist, wolte am liebsten das seine Mait. mit den Teutschen fursten befreien det.'

2. Unless otherwise noted, this and all subsequent citations are from the Convocation when it considered the validity of the Cleves marriage in July 1540. The depositions are printed in J. Strype, *Ecclesiastical Memorials*, 3 vols. (Oxford, 1822) I ii, pp.452-62 (*LP* XV, 850).

3. H. Ellis, ed., *Original Letters Illustrative of English History*, 11 vols (1824-46) I, pp. 201-2; *LP* XVI, 1409/3.

Henry VIII and Mapmaking by Peter Barber

1. The themes in this essay are developed and documented in greater detail in the first chapter of my 'Monarchs, ministers and maps in England 1485-1625'; in David Buisseret, ed., *Maps and Monarchs in early modern Europe* (forthcoming).

2. S. Anglo, *Spectacle, Pageantry and Early Tudor Policy* (Oxford, 1969) pp. 77, 82, 140-1, 160, 163, 196-7; P. M. Barber, 'Visual Encyclopedias: The Hereford and other Mappae Mundi', *The Map Collector* 48 (autumn 1989), pp. 2-8.

3. Rodney Shirley, *The Mapping of the World, 1472-1700* (1984), pp. 1-50.

4. P. D. A. Harvey and R. A. Skelton, eds., *Maps and Plans from Medieval England* (Oxford, 1986); E. J. S. Parsons, *The Map of Great Britain circa 1360 known as The Gough Map. An Introduction to the Facsimile* (Oxford, 1970).

5. David Starkey, *The Reign of Henry VIII: Personalities and politics* (1985), pp. 37-51.

6. D. B. and A. M. Quinn, eds., *New American World* (New York, 1979) I, p. 123 item 92.

7. There is no evidence of maps in C. G. Cruikshank, *The English Occupation of Tournai* (1971) or in *HKW* III, pp. 375-82 (Tournai) and pp. 383-93 (Boulogne).

8. P. D. A. Harvey, *Topographical Maps: Symbols, Pictures and Surveys* (1980), pp. 93-6.

9. James A. Williamson, *The Cabot Voyages and Bristol Discovery under Henry VII* (Cambridge, 1962); P. M. Barber, 'Old Encounters New: The Aslake World Map', in M. Pelletier, *Géographie du Monde au moyen age et à la Renaissance* (Paris, 1989), 69-88, pp. 84-8.

10. S. Anglo, *Spectacle, Pageantry*, pp. 141, 144, and see discussion of V.10-11.

11. John D. North, 'Nicolaus Kratzer - the King's Astronomer', in *Science and History: studies in honour of Edward Rosen*, Studia Copernicana 16 (Wroclaw, 1978), particularly pp. 217-222, 225-6.

12. L. Bagrow and R. A. Skelton, *History of Cartography* (1964),

pp. 147-50; P. D. A. Harvey, *Topographical Maps*, pp. 80-2, 88, 146-52.
13. Kratzer to A. Dürer, London, 24 October 1524 in Ernst Ullmann and Elvira Pradel, eds., Albrecht Dürer's *Schriften und Briefe* (Leipzig, 1973), pp. 142-3.
14. R. W. Chambers, *Thomas More* (1963), pp. 48-9; S. Anglo, *Spectacle, Pageantry*, pp. 166, 219; E. G. R. Taylor, *The Mathematical Practitioners of Tudor and Stuart England* (Cambridge, 1954), p. 312.
15. S. Anglo, *Spectacle, Pageantry*, pp. 211-24.
16. In *L'Arte della Guerra* (1521) and *Il Cortegiano* (1528).
17. T. Elyot, *The Book Named the Governor* (Everyman Edition, 1962), pp. 23-4.
18. *HKW* IV, pp. 367, 418, 731-2.
19. *HKW* III, pp. 13, 14, 352; IV, pp. 380, 410-11, 617. 630. 689, 743, 746-7; L.R. Shelby, *John Rogers: Tudor Military Engineer* (Oxford, 1967).
20. *HKW* IV, pp. 378-9, 392-3; Shelby, *John Rogers*, pp. 5-8, 127-44, 151-7.
21. *HKW* III, pp. 14 n.2, 352.
22. *HKW* IV, pp. 367-71.
23. Helen Wallis, ed., *The Maps and Text of the 'Boke of Idrography' presented by Jean Rotz to Henry VIII* (Oxford, 1981), particularly pp. 15-16.
24. A. Ruddock, 'The earliest original English seaman's chart and pilot's rutter', *The Journal of the Institute of Navigation* 14 (1961), pp. 409-31.
25. Shelby, *John Rogers*; *HKW*, III and IV passim.
26. *HKW* III, p. 374 and pl. 29.
27. S. Tyacke, ed., *English Mapmaking 1500-1650* (1983), p. 16; PRO, MPC 64; MPB 49, 51 (York).
28. Shelby, *John Rogers*, pp. 94-101.
29. P. D. A. Harvey, 'The Portsmouth map of 1545 and the introduction of Scale Maps into England' in *Hampshire Studies presented to Dorothy Dymond* (Portsmouth, 1981), pp. 33-49.
30. Wallis, *Boke of Idrography*, pp. 9-12 and Marcus Merriman, 'Italian military engineers in Britain in the 1540s', in Tyacke, *English Mapmaking*, pp. 57-67.
31. BL, Harley MS 1419 A, fos. 186-8.
32. Shelby, *John Rogers*, pp. 76-8; *HKW* IV, pp. 367-94.
33. Helen Wallis, 'The royal map collections of England', Revista da Univeerstiade de Coimbra 28 (1980), pp. 461-8.

Greenwich and Henry VIII's Royal Library by James Carley

1. Cited in N. Barker et al., *Treasures of the British Library* (1988), p. 25.
2. John Bale, *The Laboryouse Journey and Serche of Johan Leylande for Englandes Antiquitees* (1549), cited in Barker, *Treasures*, p. 27.
3. *Calendar of Patent Rolls, Henry VII* I (1485-94), p. 378; *LP* I i, 190/27.
4. Henri Omont, 'Les manuscrits français des rois d'Angleterre au château de Richmond' in *Etudes romanes dédiées à Gaston Paris* (Paris, 1891), pp. 1- 13.
5. BL, Harley MS 1419A, fo. 62v.
6. J. W. Clark, *The Care of Books* (Cambridge, 1901), pp. 299-302.
7. Cf. J. Carley, 'John Leland and the Contents of the English Pre-Dissolution Libraries: Lincolnshire', *Transactions of the Cambridge Bibliographical Society* 9 (1989), pp. 330-57.
8. J. Carley, 'John Leland and the Foundation of the Royal Library: the Westminster Inventory of 1542', *Bulletin of the Society for Renaissance Studies* 7 (1989) 13-20, pp. 13-14.
9. Bale, *Laboryouse Journey*, sig. C ii(r).
10. Cambridge University Library, MS Ee V 14, pp. 335-6.
11. PRO,E 315/160, fos. 107v-120.
12. Carley, 'John Leland and the Foundation of the Royal Library', pp.17-19.
13. Ibid. p. 15.
14. Trinity College, Oxford, MSS 25, 26, 31, 50, 55, 58, 66, 70.
15. Ibid. MS 26.
16. Cf. Carley, 'Lincolnshire', and J. R. Liddell, '"Leland's" Lists of Manuscripts in Lincolnshire Monasteries', *English Historical Revue* 54 (1939), pp. 88-95.
17. Bodleian Library, Oxford, Bodley MS 419: T. A. Birrell, *English Monarchs and their Books from Henry VIII to Charles II* (1987), p. 9.
18. Ibid. Bodley MSS 245, 458.
19. Ibid. Bodley MS 354; H. M. Nixon, 'Early English Gold-Tooled Bindings' in *Studia di Bibliografia e di Storia in Onore di Tammaro de Marinis*, 4 vols. (Vatican City, 1964) 283-308, pp. 289-90.
20. G. D. Hobson, *Bindings in Cambridge Libraries* (Cambridge, 1929), p. 66.
21. E.g. Bodleian Library, Oxford, Bodley MSS 284, 354.

The Sports of Kings by Simon Thurley

1. B. Castiglione, *The Book of The Courtier*, trans., G. Bull, (Harmondsworth, 1967), p.118.
2. Sir Thomas Elyot, *The Boke Named the Governour*, ed. H.H.S. Croft, 2 vols. (1883) I, p. 169; A. Boorde, *A Compendyous Regyment or a Dyetary of Helth*, ed. F. J. Furnivall, Early English Text Society, e.s.10 (1870), p. 248.
3. D.A.L. Morgan, 'The House of Policy' in David Starkey, ed., *The English Court* (1987), pp. 25-70.
4. *HKW* IV, p.228.
5. Cited in M. L. Bruce, *The Making of Henry VIII* (1977), p.89.
6. S. Anglo, *The Great Tournament Roll of Westminster*, (Oxford, 1968), appendix V.
7. For a discussion of the individual complexes see the following: Whitehall: H.J.M. Green and S.J. Thurley, 'Excavations on the West side of Whitehall 1960-62', *Transactions of the London and Middlesex Archaeological Society* (1990), pp.61-132; Hampton Court: S.J. Thurley, 'Henry VIII and the Building of Hampton Court', *Architectural History* 31 (1988), 1-51, pp.12-13, 29, Figs 1-2.
8. Green and Thurley, 'Excavations on the West side of Whitehall'.
9. PRO, E36/215, fos. 16v, 24v, 30, 39v, 65, 83, 97v, l99v, 260.
10. Ibid. fo. 230.
11. PRO. E36/216, fos. llv, 14v, 17, l9v.
12. Bodleian Library, Rawlinson MS, D 776, fos. 76, 88; D 775, fo. 51v.
13. Ibid. D 777, fo. 162v. Nottingham University Library MS, Ne. 02, fo. 134.
14. 'A dore goyng in to the freyers yard upon the baksyd of the tenyes playe' (Bodleian Library Rawlinson MS, D 777, fo. 191v). 'The lodgings frome the said tennys playe unto the quenes privy stayre' (Ibid. D 775, fo. 51v).
15. Ibid. D 775, fo. 55; N.H. Nicolas, *The Privy Purse Expenses of King Henry the Eighth* (1827), p. 206.
16. Bodleian Library, Rawlinson MS, D 775 fos. 41, 56.
17. Ibid. D 776 fos. 2, 2v, 3, 8; *State Papers: Henry VIII* (1830-52) VI, p. 58 (*LP* III i, 748).
18. Bodleian Library, Rawlinson MS, D 781, fo. 34; *HKW* IV, p.106.

Henry VIII: the Real Founder of the Navy? by David Loades

1. M. Oppenheim, *A History of the Administration of the Royal Navy, 1509-1660* (1896), pp.49-52.
2. C.S.L. Davies, 'The administration of the Royal Navy under Henry VIII: the Origins of the Navy Board', *English Historical Review* 78 (1965), pp. 268-286.
3. H. Schubert, 'The first cast iron canon made in England', *Journal of the Iron and Steel Institute* 146 (1942), p. 13.
4. Tradition maintains that the first guns cast in one piece in England were made in 1543 by William Levet. A double furnace was opened in 1546 at Worth, near Sheffield. In 1545 Henry placed an order with Levet for 200 guns, which took two years to complete. Schubert. 'The first cast iron canon'.
5. P. Padfield, *Guns at Sea* (1973).
6. G.F. Howard, 'Gunport lids', *Mariners Mirror* 67 (1981), p. 64.
7. Oppenheim, *Administration of Royal Navy*, p. 49.
8. De Bapaume to Louise of Savoy, 6 November 1515: *LP* II i, 1113.
9. Ibid.
10. Andrea Badoer and Sebastian Guistinian to the Doge and Senate, 29 October 1515: *CSP Ven.* II (1509-19), pp. 267-8.
11. Ibid.
12. Eustace Chapuys to Charles V, 16 July 1541: *LP* XVI, 1005.
13. *Acts of the Privy Council*, ed. J.R. Dasent et al. (1890-1907) I, p. 381.
14. Edward Echyngham to Wolsey, 5 May 1513: *Letters and Papers relating to the War with France, 1512-13*, ed. A. Spont (Navy Records Sociey, 1897), pp. 145-53; Thomas Howard to Henry VIII, 7 May 1513; ibid, 154-9.
15. Henry VIII to Lord Lisle, 8 January 1543: *LP* XVIII, 19.
16. *Fighting Instructions, 1530-1816*, ed. J.S. Corbett (Navy Records Society, 1905) pp. 160-7; Padfield, op.cit.
17. cited by J.A. Williamson, *Maritime Enterprise* (Oxford, 1913).
18. Ibid.
19. *LP* IV, 5101; *Calendar of State Papers, Domestic; Addenda 1547-65*, ed. M.A.E. Green (1870), p. 426.
20. G. Connell-Smith, *Forerunners of Drake* (1954), pp. 174-97.
21. Statute 28 Henry VIII, cap. 15: *Statutes of the Realm*, III, pp. 671-2.
22. Statute 8 Elizabeth cap. 13: *Statutes of the Realm*, IV, i, pp. 496-7; G.G. Harris, *The Trinity House of Deptford*, 1514-1660 (1969).
23. *HKW* IV, pp. 729-64.

Index

Roman numerals refer to catalogue entries

Abergavenny, George Neville, 5th
    baron II.2
Abington, Dorothy VII.21
Aborough, John XI.11, 12
Admiralty courts 178
Albany, John Stewart, 2nd duke of 82
Almains, craftsmen 44, 45
Almaire, Pierre 105
Altdorfer, Albrecht IX.12
Alwaye, Thomas 110
Amadas, Robert 132; VII.18
Ambry XI.29
Amelia of Cleves 138
Amicable Grant (1525) 78, 81
Amiens 54, 74, 81, 83, 94
Anne Boleyn, 2nd queen consort of
    Henry VIII 12, 13, 30, 61, 81, 100,
    102, 107, 110, 120, 121 123, 160,
    161; V.3, 22; VII.8-11, 17,23; IX.4,
    11; XI.17, 44
    coronation 10, 65, 100
    gift IX.16
    marriage 100
    patronage 100, 105, 107-11; VII.7
    piety 107, 108, 110
    portrait(s) V.49; VII.3
Anne of Cleves, 4th queen consort of
    Henry VIII 13, 31, 136, 138-44, 150;
    XI.2, 3, 11, 12; XII.9
    marriage 106, 138-44
    portrait(s) 61-2, 138, 140; XI.3;
      Figure 9
Annebault, Claude de XII.4
Annesley, Edward 46
Anthony, Anthony 173; roll 173; XII.2;
    Figures 12, 13
Antwerp 83, 108, 114, 178; merchants 16
Antwerpen, Hans von 113, 114;
    VII.15, 16; IX.14
Appianus, Peter XII.6; *Astronomicum*
    Caesarem XII.6
Aragon, Catherine of *see* Catherine of
    Aragon
Ardres 50
Armour 42-6; III.1, 2; IV.2, 3; V.7
Arms 8; III.3, 4; XI.37, 38
Arrighi, Ludovico degli II.15
Arthur, prince of Wales, elder brother
    of Henry VIII 11, 26, 36, 40
Arundel, Sir Thomas 134
Ashdown Forest 172
Astrolabe XI.16
Attavanti, Attavante degli II.15

Bacon, Francis 12
Badoer, Andrea 77
Bale, John 8, 155
    The laboryouse Journey and Serche of
    Johan Lelande for Englandes
    Antiquitees XI.24
Barlow, Roger 178
Barton, Sir Andrew 176
Basel 58, 61-3
Basingstoke (Hants.), Chapel of the
    Holy Ghost 29

Bassano family 106
Batman, Stephen, Dr I.5
Baynton, Sir Edward 110, 118; VII.9
Bayse, Henry V.54
Beaufort, Margaret, Lady,
    grandmother of Henry VIII 160;
    II.22; V.19
    cup 112
    tomb 32
Beddington Place (Surr.) XI.41
Bedford, Sir John Russell, 1st earl
    of 126, 128, 176; II.4, 6; IX.4, 8
Benese, Richard XI.10
Bermondsey Abbey (Kent) 15; I.3
Berners, John Bourchier, Lord 36; II.23
Berthelet, Thomas XI.26
Berwick (Northumb.) 172
Bill William 110
Birago, Giovan Pietro V.42
Bishop's Waltham (Hants.) 118
Blackheath 11
Blewbery, yeoman of the Armoury 43
Boleyn, Anne, *see* Anne Boleyn
Boleyn, Sir James 108
Boleyn, Mary V.3
Boleyn, Thomas V.38
Bona of Savoy V.42; Hours 88; V.42
Bonde, Richard 28
Books 138
Books:
    Book of Hours II.17
    The Castle of Love II.23
    Genesis 111
    Hours of Bona Sforza 88; V.42
    Huon of Bordeaux II.23
    Tidal Almanack XII.8; *see also*
      under authors
Boorde, Andrew, *A Compendyous*
    Regyment or a Dyetary of Health 163
Bordeaux, merchants 16
Boreham (Essex), New Hall 29
Bosworth, battle of (1485) V.19
Boulogne 10, 145, 150; XI.33
Bourbon, Nicolas 109, 110; VII.9
    Nugae VII.9
Bray, Sir Reginald 94
Brest 176; XII.9
Brinon, Jean 78, 82
Bristol (Glos.) 118, 120
Broikwy, A., *In Quatuor Evangelia*
    Enarrationes XI.26
Bromham (Wilts.) 118
Brosamer, Hans IX.12
Browne, Sir Anthony 94-5, 136, 138,
    141; V.6; VI 9,10
Brun, Loys de 108
Brussels 42, 61
Bruyn, Barthel, the elder 140; XI.3
Bryan, Sir Francis 47, 177
Buckden Palace (Cambs.) 21
Buckingham, Edward Stafford, 3rd
    duke of 132
Burgundy, court 163; influence of 21
Burgundy, Charles, archduke of *see*
    Charles V
Burgundy, Philip the Fair, archduke
    of 26; III.1
Burton, Avery 105

Butts, William, Dr 13, 110,143; VII.9;
    XI.4
Cabot, Sebastian 145
Caesar, Julius V.40
Caias, Diego de XI.33
Calais 8, 50, 176; V.22; XI.12; XII.9
Calepino, Ambrogio, *Dictionarium*
    XI.25
Cambrai 83
Cambridge (Cambs.) II.19
    Christ's College 112
    Emmanuel College 114
Canterbury and York, united
    convocations XI.6
Cape Breton Island XII.5
Carew, Elizabeth II.23
Carew, Sir Gawen XII.10
Carew, Sir George XII.10
Carew, Sir Nicholas 40, 47, 54, 57; V.6;
    XI.41
Carey, Henry 110
Carey, William 57; V.3
Castiglione, Baldesar 11, 26, 35, 36,
    104, 147; II.14
    Book of the Courtier 163
Castillon, battle of (1453) 83
Castles:
    Basing (Hants.) 118
    Deal (Kent) XI.10
    Tower of London *see* London,
      Tower of
    Raglan (Gwent) 22
    Sandown (Kent) XI.10
    Southsea (Hants.) XII.4
    Tattershall (Lincs.) 21
    Walmer (Kent) XI.10
Catherine Howard, 5th queen consort
    of Henry VIII 30, 143, 160; VII.1;
    XI.1
Catherine of Aragon, 1st queen
    consort of Henry VIII 11, 12, 26,
    28, 30, 40, 81, 90, 121, 133, 160,
    175: I.4; V.2; XI.34
    coronation II.21
    image 89
    marriage 12, 13; III.1; XI.22
    patronage 105
    portrait(s) 90; V.45
Catherine Parr, 6th queen consort of
    Henry VIII 133, 161
Cave, Prudentia V.43
Cavendish, George 94
    Life of Cardinal Wolsey I.5
Cavendish, Richard 178
Cellini, Benvenuto 113; V.55
Chamber, Geoffrey II.15
Chambers, John, Dr XI.4, 6
Chapuys, imperial ambassador 111
Charles II, king 25
Charles V, Holy Roman Emperor,
    previously Archduke of
    Burgundy 40, 44, 56, 77, 78, 81, 83,
    89, 121, 142, 160, 161; V.1, 2, 25,
    40, 42, 44, 47; XI.11
    portraits V.1, 48
Cheke, John 110, 111
Chios 178
Christina of Denmark 61

Cirencester (Glos.), parish church IX.11
Clement VII, pope 73, 77, 83, 161; V.2; XII.5
Clement, William XI.10
Clement of Llanthony, *Concordia evangelistarum* 157
Cleves XI.11
    ambassadors 138; XI.12
    duke of 142
Cleves, Anne of, *see* Anne of Cleves
Clocks and watches 138; VI.9; XI.17-21
Clouet, Jean 89; V.32, 41, 44, 52
Coecke, Pieter, the younger 29
Colet, John, dean of St Paul's 32, 35; II.13
Collenuccio, Pandolfo, *Apologues* II.15
Cologne 70
Compiègne VI.1
Copenhagen 178
Copt Hall (Essex) 29
Cornish, William 105
Couche, Richard XI.11
Council, the 138
Council for Marine Causes 177
Cowick (Devon) II.4, 6
Cranmer, Thomas, archbishop of Canterbury 28, 103, 133, 142, 161, 162; VII.2; XI.6
Croke, John V.43
Cromwell, Richard 121
Cromwell, (Sir) Thomas Cromwell, lord 8, 10, 13, 106, 113, 118, 126, 128, 136, 138, 141-3, 148, 161, 178; VII.1, 19; IX.8; IX.25

Danzig 178
Darcy, Thomas Darcy, lord 15
Dartmouth (Devon) 178
Daunce, Sir John 42
Demoron, Lewis 59
Dego XI.30
Denmark 177
Denny, (Sir) Anthony 156; IX.15, 25
Deptford (Kent) 14,15; I.3
    dockyard 14, 172, 176, 180
    Guild or Brotherhood of the Most Glorious Trinity and St Clement 15, 178
Descharges, Breton shipwright 174
Devon, Henry Courtenay 10th earl of 14-17, 19; I.4; II.12
Dickenson, Christopher XI.10
Dinteville, Jean de 73
Dorset, Henry Grey, 3rd marquess of 138
Dorset, Thomas Grey, 2nd marquess of IV.1
Dorset, Margaret Grey, dowager marchioness of 100; VII.6
Douglas, Margaret, niece of Henry VIII 108-9
Dover (Kent) 50, 148, 178; VI.2; XI.8, 9, 11; XII.3
Dover road 11, 14
du Moulin François, *Les Commentaires de la Guerre Gallique* V.40,41
Dürer, Albrecht V.10; *Melancholia* V.4
Durham, bishop of 175
Düsseldorf 140
Duwes, Gilles 155

Dyest, Arnoldus de, abbot of Tongerlo 114
East Harling (Norf.) II.10
Ecouen, château de XI.29
Edinburgh XI.9
Edward III, king 94; VI.5
Edward IV, king, grandfather of Henry VIII 23, 26, 94, 155; queen of 120
Edward, prince of Wales, son of Henry VIII, later King Edward VI 8, 19, 31, 46; II.8
Edward VI, state paper chest XI.46
Eleanor, sister of Emperor Charles V 82
Elizabeth, princess, daughter of Henry VIII, later Queen Elizabeth I 8, 13, 46, 61, 104; VII.8
    christening 100, 102, 103; VII.4-6
Elizabeth of York, queen consort of Henry VII, mother of Henry VIII 120
    tomb 32; II.11, 12; XI.55
Elyot, Sir Thomas 36, 104, 150; Figure 10
    The Boke Named the Governour 147, 148, 163; XI.10; Figure 10
    The Dictionary XI.25
Empire, ambassador 40, 118; III.6
Erasmus 11, 26, 36, 58, 70, 77; II.19, 20; V.4, 21; IX.6
    Enconium Morae II.20
Erith (Kent), dockyard 174, 180
Essex, Henry Bourchier, 2nd earl of IV.1
Este, Isabella de, marchioness of Mantua 12

Falmouth (Cornw.) 178
Faversham, Kent XI.7
Fayrfax, Robert 105
Fevess, Peter 42
Field of Cloth of Gold (1520) 12, 45, 48, 50-54, 81, 121, 146, 175; IV.1, 2, 4
Fish, Simon, *Supplication for the Beggars* 111
Fisher, John 160
Fitzwilliam, Sir William *see* Southampton
Flanders 88
Fleet, river 18
Fleuranges, Robert III de la Marck, seigneur de 51, IV.3
Flicke, Gerlach, *Sir William Palmer* X.2
Floriano, Benedetto VII.8
Flower, Barnard, King's glazier 28
Foiz, Odet de, lord of Lautrec, marshal 83
Formigny, battle of (1450) 83
Fowey (Cornw.) 178
Fox, Richard, bishop of Winchester 26
Foxe, John 111
France 40, 58, 74
    ambassador(s) 40, 100, 165
    gentilshommes de la chambre 13
    influence of 12-13
Francis I, king of France 10, 12, 40, 48, 50, 54, 56, 74, 81-3, 94, 102, 112, 121, 142, 160, 175; IV.1-3; V.3, 22, 24, 25, 30, 32, 33, 35, 39-41, 44, 47; VI.2, 4; VIII.2; IX.9; XI.11, 14, 31; XII.5
    portrait 89
Franciscus, Andreas 16

François, dauphin of France 89; V.44; XI.33
Frisius, Gemma 73
Froissart, Jean, *Chronicle* II.23

Gainsford, Anne 111; VII.10
Gardiner, Stephen, bishop of Winchester 143
Germanus, Nicolaus XI.15
Germany, craftsmen 44
Ghent, Burgundian ducal palace 21
Gifts 131-5; *see also* New Year gifts
Giles, Peter 70
Glass:
    stained 28
    stained, heraldic 26, 28-31
    stained, heraldic arms:
        Archbishop Cranmer II.1
        5th Baron Abergavenny II.2
        Duke of Norfolk II.3
        Prince Edward II.6, 8
        Royal arms II.4, 5, 7
    stained, religious 28, 29
    Venetian II.14; VIII.3; XI.56
Gloucester, Humphrey, duke of 20
Gloucestershire 118
Gold and silverwork 112-14; VII.16, 17; IX.9-16
Gonson, William 177, 178
Grampis, Philipo de 42
Greenwich (Kent) 14, 16, 19, 172; I.1, 3, 5
Greenwich Binder XI.26, 27
Grey, Jane, lady 19
Griffith, William 15
Gringore, Pierre III.8
Guildford, Sir Edward 40, 42
Guildford, Sir Henry 54, 57-9, 105; V.5, 6; XI.23
Guildford, Lady 58
Guisnes 50; IV.1
Guistinian, Sebastian 175

Hailes Abbey (Glos.) 118
Hall, Edward 40, 48, 60, 131; V.12
    Chronicle 48
Hamburg 178; merchants 16
Hanse (Hanseatic League), merchants 18, 178
Harderwijk XI.11, 12
Harvey *see* Howard
Hayes, Cornelis 61
Hengreave Hall (Suff.) 28
Henry III, king of France 95
Henry V, king VI.5
Henry VI, king 94
Henry VII, king, father of Henry VIII 18-20, 23, 24, 40, 48, 94, 112, 120, 122, 126, 128, 155, 160, 163, 172; II.12, 17, 22
    portrait 61; II.14, 16
    tomb 26, 32; II.11, XI.55
Henry VIII, king 8, 14, 17, 18, 28, 40, 41, 43, 50, 51, 59-61, 71, 81-3, 94, 95, 102, 110, 111, 118, 120, 121, 123, 131, 133, 138; I.5; II.7, 19, 22; III.1, 5, 6, 9; IV.1; V.14, 22, 30, 42, 44-46, 48; VI.1, 3, 9, 10; VII.2, 12, 17, 24; IX.9, 10, 16, 17: XI.11-13, 16, 18, 26, 27, 38, 41, 44, XII.1, 3-6
    arms and armour 42-5; III.2, 4; IV.2; V.7